Writing Addiction

Writing Addiction:
Toward a Poetics of Desire and Its Others

edited by Béla Szabados and Kenneth G. Probert

UNIVERSITY OF
REGINA

Canadian Plains Research Center
2004

Canadian Plains Research Center
University of Regina
Regina, Saskatchewan S4S 0A2
Canada
Tel: (306) 585-4758
Fax: (306) 585-4699
e-mail: canadian.plains@uregina.ca
http://www.cprc.uregina.ca

National Library of Canada Cataloguing in Publication Data
Writing addiction : toward a poetics of desire and its others / edited by Béla Szabados and Kenneth G. Probert.

(University of Regina publications ; 11)
Includes bibliographical references and index.
ISBN 0-88977-176-6

1. Authors—Drug use. 2. Authorship—Psychological aspects. 3. Literature, Modern—History and criticism. I. Szabados, Béla, 1942- II. Probert, Kenneth Gordon. III. University of Regina. Canadian Plains Research Center. IV. Series.
HV4999.W75W75 2004   809'.933561   C2004-902312-8

We acknowledge the financial support of the Government of Canada through the Book Publishing Industry Development Program (BPIDP) for our publishing activities.

Cover design by Brian Danchuk Design, Regina, Saskatchewan
Photo credits: Béla Szabados (Heather Hodgson), Ken Probert (Don Hall)
Printed and bound in Canada by Houghton Boston, Saskatoon

— For Joan and David Givner —

The intention is one of retrieval, an attempt to uncover buried goods through rearticulation—and thereby to make these sources empower again, to bring the air back again into the half-collapsed lungs of the spirit.

Charles Taylor

Table of Contents

Acknowledgements

All of the contributions to this book were written specifically for it and are published here for the first time, with the exception of those of Crispin Sartwell and Alan Bewell, which first appeared in Æ, the electronic journal of the Canadian Society for Aesthetics (Summer 1999), and have been revised especially for this volume.

As editors, it is our pleasure to acknowledge the many forms of assistance received in the preparation of this book. Heather Hodgson, Joan Givner and Alison Strayer gave valued counsel. Dr. Nicole Côté was very kind to offer us advice about translations of Baudelaire. The University of Regina, through the offices of the Dean of Arts, Murray Knuttila, and of the Vice-President of Research, Amit Chakma, has been generous in providing initial funds for the project. Most importantly, to the authors, whose commitment is realized here, we offer public thanks.

Introduction

Béla Szabados and Ken Probert

The history of literature is replete with substance-dependent writers. Opium (including laudanum): De Quincey, Coleridge, Crabbe, Wilkie Collins, Baudelaire; Morphine: Louisa May Alcott; Heroin: William Burroughs; Cocaine: Stephen King (for a time); Alcohol: Jack London, Edna St. Vincent Millay, Hart Crane, Theodore Roethke, Delmore Schwartz, John Berryman, Randall Jarrell, Robert Lowell, Anne Sexton.

Addiction, apparently, is a hazard of the writing life. But this impressive list of names, which is a mere sample of those eligible, invites more interesting questions concerning the relationship between writing and addiction. Could the members of the *Club des Haschichins* (circa 1845), De Quincey, Jean Cocteau, Bachelard, and others be right—that potentially addictive substances stimulate the artistic imagination? What is the relationship between the desire for intoxication or euphoria and the compulsions of addiction? Is there a sense in which writing provides similar highs and compulsions? Are writing and substance addiction similar transgressive behaviours? Could it be that both writing and addiction are ways of losing control, or perhaps of losing controls?

The central begged question in this context, of course, is, what *is* addiction? We can all agree that it has some elements of compulsion and habituation. And when the addiction is to opiates, increasing tolerance and the threat of unpleasant withdrawal symptoms loom. But the point at which attraction or appetite becomes addiction is obscure, and it is clear that there is no common set of criteria that will identify all forms of substance addiction. The checklists for establishing alcoholism, for example, commonly identify negative behaviours rather than attempting to define the addiction through physiological markers, and different organizations require different numbers of negative behaviours to declare the drinker alcoholic.

In 1964 the World Health Organization replaced the term "addiction" with "drug dependence." The new dependence, however, sounds much like our old understanding of addiction:

> *A state, psychic and sometimes also physical, resulting from the*
> *interaction between a living organism and a drug, characterised*
> *by behavioural and other responses that always include a com-*
> *pulsion to take the drug on a continuous or periodic basis in*
> *order to experience its psychic effects, and sometimes to avoid the*
> *discomfort of its absence. Tolerance may or may not be present.*
> *A person may be dependent on more than one drug.*[1]

Although it resists precise definition, and though we may give it another name, then, the idea of addiction simply will not go away. In fact, the term is applied today in expanding contexts. Here are two fairly recent applications. Addiction is "any substance or process that has taken over our lives and over which we are powerless."[2] "An addiction exists when a person's attachment to a sensation, an object, or another person is such as to lessen his appreciation of and ability to deal with other things in his environment, or in himself, so that he has become increasingly dependent on that experience as his sole source of gratification."[3] And so we speak of love addiction, sex addiction, food addiction … whatever. But the definitions just cited are at once too limited and too general to generate heuristic benefits. Better, perhaps, since we are considering *writing* and addiction, to go back to the root meaning of the central term.

The word "addiction" comes from Latin. The prefix "ad" means to or toward, and the past participle of "dicere" means to say or to pronounce. In Roman law, "addiction" was a technical term; it meant a formal giving over or delivery by a sentence of a court. In that technical legal sense, the addict would be a person who, by some official act of the court, has been spoken over to a master, who has been bound to a master. So the ur-phenomenon of "addiction" in Roman law offers a rather congenial perspective on our contemporary discourse of addiction. The original literal use is now widely perceived as metaphorical, but retrieving it shows that the current uses are really quite close to the original literal meaning: a person who is addicted to X has X as a master—is a slave to it.

Notice then the particular social and political conditions under which the concept of addiction was formed: the fact of the master-slave relationship, with its attendant duties and responsibilities, its mutual resentments, and their inscription in Roman law. Thus the recent medical/psychological conception was actually fabricated from an ancient legalized process of depersonalization and disenfranchisement. Taking this picture seriously has certain implications. First, insightful extension of the concept to non-pathological uses may no longer strike us as a regrettable symptom that the word "addiction" lost whatever meaning it may have had. Rather, we may decide that instead of making invidious comparisons between the lives of addicts

---

1. Quoted in Lester Greenspoon and James Bakular, *Cocaine* (New York: Basic Books, 1976), 186.
2. A.W. Schaef and Diane Fassel, *The Addictive Organization* (San Francisco: Harper and Row, 1988), 5.
3. Stanton Peele and Archie Brodsky, *Love and Addiction* (New York: Signet, 1975), 56.

and the lives of writers/authors, we need to let the light of the depiction of the experiences of addicts illuminate our lives as writers/authors. Second, addiction may have no fixed definitional essence, but its metaphorical and extended uses are best understood by way of comparing a variety of cases in light of the master-slave relationship.

Both tasks call for a personal index. Indeed, the *first person voice* is a common thread that runs through the essays in this collection. This is not merely a narrative artifice, since there is no more compelling way of accessing experiential sources, and thus gathering the basis for relevant comparisons, than through reflective confessions and self-disclosures that reveal the writing practices of particular authors. What is more, there is a sustained attempt to integrate the idea of writing and the act of writing, as style and text become iconic of addiction with its highs and lows, its excess and lack, its longings and fears.

While the first person confessional voice is characteristic of many of the contributions, it is more pronounced in some. Consider: "I am an addict and an author… . I have been literally addicted to authorship…, I have written compulsively" (Crispin Sartwell). Even authors who disavow substance addiction nevertheless confess to and reflect on the *modern addiction to addiction*: "I'm not addicted to alcohol. I'm addicted to its story and effect, its historical punch," wanting "to measure cultural addictions" (Aritha van Herk). Nor is it the case that those authors who aim to read and explore a chosen literary figure escape personal resonance. By pretending to be in the figure's skin, by claiming their voices through filiation, these literary critics also read themselves through reading the other. These engagements in criticism may then be seen, at least to some degree, as acts of ventriloquism. The conventional view that only autobiographical writing is expressive of a personal index may suggest a pretension to privilege certain genres as hard-edged, and to denigrate *poiesis* and life-writing as exercises in entertainment or self-indulgence. However, anyone who writes about others has not only to confront the tensions in her subject's life, but also to come to terms with his own vested interests in the project, which may be as complex as the complex motivations of an autobiographer. Going the other way, poets too must always ask themselves, is what I am writing really true?[4]

The constellation of writing we present is pregnant with personal resonance and blurs sharp disciplinary lines, which have traditionally been drawn partly on the basis of "objectivity" in various kinds of writing/discourse. We witness the *recovery of particularity*, of somebody's voice, from the falsetto of the voice from nowhere that marks traditional critical/philosophical discourse. The rigid dichotomy between writer and text is deconstructed as the writer is inserted in the space of text. It is a relief to hear the lively, authentic sounds of particular writers as they retrieve and contextualize moments in the life of writing, as they make room for the writer's body in the body of writing.

---

4. See Ludwig Wittgenstein, *Culture and Value* (Oxford: Blackwell, 1998), 46. Note his qualification: "Which does not necessarily mean: 'is this how it happens in reality?'"

A new simile is like a fresh seed in the ground of discussion. If we look at these personal retrievals through the lens of the addict as the writer's *other*, fresh and nourishing affinities come into view. One shared feature is self-division or *doubling up* as intense inner conflict makes space between will and desire. Addicts are internally compelled to do what they decide not to do, as body and desire, the biological, in opposition to reason and will, articulate the self. Writers are pushed and pulled by their literary inheritance and their desire to insert themselves bodily into it, and thus rebuild. In this sense, then, both addicts and writers are out of control as traditional ideas of the controlling self as unified and free consciousness are called into question.

Discernible in this doubling up is *writing through the body*. The writer as addict or compulsive represents "the invasion of the animal into the pristine world of the pure linguistic self" (Sartwell). For van Herk, addiction involves repetition, and "the body harbours recidivism, echoes remembered pleasures." The body, it seems, craves recapitulation: "the fond of real addiction is its physical trace, its mesmeric desire to be pleasured again and again." She asks, perhaps rhetorically, "Is it addiction that pushes writing across the fine line between invention and demonstration?" We see how the writer, van Herk a case in point, is an addict: of language ("that slippery emulsifier in her private *grimoire*"), to writing, and to omnivorous reading. Dave Margoshes also evokes a biological model when he says "The creation of literature is not at all unlike the workings of biology." And Kristjana Gunnars speaks of the almost biological, desperate need in the act of writing: "It is something that rises out of utter necessity, the cessation or blockage of writing—writer's block—tantamount to drug withdrawal crisis."

If the addict is also the writer's repressed other, then a window is opened to another aspect of doubling up. *Desire and emotion* are the most palpably visceral aspects of the self, the body in the mind, as it were. This is the space of repression/suppression in the name of social norms and control. It is the space of buried sources of avoidance, denial and self-deception, of failures in self-understanding, where, as Sartwell notes, "the left hand does not know what the right hand is doing." As these vital sources of desire and emotion are retrieved, expressive creative powers are released. In this light Andrew Cunningham suggests that like the ancient Greek tragedies, "the best literature aims to capture, express, and evoke powerful emotions." Though alcohol cannot create emotion, it can grease the wheels. Writers must feel, understand and convey powerful emotion, which requires them to confront their own lives as well. In this process, alcohol can play a "preparatory, cathartic and palliative role."

Writing then is a difficult and ironic act: difficult in that even though you desire and are compelled to write, it takes you to places you want to avoid— a *terra incognita*, as De Quincey called it. It is an ironic act, too, because to keep on writing the writer must in a sense avoid writing: "The writer perfects the strategy of avoidance, which keeps her hooked on writing, because it is always necessary to give it another try" (Gunnars). This other voice emerging in writerly fragmentation is embraced by van Herk as a voice of wild nature, teeming with life and creative potential, despite risks posed: "A writer's addictions should emulate invisible plagues lurking around the back doors of cesspools and corruption and contagion. There is something sump-tuous about an unquiet habit, one that will not hide itself in the folds of a long black coat."

Self-destruction and self-creation resonate in the collection. Both addicts and authors desire relief from the sufferings of rupture as they seek a more authentic identity. So writing and addiction may be a liberating experience as authors and addicts re-create themselves using the resources provided by their struggle with the illusions and self-deceptions associated with tradition-al ideas of self and authorship. This identity may or may not be thought of in linguistic terms. Both addict and writer often yearn for romantic solitude and wholeness, for the firm and fixed identity of a thing or body. To become body, the addict ingests the chemical substance to achieve relief; the author uses the public language to forge through writing an idiosyncratic private vocabulary, thereby becoming a body of text. These are ways of shedding the dead skin of the self, as well as the dead weight of received meaning. This desire for identity as a body of work is connected by van Herk to "death's happy closures": "The most scandalous pleasure is solitariness, silence. It's fed my addiction to death's happy closures, the text's finality. The end of the story, like the end of the affair, inevitable seizure, finesse, fini, execution, discharge, fulfillment, ultimate embrace."

Transgression also lures both addicts and authors. Addict and writer attempt to break out of confining routines or forms of social life. Addicts rebel against the deadening mechanical routines of the everyday, seeking release by erasing consciousness. Writers rebel against the dead metaphors and complacent norms of ordinary language, seeking release through resisting and rewriting the body of language—participating in that struggle of, and against, language that is literature. Through acts of disobedience and trans-gression against the rule-governed social norms or public language, writers/addicts lose conventional controls. "The writer is a perpetual addict—to language... . In a lifelong battle with words, the writer becomes heretic addict, determined to make something of her dependency, returning again and again to the source, the *adytum*" (van Herk).

The themes of *modernity and post-modernity* also echo strongly here. Perhaps to be modern, in an age of late modernity, as Alan Bewell suggests, is "to be unable to talk about our addictions," to be addicted to the discourse of addiction. In a sense, this re-conceives previous conceptions of what it is to be (late) modern. In an ironic double movement, the ideals of modernity, autonomy, self-control and freedom, are critiqued and confirmed, as we compulsively talk about and confess our dependencies, how we are un-free, how we fall short of our aspirations as moderns.

The question of what addiction is arises as some authors consider the nature and scope of our *cultural addictions*. Jeanette Lynes talks about the "intrinsic link between the addictive predisposition and the rise of North American capitalism," then develops a witty yet somber meditation on the

Canadian landscape where the place and drinks are inextricably linked. As
she reflects upon the modern addiction to addiction, van Herk broaches conceptual concerns by distinguishing addiction, "serious life-threatening
dependencies," from what she terms "habituations." Thus she takes a critical view of the modern-day pathologizing of eccentric behaviour. This is the
"excuse-zone of contemporary irresponsibility, absolving the incompetent of
incompetence." Trudy Govier is even more direct as she stresses that
"Addictions are characterized not by the quality of an activity or substance
in itself, but rather by the compulsiveness of our recourse to it, and the tendency for that recourse to dominate and diminish other aspects of our lives."

This naturally leads to the idea of *writing as therapy, as a way of healing
the self*, albeit not once and for all, but as needed. How to accomplish this in
the haunting shadow of the "anxiety of influence"? Harold Bloom's "strong
poets" wrestle with their strong precursors, even to death, imaginatively
appropriating for themselves. "But nothing is got for nothing, and self-appro-
bation involves the immense anxieties of indebtedness, for what strong
maker desires the realization that he has failed to create himself."[5] This
gloomy picture of the strong poet seems to close off the possibility of a therapeutic conception of writing, since according to it the process of striving for
an original voice multiplies tensions within the self, rather than dissolving
them, as writers in a murderous frame of mind struggle with ancestral figures in their literary tradition. To resist this one-sided picture, we need to
remind ourselves of strong voices that resonate with, and are deepened by,
literary allusions expressive of appreciation of their precursors. Striking an
Atwoodian chord, we might say that such writers show us how to "negoti-
ate with the dead": how to be creative within a tradition without undue violence to the self or the community of selves.[6] Declining thus the sharp
dichotomy between strong versus weak poet allows for a different understanding of what counts as strength in *poiesis*. In any case, by writing and
reading, poets give us nourishing resources, in life and literature, for a rich-
er self-understanding and renewal.

Ellen Lansky explores a darker version of the life/literature relationship
in her analysis of how Scott and Zelda Fitzgerald used their novels to "map
out and publicize fantasies that the authors were unable to realize in their
lives." The results, however, were disappointing: "The lives ... ended as
their novels end: vague, fading, unresolved." Repeated writerly enactments
of the desire to heal the divided self bear a striking affinity to the addict's
search for a high: "To be in a heroin nod is to finally feel cured of the self,
de-fragmented. What lurks out there as the end of highs, is the extinction
of consciousness, the extinction of the self... And I have been literally
addicted to authorship in a deeply self-destructive, that is self-creative
way" (Sartwell).

5.   Harold Bloom, *The Anxiety of Influence* (New York: Oxford University Press, 1975), 5.
6.   Margaret Atwood, *Negotiating With the Dead: A Writer on Writing* (Cambridge:
     Cambridge University Press, 2002). See Chapter 6, "Descent: Negotiating With the Dead:
     Who Makes the Trip to the Underworld and Why?," 153–80.

The *ironic* and temporary nature of this "cure-all" surfaces in Cindy MacKenzie's reading of herself through reading Emily Dickinson. Even as the idea of linguistic healing is affirmed, the malaise of linguistic addiction is realized. Are we then trading off one addiction for another? For some writers, writing itself narrows down like junk, impoverishing their life as they obsessively regard life as mere material for writing, much like addicts who obsessively think of the next fix as they go on about their daily chores. In MacKenzie's words, "Within language, the repressed self, unsuccessful in its yearning for the unified self, fractures the textual landscape with disjunction, dashes and gaps, the visual wounds analogous to the fragmented self." The split in the self is exacerbated through the process of writing poetry; the euphoria of writing inevitably brings melancholy in its wake, and the intoxication brings "hangover."

Yet *poiesis* is also the only way of assuaging pain, of healing, if only temporarily, the split self. "In the end, by healing the split self through language Dickinson must sustain the terrible tensions of human experience, but by so doing, she finds a creative rather than destructive means of living with them." This approach resonates with Andrew Stubbs and Alison Strayer as they navigate, in their own ways, the line between self-destruction and self-creation. In Andrew Stubbs's reading, William Styron's *Darkness Visible* could even be seen as a "continuation of the author's addiction (figured as simultaneous attraction to and repulsion from death), expressed as a need to observe clinically while being romanced by its subject." By making madness and sanity "complicit," Styron keeps "writing—as a means of surviving—going on indefinitely." This way the tensions are negotiated between "creating a public document" that is the writing of a memoir of acute depression, and sustaining subjective involvement that is "as personal as a signature." Strayer strikes a similar chord: "Melancholy, as well as a threat to writing is also its wellspring and thus must, to some degree, be sustained… How to milk melancholy as Muse, but avoid being spoken over to it," as is the addict in addiction, the slave to the master? Her reading of Virginia Woolf gestures to an alternative way to the search for perfection: to a way of continual incompletion, continual recommencement.

The *self-reflexivity of writing* is yet another theme that runs in this family: writing is always to some degree about writing or the sources of writing. The allusion or reference to other writers, to a tradition, suggests a need for connectedness, and thus continuity, even as the writer differentiates himself or herself. This theme is prominent when the writer explores herself through reading the other. These resonances, through a desire for connectedness and filiation, add a depth to the writing that would otherwise be a single sigh or a solitary cry. It is as if the sources of writing are the sources of our birth and bodies. Addicts in every high are performing their addictiveness as if to get to the bottom of it, both in the sense of understanding it, and also in the sense of going to the very bottom—so far down that one cannot seem to go further fully into the body.

How is this body of literature to be conceived? The different ways of picturing this body of work raises the question of *particularity* and *gender in writing.* Modernity valorized the written text, at the risk of exclusion, even the death, of the writer/author, asking: What does it matter who is speaking? There is no such indifference to particularity in the present constellation of contributions. Is the connectedness with the Father's or Mother's body? Who is calling when we write? Is it the *Mother's womb* contracting to reconceive, through writing, shallow, complacent distinctions of good and evil with a view to a horizon of greater authenticity? Or is it the haunting voice of the Father calling to perform duties of justice? Even though such either/ors are too exclusive, the different ways of picturing the *body* of literature suggested in different authors who approach this issue may be seen as shedding light on different aspects of *poiesis.*

For Gunnars, "true writing is a process in which one discovers the 'raw' state of things, in which one follows the twisted roots that take you to the 'happy mingling' of both good and evil." That writing space of authenticity and need "beyond all economies," is that of *language/literature as the womb* which pre-exists the writer and into which the writer disappears even as she attempts self-assertion. "What the writer reaches towards, but cannot quite achieve, and what is so compelling that it could be called an addiction on many levels, are essentials like freedom (from all economies), understanding (also of one's own complicities), joy (the rejected), honesty, wisdom, love— and an ability to face death."

This *ethical search which resists complacency* surfaces in Margoshes and Stephen Ross Smith who make a link between words and the figure of the Father. Ross Smith's elegiac prose poem connects words and the father—or the father's body, a father totem or landscape. "My father is a roil of words"—"my father is an island"—"is a mystery I know well like a white-headed bald-eagle." The Father or his body—which seems sometimes as if it's alive and at other times as dead and buried—seems to be devoured by words, but also to be *the opaque source of words*: the disquieting turgid waters need a clarifying filter. The plenitude of writing also counterpoints loss and depletion: it is an affirmation of life as well as a tribute to the dying. In Margoshes, as the aging father introduces young Dave to a world of difference, particularity, and injustice, the boy becomes aware of the possibility of the father's death and absence. Hence the author's struggles through *poiesis* to bestow voice to the dead and the voiceless, the falsely accused; hence the compulsive desire for an unceasing re-enactment of the word, for re-creating the world through naming difference. As if the father were a source of linguistic/ethical burdens, as well as of reconciliation with past selves, with others in community. And that brings in readers.

The chord of community suggests a sense of an ending for this editorial prelude as well as a sense of a beginning: namely, reading these "uncut kicks that open out instead of narrowing down like junk."[7]

---

7. William S. Burroughs, *Junky* (New York: Viking Penguin, 1977), 152.

Section I

Confessions

1

Ladies and Escorts

Aritha van Herk

Writers are supposed to be waylaid by addiction, accomplice ampheta-
mine digressions, the swashbuckling doors of perception. We are the
test cases, the muse mousers, the canaries in the proverbial mine of bustier
fetishism. I weigh this artistic responsibility against my method and madness, my choice of lingerie, my deep-seated melancholias. Are my repeated
actions—the slight tilt of my listening, my love of spicy food, my three-times
a day toothbrush ritual—addictions? I fear not. If I suffer from habituations,
I cannot claim their repetitions as obstructions or inspirations to my writing
life. More habits than life-threatening attachments, momentary distractions
rather than obsessive sublimities, my small addictions are laughable.

At twelve midnight, on a Sunday, under the glare of fluorescent tubes, I
stroll the aisles of my local bottle shop, no longer an Alberta Liquor Control
Board store, as they were officiously called when I was growing up, the win-
dowless facades dun-coloured, the men behind the counters stern as sextons.
I notice good single malts and excellent Spanish *Riojas*, the high end of what
was once known as demon drink. But I'm not addicted to alcohol. I'm
addicted to its story and effect, its historical punch.

Surely every writer has chalk-circled her own zone of narcosis and
intoxication. We all possess chemical friends, food preferences, obsessive-
compulsive fingernail-biting, rituals that notch the quotidian terrain of repetition. We hold the paring knife a particular way, stir our coffee a set number of times, even admit to confession or prayer, deformities of season and
rhythm. I'm as provoked by resignation as I am by hysteria, as eager to frac-
ture a complacent crust as I am to skate over the surface of punctual schedule. Besides, there's little room for addiction in any bargain with life lived
according to clock and sun.

I'm dreaming about Florence Lassandra, hanged as an accessory to murder. She was a rum-runner's moll, an Italian immigrant girl caught in an
adventure that she could not predict would end with the killing of an Alberta
Provincial policeman, and with a noose necklaced around her breath. She
was addicted to Emperor Picarello, the Bottle King of the Crowsnest Pass,

driving cars with cement-reinforced bumpers to smash through roadblocks during Prohibition, rum-running a stable occupation in the 1930s. Like Florence I've taken to wearing a red tam; like Florence I am an immigrant girl with frizzy hair, standing in front of a fence with snow in my shoes, addicted to dreaming of a different life.

To tell the truth, I'm irritated at how habituation has become heroic, a cause, a grail. I'm annoyed at picayune behaviour elevated to addiction, turned into an illness that requires the soothing walls of treatment, hushed tones of understanding. A rotten little boy is no longer a rotten little boy but a child suffering from attention deficit disorder. A man who can't stop buying shoes is no longer a man with an overly generous credit card limit but a shopaholic. People claim addiction to everything from computer games to lip balm. The tendency to want to sleep with anything and everything in sight, instead of being called horniness, is elevated to sexual addiction. If that includes a preference for being on top, the desiring one can confess to full-blown neurosis. Every day eccentric behaviour is pathologized, swirled together in the same batter with serious, life-threatening dependencies. This is the excuse-zone of contemporary irresponsibility, absolving the incompetent of incompetence, who, so the *mise en abyme* would say, are incompetent because they do not know they are incompetent. Failure and poor performance have become symptoms of disorder, and even stupidity is mercantile, actions the result of a condition. Indecisive people are victims of a chemical imbalance called indecisiveness, victimhood has become an aspired-to status, with some psychological or other external cause always at fault. And so I declare myself against addiction because repetition is boring, and blame is a retromingent habit.

Under the North West Territories Act of 1875, all liquor had to be legally ordered from the east, but it arrived more readily from the south, through Whiskey Gap, near Milk River. In true Alberta fashion, the first sitting member of Parliament from Alberta was an ex-whiskey trader from Fort Whoop-Up who had to change careers after the whiskey forts were closed down by the Mounties. He became a trader of more acceptable goods and went to work for the Mounties, building their forts, then got himself elected to Ottawa. The career path of a true-blue whiskey trader.

What motivates addiction and the concomitant addiction to addiction? Reasons and causes as diverse as human ingenuity. Greed and pride, a punitive nanny, a cross-dressing father, the alphabet of orphanage, the nerves of disillusionment. Desire's rote promises to insulate the writer from distraction, addiction the source its own distraction and goal. One perfect barbiturate will surely resurrect that elusive mixture of dust and candlelight, the dreaming fingers of trees in the garden, the integument of words momentarily momentous. One quick intake of breath will marshal those obstinate memories, their sullen refusal to assist a scene or a character, coax them to come out from their game of hide and seek. Some cold elixir will separate us from ourselves, yet bring us closer to inspiration. Yes, there and there. Addiction can inspire, help with the elusive search for inspiration's terrible dictatorship.

Bars were places sporadically attacked by pontifical clergy, although tolerated as a necessary evil. A bar was a simple arrangement: a large room with a wooden counter along its length, decorated by two railings, one below to prop up a foot, one a handrail to prop up a tottering man. Weighted cuspidors at strategic places, the sawdust floors a mess of tobacco, spit, and horse manure. The air blue with smoke. The bartender couldn't refuse a drink to a man sober enough to stand.

The writer is a perpetual addict—to language—although there are writers who use that tool as conduit to a less noble addiction, known as fame. In a life-long wrestling match with words, the writer becomes heretic addict, determined to make something of her dependency, returning again and again to the source, the adytum. In the writer's *grimoire*, language—that slippery emulsifier—plays both eternal respite and eternal evasion, the artist's chronic incorrigible, duplicitous double, and unattainable grail.

Railway workers, farmers, and cowboys, all enjoyed different drinking habits, although they all drank pretty much the same poison.

The true addict/writer is also a reader, afflicted with the persistent need to devour words. When I walk into bookstores, I am surrounded by the cornucopia of my desire, the battlements of covers inviting as passion fruit. There I am close to the zone of my undoing, the mixture of dust and binding glue and ink an exhilarating perfume. I have fainted with desire in libraries, between stacks that climb upward to an infinity of print, the volumes secretive and sirenesque, emitting a low hum of temptation that will not permit me pull myself away. I will read anything. Nothing is too insulting. The *National Post*, if there is nothing else. *TV Guide*, although I never watch television. Descriptions of the habits of sled dogs. Reports on culture and imperialism. Dictionaries for a treat. Fairy tales for relaxation. The phone bill. Dictionaries, their chewed pages, their polysyllabic sonorousness, their very binding containing the whole of the human condition. Advertisements in newspapers. Birth and death announcements. Malign reports of the lives of the chemical stars in the disgraced magazines in dentists' offices. At stop lights I read signs, decipher bumper stickers, memorize license plates. Books ride in the back seat of my car, and I carry a book everywhere, in case I have to wait, in case I am waylaid.

Booze was to blame for poverty, wife-beating, and accidents. In Alberta, between 1906 and 1910, one-third of all criminal convictions were for drunkenness. Beer was 15¢ a glass; 25¢ for two. And in 1900, the Calgary Brewing and Malting Company cleared at least $50,000, an astonishing profit for the time.

My eyes will pay the price for my addiction to reading. I'll suffer for reading by flashlight under the covers, reading in dim twilights where the words on the page dance just beyond recognition and my eyes squint to trace the story. I'll pay with failing night vision, astigmatism, myopia, and cataracts. I'll brandish a combination of glasses and magnifying glasses, I'll become impatient with inadequate light bulbs, will turn my back to the glare of light through a window. My greatest fear is of a slowly darkening room and a delicious book discarded on the table, both of us immobilized. This is the parenthesis that I have opened with my biblioholic behaviour, this ritual that riddles every moment of my life. Is my addiction condemnable or commend-able—or merely a yawn to an unbookish world? Is my obsession's useless-ness, the pure self-indulgence of my addiction, symbolic of futility? It argues me conundrums, that the condition of true health is death, that addiction tempers time, that reading's slowed clock hours relieve a writer's innate fatalism.

— • —

Beer was for some time considered a health food, a barley sandwich. Plebiscites on prohibition passed and failed. A good hotel crowd could make or break an election, and politics and liquor were friends. Every Canadian knows that Macdonald was a drunk, although fewer hear how the upright Mounties went on binges. They were supposed to spill seized booze, but they didn't always dump it all.

The truth is that I would like to give my characters addictions, sexy habits, symbolic routines. I want them to drink too much, to smoke ciga-rettes, to gobble doughnuts. But between my pen and the page they turn into purists who cite the foulness of overflowing ashtrays, the petulant breath of stale smoke. They fastidiously step past the butt-strewn doorways of non-smoking buildings, with a small grimace of distaste. They will sip at itinerant martinis, but they refuse to tap kegs of beer, and haven't got the money for expensive single malt or even good Chardonnay. And as for eat-ing, my failure to write breakfast or lunch or dinner scenes brings me close to tears. I can cook a fine roast of beef but never transform it into the dish Virginia Woolf serves up in *To the Lighthouse*, Mrs. Ramsay's triumphant *Boeuf en Daube*.

The first wars were between the "drys" and the "wets," but that soon changed to a fight between temperance and prohibition. Temperance meant drinking in moderation; prohibition meant no drinking at all. In the ultimate measurement, prohibition meant blind pigs and grain alcohol and wild intemperance. Too much forbidden fruit.

The physical world tests metaphors while addictions test the seductions of repression. This is the district of sexual desire, the body needing repeat-ed surveillance. I start to believe that the fond of real addiction is its physi-cal trace, its mesmeric desire to be pleasured again and again. Such assigna-tions must reach farther than rituals, push past reductive demands, how some are addicted to the phone, others to the faint smell of bleach in just-cleaned bathrooms, and only a minority remember the texture of new grass on bare feet. The body harbours recidivism, echos remembered pleasures, a syphilis of habit, a consumption of rote, a cholera of schedule that rules out accident. All that remains is the time between cigarettes and shot glasses, need pacing itself like a metronome, inescapable and utterly relentless in its petulant demands. In short, a boring calendar by which to engage desire.

Alcohol pre-dated almost everything that the infiltrators and invaders and traders and settlers brought west. It was a trading commodity, medicine, comfort, painkiller, and companion. It prescribed a new vernacular.

I wake to a hot and cloudless morning, and let my hand fall to the stack of books beside my bed. *Secrets of the Flesh: A Life of Colette*. In seconds I am deep inside Colette's *fin de siècle*, her battle with purity, her amours and her jealousies, her insistent self-deceptions. Judith Thurman's biography persuades me to unearth Colette's stories, and I am carried off on a cruise with that coquette, visiting her psychics, odalisque and bitter, and writing, always writing as hard as she lived. I read Colette and about Colette until I am surfeited, my life no parallel to her hyperbolic dramas. She was addicted to her own innocence and its repeated loss. Forever a girl with a dirty face, she revelled in her monstrous innocence, flouting and flaunting taboo, expectation, decency. Colette pursued the body as addiction, her body its own incestuous semaphore. Colette would persuade any writer to entertain the navel as a novel—eager to suffer a romantic disease, a worthy illness, one to treasure for the comfort of discomfort. Sickness an addiction which enjoys ill-health, the lugubrious pronouncement of symptoms and stigmata. Or should I read the life of Colette as an addiction to drama, the heightened tension of argument, the delicious fall-out of fights, old lovers in tears and new lovers wooing with all of courtship's heady endorphins? I am back to the body, the blackboard that invites the transgression of formula, the subject and object of pleasure and its double-back.

When the CPR started stitching track across this imaginary country, the presence of alcohol underlined the body politic. The truth was, navvies and crews had to drink to survive.

Peter Brooks claims that the body is "the uncontrollable agent of pain and the revolt against reason—and the vehicle of mortality" (1). The vehicle of mortality. To live is to suffer. The shiver of pain becomes the addict's irreparable destination, the mixed adage of punishment and endurance. Is every addiction accomplished *sui generis*, unique? Yes, the writer craves suffering, some distinction that will separate her life from all others. Affliction will annoint the gifted writer, declare who should be taken seriously, caressed with the soft tones of CBC announcers who adore childhood torments, recurrent eczemas, subtle dyspepsias. This is an age of vanquished affliction, curious observers bent over the panoptica of newer and newer illnesses. Audiences love a hypochondriac plot, neuralgia's infinite remorse, unsettled digestion, hives and allergies, insomnia and kyphosis. The watching world craves deformity, aesthetic injury, convulsive thought.

Hotels were heavy on booze and light on rooms. Whiskey Row, which followed Calgary's Ninth Avenue from Third Street East to First Street West, provided cheap rooms and good liquor at 15¢ a shot. The Mounties were supposed to control both rooms and booze. They looked away.

I suffer from impaired vision, that unsightly requirement for correction. Put on a pair of glasses. Pinch *nez*. Oh I want a photographable head, a congruent body, attractively grotesque. A writer pares her body to suit her text, and this enslavement then, to strangeness, to illness, to a perfidious uncommonality, trounces addictions to beauty. The larger the writing voice, the more the writer's body wears the weight of words. Expectant readers are offended at the short stature of one poet, the corpulence of another. Novelists, think readers, must be tall and imposing, with salt and pepper beards, miens of benign sternness. Smoking elegantly thin cigarettes.

Coffin varnish was raw alcohol watered down with tobacco, brown sugar, and bluestone. Bluestone was blue vitriol, caustic, injurious.

Reading then, glasses on my nose, I crave a threatening narrative and dive into American expectorate, DeLillo, that Donald—wait, is he a Donald or a Don, and is the play on his name intended to point to the man at the head, the figure waiting for remonstrance? I too am interested in the narrative structure of terrorist acts, the terrorist structure of narrative acts, assemblages of historical junk, the Americanesque underworld that precedes vendors hawking hot dogs and cheap rain slickers, the millenium that has already become cliché. *Mao II* and *Libra* quicksand my attention, manifesto my search. The 800 pages of *Underworld* are insufficient for my thirst, I want this labyrinth to continue, even if I hate baseball and its pretensions, even if I mistrust the internet and all computer-generated data. There is, at the centre of this well of time-bound words, a stillness, the writer within the cage of page, the writing within the cage of context, events which once took place.

The North West Mounted Police once had total power over liquor in the west. They could search without a warrant, fine with impunity, and pocket half the fine. Purloining the spoils of addiction.

I return to these addictive resurrections, alert to the flare of a match on a darkened set, the thickened lump of a vein under the skin at the crook of an arm. Is it addiction that pushes writing across the fine line between invention and demonstration, secrets that inveigle, camouflage, burn haystacks of waiting lies, trounce knights of air, evade the yawn of graves? Do I crave only words, reading for the act's sake? Desire designs its own banality, apportioned as if it were fiduciary, unimpeachable, a gullible cornucopia. I hug my writerly wishes close to my chest, keep them secret, *escalier dérobé*, where they can bloom and grow a lush orchidaceous scent. A writer's addictions should emulate invisible plagues lurking around the back doors of cesspools and corruption and contagion. There is something sumptuous about an unquiet habit, one that will not hide itself in the folds of a long black coat.

Whiskey was the preferred drink. Friends treated one another—two drinks were 25¢—and whiskey was cheaper than beer. Then there were the bones, the dice, the fights. The fun.

I have no addictions, except to driving, the quick thrum of the steering wheel under my hands, my foot poised above the clutch to shift, rev the engine up a notch, hot wind through the open window declaring the happiness of escape. I speed toward the territory of transgression, the promise of chaos. I follow roads that lead nowhere, that double back on themselves, that turn into gravel and then dirt, that become correction line trails. I refuse to read the signs, take unmarked detours, even cross into fields that circle rows of mowed hay. A mere habit, bootlegger's *vitesse*.

The Alberta Temperance and Moral Reform League was formed in 1907 by the Reverend W.G.W. Fortune. Fortune was one of those clergymen who claimed that hotel proprietors doped liquor and picked their customers' pockets, as if drinking were merely ancillary sin. A true zealot, he scoured the province reporting liquor infractions to the Attorney General, who averted his eyes.

Addiction cousins rote and its consequences. Repetition is good for poets, but not for the snarl of narrative. Duplicity plays curative against harm, pleasure against danger, the relaxing against the stimulating. The plot I flee is Ariadne's thread, the story a dodge of follow and replay. Bring out the artificial smoke, show the props for what they are, not dangerous devices but slaves to their own inarticulate and trenchant iteration. The restless writer is archaic as Graham Greene's craving for physical excitement, sensation even to the edge of pain. Every writer knows how Greene was so bored that he fabricated a toothache, went to a dentist and had a perfectly good tooth pulled, all in order to dispel a terrible case of boredom.

The Women's Christian Temperance Union fought hard to ban alcohol in cough syrup and liquor-filled chocolates. They promoted the signing of abstinence pledge cards. If the victim wasn't ready to give up drinking, he could sign an anti-treating card, promising he would never again buy a round for his friends. Bring on consumption's lonely, friendless death.

I'm cynical enough to measure cultural addictions. The present is thirsty for entertainments, with a passive fondness for excitement one notch above the censorship scale. We linger in the hallways of prurience, quick to slide toward critique if the gossip is not salacious enough or the slander not nasty enough. This is the latest addiction—cruelty. Cruelty practiced with terrible and repetitive stupidity, a determination poisonous as it is superficial, disgust and its leanings poised to interject between generosity and gratitude. The model is the lifeboat game, *Survival*, *The Weakest Link*, artificial estrangements, damning indictments of human mean-spiritedness. This craven love of cruelty, the ghastly zeal with which we wish for the least manipulative to fail, the traps laid for the unwary, is recreant habit.

Who were the women of the WCTU? White ribboners, humourless, full of zeal. No tolerance for a tipple, but smiling, seductive, they modelled delicious hats and fur neckpieces and wondrous muffs, rewarding themselves with a little of the say that they were so seldom given. Besides, the WCTU gave them excuses for tea parties, parades and speeches, the temptations and delights of public performance. They'd been quiet, long-suffering, and here was a chance to let some of that pent-up energy rip, exert some influence on a world eager to embrace change.

In a novel, addiction feels too staged, as if it were a Superman costume, patched together with prefigured phrases of daily speech. I long to meet Orwell, to ask him why he chose his *nom de plume*, his Eric Blair, his aspidistras. I imagine he wore a cigarette dangling from his lower lip, just like Jimmy Dean, hostile to operatic mimesis. He lessoned how to enjoy excess, an elegiac attachment to what is bad for us and worse for others. Epidemic debilitation, the wasteland of love and loss, with its attendant desire for drama. The high sentence of meeting, mergence and then disintegration, coming together only to split up, sadness and rejection heady as love. This addiction to falling in love, being in love, unrequited love, unbalanced love, broken love, the agreeable madhouse of love, the promised asylum of ecstasy. No wonder there's a swamp of newspaper ads, dating services, meet and melt matchmakers.

Bring out the pharmacopoeia for feelings.

Crusaders condemned the liquor traffic as the curse of the cradle, the nightmare of the marriage bed. There were weeping women and anguished children and fat bootleggers. There were hip flasks and parades and speeches and the evening before prohibition came into effect, June 30, 1916, everyone bellied up to the bar and savoured the last long sip.

The cure for sentiment is to invest in the brooding side of things, the humours of the blood gone slow and turgid, the sludge of hope drifting under low-slung bridges across rivers that refuse all glacial parentage. The temptations of gloominess tinge a delicious mourning, the black armband of incipient gloom, the slow erosion of morose shadow. The melancholy are tempted by windows, knives, lengths of rope, deep and shallow lakes, concrete abutments, the raw grate of poison cooling the blood, the warm embrace of snow in the dark of winter, the gamble of a gun, the body lurching in front of a train. So much for the bloat of frustration and depression, how anxiety interposes itself between act and consequences, wish and fulfillment, poison and its workings. Madame Bovary was addicted to books; so was Anna Karenina. The words merely brought them face to face with desires more lethal and unforgiving than love. They were taken with the mystery and paradox of addiction, its push and pull. Consume and consummate are doubles, but does satiety efface the taste that aroused both hunger and priapism? Debilitation, debt, the juice of arousal bewitched by danger, disorder its own seduction. Until that very bewitchment becomes tedious, not dangerous but merely repetitive. We love what makes us sick. And thus we are sick. And not roses either.

Alberta resisted being dry. However many liquor laws were introduced, there were always loopholes. Breweries never stop fermenting, and during prohibition Albertans could order booze through the mail. Strong drink was responsible for squalor and initiative, iniquity and vice. During the dry period, Edmonton's Strathcona Hotel served as the Westminster Ladies College. Imagine what they learned.

What real addiction am I capable of? I fall asleep after one glass of wine, can't bear the tyranny of gambling machines, and find the taste and smell of cigarettes repulsive. If I succumb to anything, it is to the macabre, stories of interesting deaths, murderous accidents, decapitations, ghoulish undoings. Mistakes that were made fifty years ago fascinate me, suicides make my mouth water. I am addicted to solitude, addicted to gossip, addicted to witches, addicted to adversity, addicted to howling winds, to bolts of thunder, to doing laundry, to driving too fast, to the sound of the cello, to sex in the morning, to bouquets of sage, to the sound of snow underfoot. For a few weeks this summer I find I am addicted to the Latin names for prairie birds. The crows thump across my roof in the mornings, eager to waken me. *Quiscalus quiscula* is the name of a large blackbird common to Alberta, not to be confused with *Corvus brachyrhynchos*, the common American Crow, which haunts Alberta's skies with its mocking caw, caw, caw, and which eats anything and everything, from carrion to grain.

Prohibition devoured the raucous west. Men could blame women for taking away their whiskey, but men—and not just parsons and nervous politicians—voted prohibition in. Still, there was plenty of drinking. Making alcohol was not prohibited, only its in-province sale, so people in Humboldt, Saskatchewan ordered booze from Edmonton and people in Lethbridge, Alberta ordered booze from Fernie, BC, an exchange that went on until Ottawa, smelling some missing taxes, outlawed alcohol's manufacture.

The most scandalous pleasure is solitariness, silence. It's fed my addiction to death's happy closures, the text's finality. The end of the story, like the end of the affair, inevitable seizure, finesse, fini, execution, discharge, fulfillment, ultimate embrace. I contemplate writing a book about ways to die in Alberta, begin to make a list of possibilities. Death by drowning—in flooded rivers, deceptive creeks, elegant bathtubs. Death by animal—the crushing weight of a horse falling on its rider, the leap of a hungry cougar, the quick rush of a biting dog, the trample of a buffalo. Death by snow, its cold arms holding out a promise of sleep. Death by strangulation, asphixiation, suffocation. Death by the virulent, the pernicious, the baleful. Death by loneliness, the coyote's howl floating through frosty dawns, the implacable sky an overturned bowl. Death by marriage and children. Death by politics, death by radio, death by railway track. Death by drinking.

Even after prohibition, nobody stopped drinking. Druggists and doctors, who could prescribe alcohol, became the most popular members of the community. Prescription scrips were worth gold—until some civil servant realized their black market potential and limited doctors to writing 150 alcohol prescriptions per month. There was a booming business in counterfeit scrips.

It could be the Calvinist in me, but I am fond of characters who subvert their good behaviour and flee fulfillment. I'm jealous of those who resist the brisk detonation of the alarm clock, those who can work at night and sleep all day, who refuse the 24-hour signal, who swipe aside clocked habit. The ones who turn a blind ear to the crack of icecubes and "Hurry up please, it's time," those who know where to find after-hours speakeasies and jazz clubs.

Those in charge of policing prohibition were often tempted by the goods they were supposed to confiscate, and many a policeman spent a happy hour singing over the alcohol he was expected to spill. One zealous group of policemen drank everything they had seized at a local still. Waking the next morning, hung over, they realized they needed some hair of the dog, both to face the day and because all the evidence against the man they had arrested was gone. They had to go to another bootlegger to put some liquor in the barrels so that the first could be charged in court.

I succumb to a case of Baudelaire, old translations, new translations, editions and their dignities, their demonic profundities, the dying threads of what was poetry now a pretension utterly debased, sickened and profligate, words detached from both espionage and verity. For a few days I board with Baudelaire, rent cheap rooms on the *Ile Saint Louis* with him, scrub the bare boards on my hands and knees to assuage his ill temper, sea voyages already memories, improvidence a habit sick with the misery of funeral expenses, their pomp and velvet cords, let there be quarrels and restitutions, we are obsessed with the *nouveau*, Gautier and Paradis and Delacroix, enthusiastic syphilis, health and finances together spiralling down, down, the long toilet of time, and in the same year that Canada becomes a country, Baudelaire dies in his mother's arms. The bad boys always do, renounce their profligate addictions for their mothers, while their true addictions are to their mothers. Let that be a lesson to all virgins, demons, monsters, martyrs, wives and lovers, I've drunk too long at his fountain, the not-so-old reprobate, and I stumble out into the sunlight, blinded and weak, reeling from my bender, the intoxications of those rank and festering flowers rotting in their vases.

There were loopholes as big as barn doors. People invented liquor, stockpiled liquor, imported liquor, and the breweries of Alberta corked bottles and shipped them off to B.C. and Saskatchewan, while Saskatchewan and B.C. shipped bottles to Alberta. Bootleggers were making a good living and the Alberta Provincial Police declared that it was impossible to enforce the damned law, moral suasion be damned.

Addictions come from boredom, the indifference of time to the urgencies of departing trains and lines of traffic, the thick swell of summer midnights demanding recompense for their darkness. Habit's a cousin to selfabsorption, sociopathy's an eager score, warnings are siren calls, and the worse the effects the greater their desirability. I arrive at a hypothesis. Only when we reach the zenith of how much we love something or someone, only when we understand how utterly in thrall we are, can we give up the addictive substance or person. The double benefits of double negatives. Knowing how much I love, I am finally able to resist, refuse my shackles and turn toward the beacon of an alternate addiction. Survival or consolation, the bone-deep thrum of capitulation. Love stories so chronic are rare now; they've become simulacra, tinged by seduction and agreement.

Everybody got tired of the game, the lying and smuggling and bartering and chasing and enforcing, although drinking's attraction increased with its forbidden state. Women drank, teenagers drank, horses drank. Drinking was the forbidden zone that tested the adventurous.

We take our marching orders from the technology of repetition, habituation's illness. Farewell to the distant shadow world, the world away from worlds, and welcome to recovery. As if cure were a destination, a similarity disorder. This *ostranenie* will make strange, break the need to see events the same again and again, spectatorship broken out of expectation. Alienation transforms addiction to an aesthetic transcending dependence, craving, habit, tolerance, chronic or acute behaviour, trauma, narcotic, analgesic, transportation. Inveterate, *comme d'habitude*, implanted, instilled, inculcated, routine. A fashion.

Wet and Dry camps faced each other across the coulee of difference, until those in favour of a nip or two discovered the word "moderation," and Moderation Leagues, backed by breweries, began to lobby for change, claiming that 30% of the population was trying to control the other 70%, and that the effect of this imbalance was to make the bootlegger, that outlaw producer, a sympathetic romantic figure bent over copper coiling in a little bush shack, the real hero of the story.

Resorting to escapade, I pick up Marian Engel (not as famous as Richler and Purdy, the now-eulogized booze-boys), a breath almost forgotten. In Engel's brilliant short story "The Tattooed Woman," the character wants her age and life experience to be recognized. When her husband dumps her for a younger version of herself, neat and unmarked, she is calm but incensed. Once addicted to her own self-abnegation, the discarded wife becomes an artist addicted to carving small stars on her forehead, slashes on her cheeks, arabesques on her breasts. Of course, her addiction arouses disgust, curative impulses, doctors, shrinks, although the perfect doctor finally tells her that she should travel to a tropical destination because the scars will result in a striking tan, a badge of honour.

Clause D of the referendum—"Government Sale of all Liquors, Meaning thereby the Sale of all Liquors by or through Government Vendors. Beer to be consumed on Licensed Premises and in Private Residences. Wines and Spirits to be purchased in limited quantities under permit issued by the Government, under Government Control and Regulation"—repealed prohibition. The government had figured out that the liquor traffic was a financial asset, and government-sponsored and controlled liquor vendors were the solution. The Alberta Liquor Control Board, a body that still imports alcohol, grant permits, licenses premises and outlets, was born, wielding an omnibus of clauses, from fines for drunkenness to licence fees to hours of purchase. Hotels selling beer had to sport a certain number of bedrooms. Female employees were not allowed in bars. Entering a designated Alberta Liquor Control Board Vendors Store became a public declaration, frowned on by nosy neighbours. Premises seeking a license had to provide good character references. Interdict lists were kept, and drunkenness was strictly monitored. Any place caught with "disreputable women" on the premises would have its license revoked. "Ladies and Escorts" policed sexual morality and public bars were as low-ceilinged, hard-chaired, and uncomfortable as possible. If drinking was to be a recreation, it was best a recreation to be suffered.

She peers out from behind my fascinations, the addictive one, my double, my other. A woman like me, with different-coloured eyes, the first marking of my sinister affection. Face separated from its halved denunciation, the twinge of a person who is and lives in the world, but always more eager to read about living than to live. The stasis of the page marking the coffin that waits for all writers, the celebrated self-transcendence of the texted affection, more than the first kiss or the curled lip of suspense. Defeat is built into every desire. To exorcise addiction is a fond hope, an amulet against the parallels of experience, Circean ordination. I am as desperate for a page as others are for a drink.

Works Cited

Brooks, Peter. 1993. *Body Work: Objects of Desire in Modern Narrative*. Cambridge: Harvard University Press.

Baudelaire, Charles. 1982. *Les Fleurs du Mal*. Boston: David R. Godine.

Colette, *Collected Works*.

Engel, Marian. 1985. *The Tattooed Woman*. Markham: Penguin.

DeLillo, Don. 1997. *Underworld*. New York: Scribner.

——. 1991. *Mao II*. New York: Viking.

——. 1988. *Libra*. Toronto: Lester & Orpen Dennys.

Thurman, Judith. 1999. *Secrets of the Flesh: A Life of Colette*. New York: Knopf.

Woolf, Virginia. 1937. *To the Lighthouse*. New York: The Modern Library.

2

Junky

Dave Margoshes

> *"Writing only leads to more writing."*
> — Colette

You lie in the dark. You float on your back in bed but sleep is not your friend. Your eyes are wide open, staring up at where you know, beyond the darkness, is the ceiling, each crack in the paint, each water stain, each corner cobweb, intimately known to you. Yes, you have lain this way, open-eyed and staring, in daylight too, trying to remember something, trying to forget something.

Moments before, just as you were about to sleep, the poem came to your campfire and began to howl, just outside the reflections of light, in the darkness where you could not see it but could hear it, could feel it. It howled and snapped at the scraps you threw to it, but it wasn't satisfied. Now it is in your mind, no longer a wolf but an amoeba, a jellyfish, that amorphous, changing shape, refusing to take shape.

For it to do so, you know, you must rise, as silent as you can in the depth of night the partner of your bed has no desire to know, you must creep upstairs to the room where your computer hunches in the dark like a wild animal daring you to tame it. You must lasso that beast, throw a bridle on it, and stare, your eyes becoming adjusted to the light, at its gleaming eye.

Then, only then, if your memory has not failed you, will the poem begin to take shape, tearing itself from your mind like a breech birth, coming feet first and howling again into this world from its own.

Thus is your hunger satisfied, and only thus. And only then, later, will you be able to sleep.

The poem—no, the tale the poem tells, the elusive tail of the narrative waiting to be seized—is a fever. It is a sweat. It inhabits you, soaks you, leaves you dry, your mouth and eyes dry. It is cold turkey for supper every day, wanting to come into this world, yet wanting only its own privacy. It makes you howl outside the ring of light of the campfire, begging for its scraps. Why do we pursue it? Better to ask why it pursues us.

Is the writer an addict? The question is naïve. Yes, the writer must write—just as the painter must paint, the dancer must dance—in a way the accountant does not have to crunch numbers, the fireman does not have to quench flame. The critic does not have to analyze, but the poet must create poetry. To not do so is not so simple a thing as to change career or vocation, it is to deny what the poet is, as much, say, as the homosexual denies who he is by pretending to be straight. As much as the junky can ignore his junk.

In truth—and here, I muster a deep breath—artists are the homosexuals of the vocational world, the queers who cannot properly fit in, who strut and wail from the margins. Addicted to what we do as any junky is to his dope, so too are we as shunned by society as any junky, because we are abnormal. It is the nature of the human beast to do, not to create, and those who do create upset the equilibrium, the status quo, just as the queer does with his aberrant sexuality that seeks only recreation, not procreation. They may be valued, but they aren't to be trusted. Who knows what they may be up to next, what havoc they may wreak? Celebrated, sometimes; honoured, occasionally; prodded, probed and analyzed often, still we are shunned. And rightly so. Poor conversationalists, we don't make good dinner party company. Self-absorbed, we make lousy lovers.

Of course, I'm talking of artists, not entertainers, not "recording artists" of pop pap, not action actors, not circus jugglers or talk show exhibitionists. They too, many of them, are addicts—addicted to celebrity—but they are certainly not shunned. Indeed their celebrity casts a shadow beneath which artists shiver. The superior race is worthy, but their primary concerns are other than the creation of art, though many of them are also artists. They are addicted to applause. And, while artists are by inclination mind-blowers, entertainers are mind-numbers; they lull people to sleep, while artists, sleepless themselves, wake them up.

Artists are much akin to athletes, always pushing themselves, stretching, challenging themselves to new personal bests. Athletes, too, are addicts, of course, sweat junkies, who always want to run another mile, hit another ball, take one more lap, to go faster, jump higher. Like the poet agonizing over a comma, athletes too are preoccupied with minute detail, a hundredth of a second. At night, though, they sleep soundly, dreaming of their own exertion; unlike artists, they have no need for the sleepless night because they have no need to create—they are their own creations.

— • —

As I sit at my keyboard, more often than not gazing out my window as the sticks and stones of the story I am seeking to tell coyly refuse to take shape on the page, I often compare my efforts to that of Mother Nature, that most consummate of artists, that Ultimate Junkie. The creation of literature (not to put too pretentious a name to what I do) is not all that unlike the workings of biology. A novel is much like an elephant, a short story like a fox, a poem a butterfly, a venomous spider. All these animals are miracles of biology, the particular form taken to its maximum, its logical extreme. Like the writings I compare them to, all embody equal parts of craft, logistics, imagination and inspiration. As her biographer, Darwin, makes clear, Nature works determinedly, single-mindedly, compulsively to evolve her creatures, to bring them to their highest form, casting away the failures, recreating the successes, honing, polishing. Like Wilde, who remarked famously that he'd spent the morning putting in a comma and the afternoon taking it out, so Mother Nature tinkers, hones, polishes, one compulsive draft after another.

In an essay in *The Globe and Mail* recently,[1] in which he ruminates on the rigours of novel writing as opposed to the relaxed pace of creating poems, Steven Heighton refers to "the narcotic properties of overwork—the exhilaration of constant, aimful activity, the sugary gut-rush of adrenaline, the addictive sense of self-importance... . A novel alters your metabolism. You become hooked on executing, applying, focussing—in a word, on doing."

That's certainly a nice way of putting it, but I'd say the doing involved in novel-making is not measurably different from the doing of surgery for a physician, of arguing before a jury for a lawyer, of poring over his blueprints for an architect, or, for that matter, the intense concentration required of an assembly line worker or computer programmer, the intense physical activity of the steeplejack, the mechanic, the carpenter, the labourer. Doing can always be addictive while you're doing it. But what keeps bringing people back to the doing? For most, it is the security of the paycheque and the habitual aspects of the network of social relationships that accompany most occupational activity.

For the artist, whose pay is often low, who often works in isolation, it's the addiction itself that keeps the doing doing.

This is particularly true for the writer. Consider how much rejection is a part of the writer's life, more so than for most other artists, I think, and much more than people in most other occupations. It's absurd, impossible, to imagine a lawyer who loses as many cases as a writer's normal collection of rejection slips. Could a doctor survive as many deaths in his practice? A teacher as many students who fail? An accountant as many audited tax returns? Even other artists don't have to deal with rejection to the extent writers do. It has to do with the economics and logistics of the various art forms. A singer or band doesn't go seeking a record contract till a body of work is done; it's the same with a painter seeking a gallery. But a writer, who sends out individual stories or batches of poems to magazines, gets rejections on a regular basis. Comparable, maybe, is an actor going to auditions, failing time after time to get a part. But once he does get a part, then he's out of the cattle call for a while. A writer who gets accepted keeps on sending out his work, so the occasional acceptance doesn't do anything to stop the steady stream of rejection. I know there are some writers who click immediately and have nothing but wild success—rave reviews, prestigious prizes, big box-office. But for every one like that there are hundreds, maybe thousands, for whom the writing life is dominated by three negative icons: rejection slips

---

1. *The Globe and Mail*, May 27, 2000, Books, D-22.

prior to publication, bad reviews and disappointing royalty statements afterwards. And yet we go on, cheerfully much of the time, loving what we do most of the time.

— • —

I started writing when I was about 10 but it wasn't until I was 13 that I became a writer.

When I was 10, I was very much in the thrall of Albert Peyson Terhune, who wrote wonderful stories and novels about dogs, mostly collies, that most elegant, intelligent and noble of breeds. The stories I wrote, sometimes actually scribbled on paper but mostly in my head, were also about dogs, usually collies, and sometimes about horses, which I was also crazy about.

When I was 11 or so, I devoured all the *Topper* novels by Thorne Smith—Topper was a very debonair, elderly ghost who took up with a young, very-much-alive couple. Very droll. I started writing stories about ghosts.

When I was 12, I became enamoured of *Penrod*, by Booth Tarkington. Penrod was a boy of about 12 who did all sorts of fun stuff, the best of which was dress up in a trenchcoat and play private eye. Somehow I managed to convince my folks into getting me a trenchcoat for my birthday or Christmas and I took to following people on the street and making up stories about them. Making up stories. It seemed innocent enough.

Something significant in my development as a writer happened to me the spring I was 13. My father was a newspaper reporter and he used to go out of town occasionally on assignments. This year, he had to go away for a week to cover a convention, and he asked me if I'd like to join him for the weekend. Of course, I was thrilled, and on a Friday I took the subway from Brooklyn, where we lived, into Manhattan to the Port Authority Building, where I caught a bus to Atlantic City. This was heady stuff: being on my own, riding the bus, joining my father, staying at a hotel, eating in a restaurant—I remember I had my first club sandwich—being introduced to people by my father as "my son."

This was the first time, I think, that I'd ever been around so many strange adults. Children live in a child's world—the only adults they know, usually, are parents, relatives, neighbours, teachers—people they take for granted and don't find very interesting. Now I found myself sitting in the hotel coffee shop with my father and his friends, reporters and labour leaders. There was, I remember, a man who had lost a hand while fighting in the Spanish Civil War. There was a man who had been a communist and now, my father said—this was his phrase—a "rabid anti-communist." There was a man who'd been a gangster and earned a reputation breaking strikes but now worked for a union and was, my father said, "a pretty decent chap." There was a reporter who I remembered reading about, a man who'd been blinded when gangsters threw acid in his face. There was a man and a woman holding hands—the woman a lovely blonde with very sad eyes—who my father told me only met at gatherings like this because they each had families at home. "They married the wrong people," said my father with a wink.

I started thinking about these people, of course, and, inevitably, started to write stories about them in my head. I had a notebook with me and I jotted down ideas and descriptions and, on Sunday night, on the long bus ride home, I began writing a story about one of these people I'd met—several of them, actually. Somehow, in the sluice of my imagination, the former communist and the married man who loved the married woman merged and became one character, and the former gangster and the blinded columnist developed a grudging friendship. It was a fanciful story but a story completely different from anything I'd written before, about real people, doing real things. That's more or less what I've been doing ever since, as helpless now before the addictive power of the story as I was then.

But that wasn't the most remarkable thing that happened to me that weekend.

My father and I shared a hotel room—there were twin beds—and let me immediately disappoint anybody who thinks this is going to be a child abuse story. Quite the opposite. I had never been alone for so long with my father and I'd never been so close to him. This was the first time since I'd been little that I'd slept in the same room as my father. We undressed for bed together, and that too was a first.

I should mention here, because detail is important to any story, that my father had married late and that I was the last of my parents' children, so my father was about 50 when I was born and on this weekend, he was already in his 60s, his body going soft, his hair thin and grey.

I saw that body in a new light that night in the hotel room and, as we lay in our beds in the darkness, my father's voice drifting disembodied in the air above us, I was struck suddenly and sharply by the certain and unexpected knowledge that he would die, and I was washed over with a powerful, ineffable sense of sadness and loss, almost as if the loss had already occurred. It was absolutely the strongest emotion I'd ever had in relation to my father and it shook me.

But—and here's why I said this incident was a significant development in my life as a writer—at the very same time I was feeling this inexpressible sadness, I was also thinking about writing about the experience and the feeling, about finding a way, somehow, of expressing what seemed to be inexpressible, and I was already, in my head, actually starting to do just that.

"'Tomorrow we'll walk on the boardwalk and watch the waves,'" the man said in the darkness," I wrote in my mind.

"'That will be good,'" I had the son respond, somewhat woodenly.

"Goodnight, son."

"Goodnight, Dad."

Was that my father and I speaking—actual voices hurling words into the darkness of the humming air-conditioned hotel room—or the father and son I was creating, the creatures of my imagination? I didn't know.

Up until that point, I realized—not then, but later—I had been attracted to writing because of the writing itself, the thrill of manipulating language—

what at writers' conferences and university creative writing programs we call craft, although, as I've already mentioned, I didn't have much of it at the time. But there's another important part to writing and I had just stumbled into it: I now had something very specific I wanted to write about.

My father was talking—a real person, saying real words—but in my head, I was turning him into a character, turning his words into dialogue, thinking about how to get it right.

I've been doing that ever since.

— • —

In morning's harsh light, the poem that held so much promise in predawn darkness seems an unlikely candidate for inclusion. It's flat, pedantic, lifeless, meaningless. Worse, it's hostile, hissing like a coiled snake as you approach. It wants no part of your attempts to poke and prod it, to understand it, to modify its genes.

But it is yours and it requires attention. You don gloves and a mask to protect yourself against its venom, plug your ears against its cries of protest, its shouts of alarm, its vituperative screams. This is a child refusing its medicine, a sulky colt balking at the sight of a halter. You know better, you have a responsibility, a charge. The poem, after all, is merely a poem, you are the poet, and it is your will that must prevail. If the poem writes itself, then where is the art?

The poem is a colicky baby, a headstrong child digging in his heels at bedtime, a sullen teenager dreaming of a place of her own, but the poet is the parent; it is the poem's life, most assuredly, but the poet's job to steer the course of that life.

The words cry out, to be stroked, massaged, manipulated. Each comma and dash mewls for attention, every metaphor struts on the page like a peacock, demanding attention. But even above their cacophony can be heard the plaintive cry of the characters, calling out in their loneliness for the helping hand of the author. Beware the author who insists, disingenuously, to having no responsibility for the written product: "I just started typing and the characters took over, did their own thing." There may be an occasional writer who really believes this, but most who adhere to this theory of the creative process are either naïve or mischievous.

In truth, we can't keep our hands off our characters because we know it is they who carry the stories we seek to tell. We mould their bodies—in our own image or the image of some other, lesser, god; we clothe them, give them bad habits, moral creeds, nervous tics. We put words in their mouths, thoughts in their heads, stir their loins. It is with our characters, perhaps, that our addiction is most ruthless, most demanding. Forever fussing, straightening their ties, primping their hair, correcting their grammar, we just can't let them alone, any more than our addiction can leave us alone. They are our plaything; we are the plaything of our habit.

And sometimes, like any junky, we are seduced by our addiction into less-than-exemplary behaviour, reduced by it to sullen ruffians. Poor company. Unresponsive lovers. It's hard to be civil with a monkey on your back.

Confession

Steven Ross Smith

i.

looking up from scribing in this mossfringed grove i see an eagle circling. she stretches a talon to scratch her underwing, plucking, from her body, setting adrift, a single white feather. feather floating. dropping, as she thermals up, loss-adorned. feather, current-borne— cleft, wordless, hollow-shafted.

utterance is loss. and prop. squirming on this page. my father a roil of words. words attempt. are a crumbling shore. a breaking sky. i forage. i store them in my pockets, in my satchel, in every room of my house. they fall from me. from every edge. levied. verged. a phrasing of birds a-wing in my grove. wrentit chatter-rattles incessantly. chickadee, warbler, towhee scuffle and cheep. my ears tingle with twitter and trill. i sit still. wordless. whisper of eagle-shadow brushes moss and fern. i imagine unknowable eagle-thought. i know my father well, but he is a mystery. so too the white-headed minds of baldies skirting islands and coastlines. writing, i am coastal, edging. hunger draws me to it.

wave-worn rock, the pressured surround. the strand/ed choice. islanded. skittery. at sea, pretending calm. sea, steely blue almost white, at high tide, licking rocky outcrops. land-limbs. my arm jars the cup. coffee spatters. such staining, and words. miles away in a hard glinty room Grandma Evelyn is hardly eating or speaking. her voice chemo'd, empty. i am bereft. without ideas for her. i am a beggar, circling a lack.

trawling, i want diction, syntax. coarse or airy. wordpour. currentflow. feather-drift. white-crowned sparrow, high in spruce, trills over chain saw's biting descant. the ferry queen hovers and spills passengers. hollow rumble in my head. island full of dream-balm mulled from twenty-six herbs and stones. i have spun. am dizzied by water's surround. her voice a bare whisper my father cannot hear. loss-fringed. lapping deficit. he strains after syllables vanishing into the dark unheard. waterwords whisper *drink me*. i am his blood but not his cochlea. can't hear for him. i strain. salt grits the furrows of my forehead, the creases of my neck. parched mouth. not reading.

lips or symbols. am stranded. nowhere to go but north and south. looping. guzzling directories, rumpled lists. scavenging an inkdrop, squeezing feath-erdry alphabets for juice.

ii

chainsaw gnaws its whiny raga. from the path dogs spill, and strangers with questions and accents. Norwegian perhaps. i am discreet. restrained. cover my name. under tongue cover we invent identities. *nice day*. decipher, hedge. we are characters. read of gamblers, of penchants for confession, asphyxia. I'd be reading right now but for this, but for you, now reading. but for strangers. letters dangle. serif-hook. dog-slouch. i'm Gullivered by stakes and loops. loss-adorned. the pressured surround. i squirm, beg mercy. i search and search for myself in the mystery of patterning that might reveal. blind turning. the hand slackens. the game stacks. recombinant DNAlphabet derives me. drives. desires me. i am ravished by erased codes. cast neither this nor that way, by my own encryption. the maze, a white-tipped sea. dog-tail wagging farewell through the gate.

marker day. transition. trace. five and one half decades falling away. enu-meration. annum versary. this scribble. talon-scratch. poke of dark symbols across the island i am. surrounded by years, self-looped in trees. bush and moss cushion my shores. and here, a stump, a rock. grazed shin. i am amazed in the philosopher's grove. words should come to ease, shaped as great thoughts. islanded among salal and cedar. near foxglove and yellow warbler. i'm a-buzz, a travelling thought-pulse, sputtering from a small space. sur-rounded by sea and flesh and land that falls away. a fallen tree is an archway. a lover's arching back, a vowel. the tongued exchange slips through in mem-ory. and time. through and up. slope-climber. peaked. stunned and ecstatic. i cry out—life-vowel of breath. i land. am island. circling self. i can't remem-ber a quarter century. can circle the day. on a grid. in mind. one half decade back, the recallable scene. see my son born and self-in-him borne into this world and see the island forming from the sea and see himself becoming and myself and his struggling miraculous mother and forget all loss. buoyed and wordless. boyed. and above, a circling of eagles.

i am older. the buzzing itself is not annoying. i am usually waking up about now. sun is a low blaze, breaking through the trees. i have read a few thousand words since rising. freed them. was it wind calling? tires on the gravel road? the pressured surround. between two mountains. here on the slope of one, looking up i see the cedar with a forking trunk. from a strange perspective far below the branching. syntax should adapt like that. avoiding the prescribed. you can forget sex. almost.

concentration is avoidance, or avowal. point of view. Grandma Evelyn is surrounded by machines. anchor-weight, down-draft. she's eating little. a friend of mine doesn't eat, but she is young and her body keeps going. hunger is primal. air is a tough suck. not everyone eats. my father has said he will not. if you can't hear your lover, why eat? replace food with emptiness, but hunger never lets you forget. a sizzle of chestnut-backed chickadees buzzes my head while anna's hummingbird rests on a blossom-less broom branch. i have not been cycling. pelvis static, legs longing for motion. i am a still island lapped by birds. moss is a furry coat on this log, buffed by fern fronds.

my word account hungers. yet i owe. sometimes i am silent with loved ones. mother, father, lover, son. feather-silent, in partial amnesia, we are hungry, desperate. deny, then gulp at every offering. can't stop the whispers, the dark drift. i tried avoidance. but all is erasings. blade-bite. gum-rubber crumbs.

iii.

it wasn't so much, as i said, the buzzing, as the idea. bees, after all, need the nectar of the salal bud. salal is prodigious, leather-leafed and berried. idea of sting. not as bad as stung. but unnerving. i'm using almost ordinary speech. am i? poetic tongue and fibre set aside. or is it play that grips? the difference a letter trips. this premise a promise. does it achieve acuity? promiscuity? it's not easy, with words. nectar-suckers. feather shafts.

i know my father well but he is a mystery. inside each of us a secret. hidden earmarks and coverts. flashes seen. taking off. coming down. you know by now of my regard for my father, and that i seek birds, their habitats, identities. traits challenge. flipping through guide books. forgetting to look in the need to name. hunting like mad through glossary, index. i cannot live a day without identification. the pattern of, clue to, the veiled, greater scheme. sometimes speech blinds me. can't find the words, their vanishing syllables. how they fly our longing with such ease. *don't leave me*, in dad's diction. in his mouth. as if through a hollow. well-deep. farewell-deep.

disappointment perhaps. deep, unparsable desolation. fear of. or fending off. loss. desire and dream turned on themselves. a bent way. the crush. circling in obsession. the pressured surround. wish for control. hangover, withdrawal, letter-quiver. hovering ideas. high hopes, blown sky-high. shattering of hope. toxins taken in a blink. allergen-bite. anaphylaxis. air is a tough suck.

iv.

my eyes blink to a cathedral of fir and cedar. to my left the fallen mother-trunk, ahead the sunbathed meadow. anguish is primal, loss-adorned. danger game. strokes and whorls and spars that never cease to swirl me. letter-forest. ecology is not the issue. or is it? a way to avoid futility. disappointment is to bemoan obsessive about anything else. or reach for the seratonin uptake inhibitor. the mystery of photosynthesis. but speak and words are sage, fall from me, wordshorn-one. words return to lap at edges. stroking bits of me away.

tangents. we tangent, me and my other. remember that word from grade ten geometry. the propositions. no ability to say no. or stop making them. the bald eagle is overhead. i am always in flight, wanting to taste everything but the allergen. to settle rarely. words let me love and leave 'em. words are promiscuous. they have other mouths. will come across for anyone. a stalk of oatgrass springs free of a clutch of salal in berry. white topsy-turvy teardrop berries reaching out beneath shiny leaves. i think deer eat them, but

I'm no authority. i first thought snow-drops. later they turn blue, the berries. i like that. the play of colour. and alphabet. its logical illogic. some people clutch convention for control. or their loved ones. i can't find a rule to suit me. an injection to fix. i am an empty wallet. wallets disappoint, empty or lost. everything at risk. toxins seek Evelyn's body's pockets as a market of exchange. deals or no, loss calls. a word is an offer i can't refuse. i am easy, wanting when propositioned by any letter. i give in. i pause, contemplate escape. read words that fly from me. words not anchored here.

v.

a fly on the page. the first ferry of the day. or have i said that? few people on-deck. those not complacent or weary. i can't hear them. hear thrumming though. and buzzing translucent wings. a black glyph surrounded by white. Grandma Evelyn on intravenous support. word ions lurking beneath any report, a sous-text. inject-text. the flat black clouds menace the mainland forty kilometres away. i am in sun. it needles my bare arms. winged glyph returns, sitting above the letter *d*. the tidal race through the pass is obviously complex, turns and turns on itself. its currents chiaroscuroed by the rising sun reflecting off riplets and pulls. my son crowns from his first sea into air. fish are sucked in the watery draw. capsizing boats, drownings. what if that *d* were the last remaining letter of the last alphabet. how would i use it? that last island surrounded by eternity. what sounded letter will be the last to fall from my lips in my slipping clutch of the glyph before i glide into tongueless white?

vi.

a basset hound has limited vocabulary. his tongue hangs, he cares not. un-self-conscious of this, or his short legs and drooping ears. letter *m*. crest and trough, white sea these strokes try to fill. the pass is a vein between islands. possibility. his bark a churr in his throat. i used to be a poet. i am writing sentences now. where is the line, drawn? feathered out. Evelyn has stabilized. her platelets were down but they gave her a transfusion of normal blood. a market of exchange. third morning ferry, *of nanaimo*, draws through the pass. queens in procession. regardless. i have nothing to say with authority. the sea. the self. that sparrow, white-crowned, singing from the same branch many words later, and days. no point resisting its song. a walking stick may aid you. a twig. or stylus. serifs hook. whatever holds you up or gets it down. seraph. needle-song. inside each, a secret. I'm no Tom Waits. nor his brother Trouble. though distress dogs me.

vii.

words are bark. are sap. are branching, root-clutch. similes are not precise. or like themselves. they eke. the dictionary is my chief supplier. or is it? (which came first?) random cut. an *oxfordized high*. high school was not. shriek of the broom-saw is too shrill for contemplation. an island is like that. you can only get so far before you're back. a small paragraph. inside each of us a mystery we circle. through the clouds, sun casts fairy-glitter on water. a feather. shadow on this page. these mornings are sacred. the miracle of pho-tosynthesis. birdsong, edges, distance, juncture of light and tissue. loss-adorned. pouring.

my father is an island. word-shored. in a roil of words. pontifications bridging, to the next and next. words, his gnaw and rah and rat-a-ta-tat. no stopping. words lap at him, lap from him, transgress his skin in all directions. he devours their black symbology. they are his hors d'oeuvres, his entrée, his bran, his dessert and beverage. they enter his eyes his ears his porous flesh. he devours them. his being, the word. his raison d'être, the word. his risk and resilience, the word. his hiding place. the pressured surround. he has stopped. weakness and silence now his mode. wind-buffed feather. the re-sign-ation. departure of signs from the unsaid. i am left with the ashes of his phrase. *under that rock on your island* he said. unsentencing.

hunger draws me to it. wet or feather-dry. diction is what i hold on to in the coming apart of things, the feathering down. i write, hollow-boned. the sea is steely blue and swallows at high tide. i cling. coffee spatters on my page. such staining and words.

— Dedicated to Evelyn, and Clarence

4

Happy Minute:
A Northern Writer's Somewhat Chronological Reflections on Addiction

Jeanette Lynes

1. Arcadia, circa 1912

Few writers understood the intrinsic link between the addictive predisposition and the rise of North American capitalism better than Stephen Leacock. The focal point of his 1914 satirical masterpiece *Arcadian Adventures With the Idle Rich* is the posh, well-appointed "Mausoleum Club," meeting place for the twentieth century's new capitalists—the Bill Gateses of soda water. Leacock, describing the "Club's" patrons, articulates an intriguing psychology of addiction:

> *You may see them sitting about in little groups of two and three under the palm trees drinking whiskey and soda; though of course the more temperate among them drink nothing but whiskey and Lithia water, and those who have important business to do in the afternoon limit themselves to whiskey and Radnor, or whiskey and Magi water. There are as many kinds of bubbling, gurgling, mineral waters in the caverns of the Mausoleum Club as ever sparkled from the rocks of Homeric Greece.* (3)

This scene possesses several addictive elements. First, its sense of aesthetic proportion is seductive: "little groups of two and three." There's syntactic balance in "whiskey *and* Lithia," "whiskey *and* Radnor," "whiskey *and* Magi water" (my emphasis). There's the allure of the simulacrum, a simulated landscape that stands in for tropical and classical worlds. "Palm trees" don't grow indoors in most parts of North America. "Homeric Greece" is about as remote as Fantasy Island. There's the linguistic glamour of high-end drinking; in other words, entry into Leacock's exclusive club of power and privilege includes the right to say "Lithia water" and "Magi water." Who would not want to say these words?

After hearing "Lithia" and "Magi," this writer can't live without them. Both her eyes and ears are addicted to their music and exoticism.

In Leacock, "liquid assets" are also discursive assets. His wealthy folks have access to every shading of linguistic variety. Now, Leacock's characters aren't writers; nevertheless, they're aware of a relationship between social standing and discursive efficacy. For instance, Leacock's satirical portrait of Mr. Rasselyer-Brown, a drinker who made a fortune on coal and wood, is a veritable happy hour of euphemism. Mr. Hyphenated-Brown's day-long parade of drinks are rationalized by renaming them: "eye-openers" (morning drink); "bracers" (support for breakfast); "something to keep out the damp"; "something to keep out the cold"; "tone-ups"; "nips" (for night-time composure, but "not really a drink") (59–61). While we might smirk at the distortion of reality, we surely admire the linguistic ingenuity. In the world of high finance, Leacock tells us, "a man has got to drink" (60). Even though Rasselyer-Brown is what we might today call a functional alcoholic, nowhere does Leacock's narrator use the A-word. In fact, we are told more than once that "there was no excess about Mr. Rasselyer-Brown's drinking" (60). His drinking is simply part of his work.

"Arcadia's" bubbling fountains of whiskey and Magi water are symptomatic of a deeper addictive dependency. As Leacock succinctly puts it: "when you have once grown used to [the gurgling caverns of the Mausoleum Club], it is as impossible to go back to plain water as it is to live again in the forgotten house in a side street that you inhabited long before you became a member" (3). Leacock's characters are hooked on upward social mobility and conspicuous consumption, yes, but underlying this is the book's deeper love affair with new technology—the machines that make the submersible pumps in the spouting fountains and the bubbles in the soda water. The machines that spawn brave new vocabularies—"Lithia" and "Magi"—spoken and swallowed. The technology of drink-making runs neck in neck with the print technology needed to ensure continued aesthetic novelty of attractive labels and names. "Mike's Hard Lemonade." "Bacardi Breezer." "Mississippi Mudslide." There's a poetry here that's difficult for a writer to ignore. Inventing names for things is part of the writer's work, too. This writer's dream job would be thinking up names for the bubbling, gurgling substances lining the shelves of the Liquor Control Board.

Where did Leacock's Mausoleum Club end up? No doubt, exclusive clubs still exist. But mainly, the club democratized into the watering holes of today's late-capitalist era. In said holes, there is still the same addiction to simulacra (whether it's Big Easy or Italian Café, neither of which really exists), and the big machines are right in your face. Take "East Side Mario's" in any-town, North America. "Mario" has a blender for the apocalypse. The size of a cement-mixer, it turns out the coldest, most seriously pulverized margaritas imaginable. It's fast and mean. It's a privilege to sit, elevated on the bar stool, in Toronto's Eaton Centre or car-dealers' strip in Thunder Bay, or whichever patch of concrete Mario has conquered. This is the new club. You get to watch the machines, and you don't even mind paying the six dollars. If "Mario's" is too crass for your taste—the peanut shells on the floor and the computer trivia game might get on your nerves—you can watch while massive vats brew your Peculiar or bitter in one of the new brew pubs. Often, you can even brush up your fake English accent.

If an electronic device, plugged into this writer's brain's pleasure center, measured the happiness level generated by a perfectly made frozen margarita and then a beautiful line of poetry, the readings would be the same.

2. The Big Chill, Later in the Twentieth Century

If Andrew Barr is to be believed, by the mid-1950s much of America was addicted to ice. The ice man, of course, was eventually replaced by refrigerators, even in the southern states. A cold brew after work became every American's God-given right. Cold became hot. Gwyn Prins, a British anthropologist, argued that Americans "were addicted to air-conditioning" because

> they wished to dissociate themselves from the poor blacks who
> sweated in hot weather in the South, and from the poor whites
> who had once labored in sweatshops in the cities of the North... .
> By indulging in air-conditioning, many people are distancing
> themselves from the primitive and brutal life of the frontier... .
> They are trying to live down a collective folk memory. (quoted in
> Barr, 59–60)

This dissociation from a sordid, undesirable past is likely not that different from the suppressed, "forgotten house in a side street" in Leacock. The more advanced the machine, the colder the drink. The colder the drink, the greater the potential for numbness, for disclaiming a world we neither believe we belong to any longer, nor to which we would wish to return. A young American writer named Scotty leaned, once, into the bitter wind of St. Paul, Minnesota. Does he want to go back there? No way.

In America, a cool, detached civilization can be simulated, for a price.

3. North to the Land of Broken Blenders

What of Canada? We're a long way from Mississippi and Homeric Greece. We have our share of collective guilt, to be sure. But can we dissociate ourselves from the frontier? Do we want to dissociate ourselves from the past? Ice is no big deal for us. We just open the window and reach for a bottle on the outside sill. Machines are everywhere. Winches winch and heavy machines hack away at the rock, but this doesn't convince us that we're a culture evolving in some great, mythic direction. The truth is, most of our machines are broken. Having tried to order margaritas at a wide range of lounges across Canada, this writer can report that the most frequent response is, "our blender doesn't work." Some grant funding would be required to hammer this empirical research down definitively, but some fairly extensive preliminary field work reveals this: we are a nation of broken blenders.

4. Singing Pencils

Canadians can't blend, merge, integrate, whirr like fury, mobilize upwardly. This is why some of us write. The poet Dennis Lee called us "the evidence

/ for downward momentum" (41). Lee understood the north. Distance, silence, breakage. The onus is on writers to bear witness to our broken, inexplicable world; to gather and map "evidence / for downward momentum." Evidence is all around us; the problem is, it would take much longer to collect and write it down than we're allotted. In the scheme of things, we have about a minute. Happy hour just got a lot shorter.

We can't live here. Too many things are broken. This is also why we write.

George Grant said we were never "here" in the first place. Because we're addicted to the big machines of the south, part of us left a long time ago. Canada is a normal enough contemporary event, a site for "the erosion of the distinction between the real and the imaginary, the true and the false ... the real and the fake"—like "every contemporary event," "a mixture of the real and the imaginary" (Ritzer, 95). A few miles away from where these words are being keyboarded into little ghosts, tourists gather at a site commemorating the Acadian heroine Evangeline. They can't tell if she's real or not.

We've seen the limits of our own simple technology, how quickly, soundlessly, a canoe carrying an artist can disappear forever. We know what happened to the *Edmund Fitzgerald*. We depend on American software technology to record our unblended separateness. Who among us has not been seduced by Microsoft? Those who write with that crude object called a pencil are practically an official endangered species. Even pencils have lost their innocence. This writer owns a pencil that glows in the dark and sings Merry Christmas. This writer shakes with withdrawal when her word-processor doesn't work, hyperventilates when it sends her a "fatal error" message. It's the same distraught, bereft pang as arriving at the Liquor Control Board five minutes after closing and the pyramids of gold and blue bottles gleam through the window but can't be touched and tomorrow is Sunday a thousand miles from nowhere.

We're pebbles without applause.

5. The Pangs of Sunday

The poet Sharon Thesen invented "the pangs of Sunday." She knew. Because it's Sunday on the frontier, there's nothing to do if you don't curl or own a snow machine—that crummy old world of the past is starting to look pretty good. What is being referred to here is not Prins's "collective folk memory," but the unblended, discrete shots from a writer's past. The happy minutes that stand alone, that cannot be pureed in a big glass bowl and sold for six dollars a goblet. Sometimes, this writer would rather be back there than here. The question is, how to get "back there?" Luckily, nearly every northern house has some untapped octane. That bottled vileness friends brought back from Greece. A small airplane-portion of Wild Turkey kept as a souvenir. Up here, we hang on to our pasts. Past-rats. Here's to Freud, for saying that childhood is bottle-shaped, and for being right about that one thing (Gilmore, 150).

Now you're ready to go back. Tap the heels of your skidoo boots together three times and repeat, until you feel yourself going in a reverse direction: "there is no such thing as upward social mobility." When you wake up, you'll feel dehydrated. Don't be alarmed. This is normal, will pass. If possible, take Lithia water.

p.s. If in Alberta, there are "off-sales," an option that may reduce the pangs significantly.

6. Happy Minutes

Dandelion Fields, 1969

This writer was heavily under her mother's influence. An early capitalist, her mother had a good grasp of the concept of goods and services exchange. A neighbouring farmer would clear the laneway with his snowblower in exchange for some of her homemade dandelion wine. His big blade scraped through its gravel's skinny, jagged line even when it didn't snow. Happily, in that age of agrarian decline, dandelions were the best crop. The mother sent the little writer out into the yellow fields with a cardboard box to collect evidence of the dying farm. The writer didn't know it was dying, at the time. It was a manager's secret, of sorts. All she knew was her fingers stained with summer. The same fingers that today tear across the keyboard, chased by spirits.

The Cardinal Motor Inn

This writer had a job, once, waiting on tables. It was 1972, and decadence was a hot beef sandwich. She showed talent and promise, so she was moved to the Dining Lounge, southwestern Ontario's version of the Mausoleum Club. The manager told her secrets. "See that man there? He's the richest guy in the county, made a fortune on a new breed of cattle—wait on him first, whatever he wants." The lounge had paper placemats covered with adorable maps of drinks. A small green dainty thing in a glass: underneath was written "Grasshopper." Or "Pink Lady." "Singapore Sling." "Tequila Sunrise." "Manhattan." The writer had never heard such lovely words. Most people drank things with plain, even ugly, names like "Export." But someone ordered something beautiful often enough to keep her happy. Remind her that she could not live without suns rising in tumblers, maraschino cherries, tiny paper umbrellas. She had one foot in the club, got to say, "another Tequila Sunrise, sir?" The fancy drinks were mixed by shaking them in a silver container. There were no machines. Manual shaking took a long time; there were always pieces of ice left floating like spring breakup. The lounge wasn't air-conditioned. The rich rancher's cattle were bony and white, their name sounded like Charlie. Those weren't the things she loved about the motel world. It was the maps. She'd give anything, now, for one of those diagrams of little coloured drinks, each its own private country, the name printed below. There was a book behind the bar, mixing instructions. Passports into each country. Why didn't she save one? She had no idea she would be so thirsty later. The silver shakers might have made good pencil jars.

Higher Learning, 1975—1985

The writer learned many new words: grog shop, saloon, cantina, road house, dive, sports bar, microbrewery, hegemony. The campus had a pub for each letter of the alphabet. She read poetry in their dark, wooden corners, imagined she was Al Purdy in the Quinte Hotel. She read *Under the Volcano*'s aching ecstasies:

> *what beauty can compare to that of a cantina in the early morn-*
> *ing? ... for not even the gates of heaven, opened wide to receive*
> *me, could fill me with such celestial complicated and hopeless joy*
> *as the iron screen that rolls up with a crash, as the unpadlocked*
> *jostling jalousies which admit those whose souls tremble with the*
> *drinks they carry unsteadily to their lips.* (quoted in Day, 346)

But closing time comes to the cantina, the big, plastic draft jugs are collected in the northern, suburban campus pub, and there is a sense of exile. Despite her best efforts to the contrary, the writer graduates, the devolution begins. In the back of her mind, a sad, little motel, a Tequila Sunrise, a child with a boxful of dandelions.

7. Late Capitalism, 1991

The writer had a job again, at a university with the largest student pub in Canada. Her office overlooked the great grain elevators of Lake Superior. But fewer and fewer ships came into port, and wrecking balls slammed through some of the elevators, leaving a scarred, lunar land of whiteness and block heaters. Neil Young drove through in a hearse one time. On the hill, Terry Fox still runs westward, cast in iron. On days with lethal forty below temperatures, the thought of the poor bastard up there in his gym shorts and his head cast back with its pained expression is enough to make you weep. Make you need a stiff one. At the other end of the sprawl of buildings called, wrongly, a city, there's a stupid fort where hungover students dressed as voyageurs act like tour guides. Their Adidas poke out from under their fake buckskin pants. On a once- prosperous street near the writer's home, sex-trade workers, kids drifted in from Winnipeg, stand on the corner, their thighs exposed even on the coldest nights. There's a hotel there: the Adanac. One night, a young Adanac patron wearing cowboy boots told the writer that he was one wrong turn away from becoming a famous rock star. He had sad cheekbones, wanted directions back to Wrong-Turn Road. There are pickled eggs on the counter in big lab-like jars. Each egg floats, suspended like a once-perfect, round white planet that got stretched by someone big who pulled hard at one end and someone bigger who pulled even harder at the other. "Adanac" is, of course, "Canada" backwards. This is the house joke, and the longer you stay, the funnier it gets. Imagine the Mausoleum Club spiraling down, down, down into its exact opposite, and step into:

> *The Adanac Hotel,*
> *Thunder Bay,*
> *Ontario, Canada,*
> *The world.*

The blender there has been busted for approximately fifteen years and you can still find someone shedding a tear for Patsy Cline. It's a sad little country, but it's a country. George Grant said that "a society only articulates itself as a nation through some common intention among its people" (68). The Adanac is nothing if not intention. Its intention is amber, the silky plum of coke mixed with rum. Spelled backwards, it's "no i tent in" (almost) and if you're absolutely stuck, the bartender will let you camp there for one night.

8. Last Call, circa 1997

A broken, northern place is an ideal place to be a writer. The slag heap of capitalist decline, dumping ground for "downward momentum," stop-over for every washed-up rock band, unofficial national skullduggery capital. In a world of low finance, a writer has got to drink. It's impossible to believe in frontier-dissociation, so a few tone-ups, nips and bracers are always in order. The North can make you very thirsty, can trick you. That's an oasis up ahead? No, it's a declining lake freighter industry. Gotcha. Is all this comedy or tragedy? When the lines begin to blur, you're ready to start writing. This isn't a clear place, will never be; the not-clearness is needed; it instills humility. So do things out there much bigger than the writer. RCMP officers with Pavarotti sirens. Sometimes the writer is spooked, doesn't go outside. She pitched a tent in her living room once, filled it with supplies, a stuffed raccoon, stayed there for three days. Her own wilderness experience without leaving home. The idea of living in a tent in a house was funny as hell. (Only thing better than a simulacrum is a silly simulacrum.) Her employer hammered at the door; she lay silently on her belly in the tent until he went away, kept thinking, "no i tent in." She hopes to write about this someday. She hopes Roots Canada eats its Olympian heart out.

The place is full of spirits. Take Thunder Bay's Inntowner—a completely midnight interior except for one light that makes white clothing glow in the dark. The place is full of walking shirts, disembodiment, reverse beauty. Consumer choice. Fourteen kinds of wine coolers, eight kinds of hard lemonade. And that's just the half of it.

In the North, you can have the apocalypse whenever you want, and if you're a writer, write about it. This is the land of negative capability, driving in the face of doubts, uncertainties, etc., when you can't even see the road. Boreal country where the Macarena drifts across a smaller lake, and you can't tell where it's coming from. This is the world of childhood. You're little here, play games like Beat the Ride Program and Spin the Bottle. Others have toys like speedboats and snow machines—way more cool than Nintendo. The computer is your literary speedboat. Wonder they don't start up a chapter of MANW here—Mothers Against Northern Writers. This is the place where nothing fits together, and it's ok.

I'm decay, you're decay.

You can sit with a bunch of Finnish skiers and drink cheap draft next to a boccie court while watching a powwow on tv. You can climb a whole mountain all by yourself. You can smuggle in pink cowboy boots from Pigeon River,

Minnesota. You can sit on the back of your student's snow machine while she drives you over an old, abandoned mine, your face freezing off. There's talk of closing down another elevator, 200 more men out of work. If this keeps on, no ships will come. Who wouldn't be homesick for all this? Who wouldn't need it like crack, like the sump pump thrubbing away in the tent inside your chest?

Summer lasts for about ten minutes.

The writer has about five minutes left.

A little something to keep out the cold?

Works Cited

Barr, Andrew. 1999. *Drink: A Social History of America*. New York: Carroll & Graff.

Day, Douglas. 1973. *Malcolm Lowry: A Biography*. New York: Oxford University Press.

Gilmore, Thomas B. 1987. *Equivocal Spirits: Alcoholism and Drinking in Twentieth-Century Literature*. Chapel Hill: University of North Carolina Press.

Grant, George. 1965. *Lament for a Nation: The Defeat of Canadian Nationalism*. Toronto: McClelland & Stewart.

Leacock, Stephen. 1969. *Arcadian Adventures With the Idle Rich*. Toronto: McClelland & Stewart.

Lee, Dennis. 1972. *Civil Elegies and Other Poems*. Rev. Ed. Toronto: Anansi.

Ritzer, George. 1997. *Postmodern Social Theory*. New York: McGraw-Hill.

Thesen, Sharon. 1990. *The Pangs of Sunday: Poems*. Toronto: McClelland & Stewart.

5

E-Mail Addiction?:
So Far and Yet So Near

Trudy Govier

It's the first step in every working day. Check the e-mail. Reply right away, get it done. One charm of e-mail is its speed. When it's business, thirty seconds of fast typing and I'm done. It feels like fun: an invitation accepted, request refused, appointment or meeting arranged, document transferred. Equally satisfying is the solicitation deleted. Do I want a free Ph.D. from a well-known non-accredited university? Viagra? Photos of hot college girls in their rooms? New drugs for weight-loss? An opportunity to earn $6,000 a month from home? Delete, delete—so much easier than trying to politely put off solicitations on the phone.

Professional chat is welcome, and provides a sense of colleagues that I cherish—I work alone a lot. For these things, I don't use the delete button and I need more than thirty seconds. Questions about past work: "Can we translate your article on trust and feminist theory into Swedish?" "What did you mean by deductivism? Do you still reject it for the same reasons?" "Can that anthology from the eighties still be obtained? Why did they let it go out of print?" "In that textbook of yours, I think there's a mistake in an example on page 320." "Here's an outline for my thesis on the logic of analogies—remember those papers you published, ten years ago?" "As to that paper you wrote on public apologies, you seem to think it makes sense for one person to apologize for the actions of other people. To me this sounds crazy; how would you reply?" "I attach my thesis on forgiveness and moral debt; can you read it for me?" Family members send messages to arrange birthday and holiday events. There are activist messages about committees, lectures, campaigns and demonstrations for a multitude of causes: environment, peace, social justice

E-mail suits my disposition to handle things quickly, get things out of the way fast, so I don't have to think about them any more. It squashes time, making life faster and faster—an effect not altogether good. In addition to speed and ease, e-mail has entrancing advantages of global reach. By e-mail,

I can contact friends and colleagues in B.C., Ontario, the United Arab Emirates, Missouri, Iqualuit, Holland, the Cook Islands and South Africa just as easily as my neighbour on our own street. Bizarrely, I can often send a message to South Africa and receive a reply more quickly than I can contact my doctor by telephone, though her office is only a few miles from my home.

There's an absorbing character to the whole thing—a distanced, yet misleadingly immediate, confirmation of one's own existence in this chaotically interactive world. I must be somebody, I must have done something—otherwise, how would I be getting all these messages? There's a kind of must-do feel to the whole thing. Could e-mail be addictive? It's got this absorbing character, a fascination hard to switch off, even for a non-tech person like myself. Grant for the sake of argument that the positives of e-mail outweigh its negatives, that e-mail is on the whole a good thing that enriches human life. That wouldn't prove e-mail is not addictive. Whether we are addicted to something doesn't depend on whether it's good or bad overall, but rather on the role it plays in our lives. Even granting that e-mail is a good thing, we could, in principle, be addicted to it. We can, after all, be addicted to something which, considered on its merits and apart from the addictive syndrome, is mostly good. For example, people can become addicted to exercise. In general terms and in moderation, exercise is supposed to be good for us; it's necessary to maintain our muscles, circulation, and general health. For someone addicted to exercise, having to cope without that regular jog or swim feels awful. What it means to say that some people are addicted to exercise is that they need it so much, miss it so acutely if they have to do without, that they organize their lives to make opportunities for it. A man who couldn't set aside time for an old friend in a state of crisis because it would mean that he missed his daily run could be said to be addicted to exercise. To be addicted to something is to have such a compulsory relation to it that it comes to occupy an entirely disproportionate role in one's life. Running may be good for you—but it shouldn't matter that much.

The idea of disproportion is crucial here. It is not simply a matter of the activity or substance playing a dominant role. Suppose that the man didn't set aside time for his old friend because he was involved in a highly passionate new love affair, and on that day, what mattered most of all to him was that he spend every possible free moment with his new love. We might think that his priorities were wrong, but we would not think the allocation of time is disproportionate the way we would if he could not see his friend because he "had to" go jogging. After all, a grand passion is an intense, meaningful, life-enriching and life-changing matter. If it dominates a person's life, in some phase, even if there are compulsive aspects in this domination, one would still not be inclined to say the passion is addictive. The reason, I think, is that the central or dominating role of such a passion can be defended as appropriate, considering what it is.

Consider alcohol, a notorious and damaging case of an addictive substance. Here too, some people are addicted to something which, in moderation and apart from compulsive need, can be considered good in its own right. Alcohol has virtues of taste and sociability, and its relaxing properties mean that in moderation it can be good for one's health. But obviously, these positive aspects don't mean there's no such a thing as alcohol addiction. We can become addicted to alcohol, and those who are have such a strong need to consume it that they will continue to do so even when costs to their health, work, and relationships are terrible and right out of bounds. People so addicted cannot—without serious reform—manage in life without alcohol, so they arrange their lives to obtain it and consume it. The results are often horrifying.

People may become addicted to cigarette smoking. Their bodies, minds, and souls have come to need nicotine, and they will tolerate considerable expense, inconvenience, health risk, and social disapproval in order to get it. People who stand outside at -30°, bare-headed, bare-handed, really need their cigarettes. Freezing in order to smoke gives real evidence of addiction to nicotine. Those addicted to heroin or cocaine have come so acutely to need the highs from these substances that they will find the money and the occasions for use, even when costs and risks are extraordinarily high.

Addictions are characterized not by the quality of an activity or substance in itself, but rather by the compulsiveness of our recourse to it, and the tendency for that recourse to dominate and diminish other aspects of our lives. To say that alcohol, heroin, cocaine, or nicotine is addictive means that there is something about these substances, and the ways many human beings use them, that makes their regular use become compulsive and too prominent in our lives as a whole.

So back to e-mail. Could a person be addicted to e-mail? Is the compulsion to get to the e-mail, see what's there, and deal with it first anything like addiction to alcohol or nicotine? Or likely to become so? Probably not. Many people on holidays manage without their e-mail and enjoy doing so. (Of course, there are others, who take lap-tops and arrange connections so they can continue to get e-mail even when they're far from home.) Perhaps an "e-mail addiction" is more metaphorical than literal. It's not a literal addiction, but more like the "addiction" that some people have to chocolate or fancy coffees. Or perhaps exercise. You might miss the e-mail a bit if you suddenly didn't have it. But that's all it would be—a slightly uncomfortable shift in routine. There's no real need, no compulsion. Millions use e-mail without feeling a compulsion to arrange their daily routine around it; millions use it without its having debilitating effects on their lives. Since millions use e-mail and few are addicted to it, it would seem that e-mail is not the kind of thing that causes or encourages addiction.

A simple conclusion it seems. But in my case, this would understate the story. For me, what has been really important about e-mail is long-distance relationships conducted by writing. Or one relationship in particular, and this is where the question of compulsiveness enters the picture. The intricacies of this relationship go deeper than solicitations, invitations, requests, and family and professional correspondence. It's a relationship I treasure, one I've come to depend on. I miss it when it's not there because my e-mail partner is ill, travelling, busy with his children, or for some other reason away from his computer and my messages. If I had several such e-mail relationships, they would intrude too much into my work and family time. Fortunately, there's only one, with a friend and colleague I write to every day. My messages to him would provide a virtual journal of the last two years, including reflections on shared professional interests, daily happenings, medical problems and anxieties, bits and pieces of reading, development of children, successes and failures, social problems and activist campaigns—just about every feature of my life during this time. I anxiously await the replies, checking first thing in the morning to see if they've come in. If this pattern amounts to an addiction, it could hardly be an addiction to e-mail itself. It would be an addiction to this relationship—or some aspects of it.

But that's too simple. The relationship itself can't be separated from the e-mail, and it's this relationship that gives me a slightly compulsive relationship to that e-mail. It wouldn't be the kind of relationship it is if we mostly communicated in person, by telephone, or by snail mail. If my friend lived down the street, or even in this town, or if we worked in the same department, we would have a very different relationship, one much more affected by the realities of daily life. "I can't talk now, I have to pick up my children." "I'll read your new essay next week if I can, I can't get to it today." "Why did you agree with that material for the calendar entry? It's really unclear." "The pipes burst and I've got to go home, so I'm going to have to cancel our coffee date again." The nature of e-mail preserves it from most such intrusions, which makes e-mail relationships seem easy and undemanding. If the relationship, or the writing that mostly defines it, has addictive qualities, its e-mail structure has a lot to do with that.

JV, my e-mail partner and electronically close friend, lives in Cape Town, South Africa, which is about as far away from southern Alberta as you can get while still remaining on this planet. I've known him for nearly four years now; our intense e-mail relationship has gone on for almost three. JV is twenty years younger than I am. He has a cherished wife and two lively children ages eight and ten. First a junior colleague, he has become perhaps my closest friend—almost all of this through e-mail. Our contact began because we were both philosophers interested in ethical issues of reconciliation, trust, and forgiveness. In 1997 I visited South Africa because somebody there was keen on my textbook on practical argument. At that time, JV was working as a staff researcher for the Truth and Reconciliation Commission. I had become interested in peace politics and related ethical questions about forgiveness and reconciliation. So my host at Rhodes University arranged for me to interview JV in his office at the Cape Town headquarters of the TRC. This first meeting lasted for one hectic hour spilling over with intense and rushed talk about the TRC, retributive and restorative justice, forgiveness, collective responsibility, and as many related themes as we could cram in. Though what we said seemed deep and important while we were saying it, and I am generally pretty good at taking notes, the results on that occasion were too chaotic to be useful. Too much was going on, too fast. Sensing a kindred spirit, I left JV's office feeling regretful and sad, thinking that I would probably never see this person again. I reckoned without e-mail.

In the peculiar non-space of cyberspace, you can establish a peculiar and intense intimacy. Strangely, perhaps sadly, that intimacy can be easier to maintain than relationships close to home. Shy people may pour out their thoughts on e-mail, reassured by the fact that they don't have to speak or look the other one in the eye, that the computer seems receptive and uncritical. Your keyboard and screen are nearly always available, whereas local friends and family members may be marking exams, sleeping, watching television, or taking a shower. You don't need to set up appointments, put on a scarf and coat, go out through the cold, drive on black ice, or find that coffee place on the other side of town. You can use the ease and speed of e-mail to become close to someone on the other side of the planet. This is what happened to us.

No it didn't "happen." To say it did would be to discount agency too much. This relationship did not simply develop or come about; it is something that we actively, deliberately created. I liked JV enormously right from the first and felt sure this was someone I wanted to know better. We had tried to say so much in that first confused and exciting hour that I was convinced we had to say more—and if there was a way to do it, sitting on the other side of the planet, I would seize the opportunity. There was a way: e-mail. When occasions came up (my organizing a conference to which he was invited, his writing parts of the TRC report and wanting help with editing) I threw myself into our correspondence. I responded quickly and in detail to his professional queries and requests, including many asides and personal comments about daily concerns. Perhaps he was surprised by these intense and prolific missives. But it seemed that JV wanted this relationship too. To my intense and detailed messages, he replied in kind. We arranged a two-week visit to do collaborative work. This first visit was to be followed by two others.

For both of us, the relationship met real professional and personal needs. At its early stages, he wanted help with editing; I'm a decent editor and was prepared to spend a lot of time on this work. I had for years been in the anomalous position of being a philosopher not based in a university department, and felt a desperate need for professional colleagues. His wife's political role and obligations, the demands of two careers, commuting, and growing children, worked to inhibit his development of intimate friendships close to home, so a long-distance friendship was attractive to him.

When our intense e-mail correspondence began, I was living in Holland during my husband's sabbatical year. To suggestions about JV's framing of points about the work of the TRC, I added details about the bike paths from our northern town of Alkmaar to the ocean—the dunes and trees, sheep, cows, and inland lakes. My husband and I returned to Canada and Calgary, which JV couldn't envision at all, so then I described the foothills and

Rockies, river pathways, and local parks—which he later saw for himself. He told of wind and heat, beaches and bombings, Afrikaner resistance to the TRC, the running paths he loved, walks on Table Mountain. After years of such communications, the result is that although I live in western Canada, part of me seems to be hovering over Cape Town. A distant world feels close, often closer than my friends here. "It's thirty below." "Really? Well I hear it's twenty-six in Cape Town, pretty hot. But it's too windy to eat outside." Due to the circumstances of his wife's work, JV may move to Dublin soon. Then I may vicariously live in Ireland.

My relationship with JV, made possible by e-mail, shaped by e-mail, nearly always conducted by e-mail, has become a fundamental part of my life. Friendly greetings; expressions of sympathy and support; references to philosophical articles about justice, punishment, or reconciliation; tales of his half-hour meeting with Desmond Tutu ("the arch") or activist efforts; family problems. It's all there, and now it's all part of my life. I can call it up on my screen, or look through the fat file I printed. Even the titles recall our sharing. "Green anti-racism." "Fluffy white stuff." "Our election." "The perils of domesticity." "Your amazing message." "Synchronicity and life and death." "Finding my river of life." I thrive on his consistent concern, sympathy, and patient interest in my ongoing problems and unorthodox projects— and I hope and believe it works both ways. ("Thanks for your clarification of the difference between cynicism and pessimism—how can you do this so early in the morning?" "My students like your paper on acknowledgement." "A philosophical novel about Kant and Königsberg? Your agent thinks it's doomed? Obscure? Persist, follow your instincts. The idea is so unique and wonderful, you just have to develop it; be true to your own self and your creative instincts." And then, again and again, "be gentle with yourself; don't be too hard on yourself.")

"I'll tell you about Trent in those early years, how it was." ("It was like that? You had that kind of collegiality once? No wonder you miss it so much. Most people never get that, ever. I've never experienced anything like that.") I try to offer what I receive. "A draft chapter of your thesis? I'll read it today and send you some comments tomorrow." "Troubles with colleagues? You're organizing a meeting where all of you can discuss the issues and how you feel about them? Gosh, I admire your courage in setting this up." "The children were grouchy and demanding? Ours turned out all right and yours probably will too, given the parents they have. Try to enjoy them as much as you can. As an older parent, I can tell you, in the end, it all goes too quickly."

Strength from afar. The months and years go by, the flavour of our visits recedes in time, there are shifts and changes and gaps, but the e-mail and the relationship it structures go on. E-mail makes this distant friend and his far-away world seem immediate, seem more a feature of my life than some of my close friends here. I am a techno-clutz—perhaps even a technophobe—yet my relationship with JV is an unexpected gift that technology has brought to my life.

This relationship began with professional interest and help. It was spurred on when we arranged visits to work collaboratively, talking intensively, then writing and editing four papers on themes of apology, forgiveness, and reconciliation. We didn't do all our work over e-mail. It was made possible by visits, two in Canada and one in South Africa. Our professional and then more intimate communications began with e-mail and continue there. When JV came to Calgary the first time, I found it confusing. We were close through e-mail, yet we had only ever met for that one hour in his office at the TRC. When I mispronounced his name, my adult daughter, ever alert to reform her mother's behaviour, jumped in to tell me this was absurd. Why had this chap come to stay with us for two weeks, when I couldn't even pronounce his name properly? He leapt to my defence, saying "we only ever met for one hour, though it doesn't feel like that." Here he was, off the screen, a real person needing breakfast and enjoying walks by the river. His in-person personality seemed different from his e-mail one; he is a slower typist than I but speaks very quickly and intensely. The balance of energy seemed to shift in our relationship when we moved from the screen to the world.

During these years my closest woman friend, MK, who lives nearby and whom I've known for more than twenty-five years, was studying Russian intensively. She had become obsessively interested in contemporary Russian politics (this was probably an obsession and not an addiction, though the point is arguable) and was undertaking important legal and administrative work in Moscow. The mother of three active teenagers, MK has been to Russia twenty-five times: she is out of town for months every year. She doesn't send me e-mail when she's travelling, and her fascination with developments in Russia is so intense that sometimes it feels as though she's in Russia even when she's not away. We have shared so much, energetically discussing philosophy and public events, chatting through pregnancies, enjoying each other's babies, sharing tales of stress with young children and then teenagers, commiserating about pitfalls in public education, working together in activist campaigns, complaining about the way men do or don't communicate. But these days, when she's home in Calgary, MK spends a lot of her time e-mailing people in Russia, where she now has other cherished friends. I sometimes resort to e-mailing her at her office here, when we can't arrange walks or coffee or visits over the phone. When she's home she's busy with her children and family life and while part of me hovers over Cape Town, some important part of her mind and spirit is off in Russia. It's an irony of globalism and post-modern communications: what is far can seem near, while what is near seems inaccessible—and in some cases, the cause is the same.

All of which suggests that e-mail relationships have their perils. We can neglect near-by relationships because we have—or think we have—deeply satisfying relationships with people far away. Some people have ruined marriages over e-mail relationships; some—and some of the same ones—have created new marriages the same way. Thinking about all this, it strikes me that e-mail relationships have peculiar temptations. The problem is, if you have an intense relationship conducted through e-mail, compared to your other intense relationships, the e-mail relationship is likely to be unannoying and undemanding in ways that are rather misleading. You can pull up your friend on the screen almost any time. If there isn't a new message, read some of his old ones. Or the ones sent to him. Or send him something new, even if he hasn't replied to your previous message. You can always do it. If you are a fast typist and enjoy expressing oneself, you easily can tell him what you were thinking about, how you felt, what you read, what you saw.

With these advantages, things are likely to hum along nicely. There's a selection, a mostly positive bias that gives elements of unreality to intense relationships conducted through this medium. Compared to family members and friends in physical space, the e-mail friend is likely to seem consistently supportive and positive, and charmingly undemanding. He won't need meals or rides; he doesn't have to cancel dates. His messy house and demanding children are far away and have no effect on you. He makes supportive noises that you love to hear, and most likely, he thinks you're great. Maybe you are great—but this guy is more likely than others to think so because he finds you at your better moments.

Perhaps for me it's my own writing in this relationship that comes closest to being addictive. What's addictive is being able, at just about any time of day or night, to so quickly and smoothly send personal messages or tentative thoughts and reflections to a sensitive person who will respond—usually quite soon. If I'm addicted to anything, it isn't e-mail as such, or this person as such, or even this relationship as conducted by e-mail. It's to my own writing of my own life, in the quasi-journal that this whole relationship-over-a-vast-distance has inspired. All this is not just writing a journal. I could certainly do that without JV or e-mail. It's writing this quasi-journal to him, to JV with the interests and ideas he has, and with the care and concern he devotes to replying. And it's writing this quasi-journal by e-mail, because that method is so quick and easy, so frequently available, and so likely to inspire quick replies.

Not that it's all perfect. You can have misunderstandings and even quarrels over e-mail. Somewhat perversely, speed and ease even contribute to the possibility. Because people write so quickly and casually on e-mail, and it's so easy to send a message, we may not be careful enough in what we say. And there is no context—no vocal tone, no body language, no expression of sudden anxiety to hint that what we are saying is somehow not right. It is words, words, more words, fast words, often too-fast words. And there's not even the personality of handwriting.

Of course, such pitfalls could be present in any correspondence. E-mail is a special case—but not unique after all. People have been writing letters, creating and sustaining intimacy in letters, and supporting each other through letters for hundreds of years; and no doubt some have become highly dependent on long distance, mostly-written-words relationships. Probably it's always been true that some factors of selective encounter give the distant friend certain advantages over those nearby. In the eighteenth century, letters were hugely popular, and good friends and colleagues often wrote each other frequently—sometimes several times daily, even when they lived nearby. The differences between this more formal correspondence and our e-mail are, after all, differences of degree. Because e-mail is so fast that messages are transmitted almost instantaneously, we have a greater range and can delude ourselves into forgetting about geography. Sometimes I feel I know more about JV than MK. I can forget that she is only a few kilometres away, while he is some 14,000.

Though people now call physical mail "snail mail," its pace is not historically so unusual. Unless correspondents were in the same city, eighteenth-century letters took many days or months to reach their destination. In his social history of eighteenth-century Germany, W.H. Bruford reports that a typical length of time for a letter from Berlin to reach Frankfurt was nine to twelve days. Today, physical letters can take a week to get to Calgary from Toronto—just as long as to Cape Town in some cases—although there are airplanes that can fly the distance in about four hours and much faster deliveries should be possible.

Eighteenth-century letters were characteristically more florid and formal than e-mail is today, though good friends dashed off short messages to each other, and some correspondents were emotionally effusive. Like e-mail, physical letters probably showed selectivity and some positive bias. When people were really ill or desperate, they were no doubt less likely to write. Letters from that time tend to be longer and more reflective than most e-mail between friends today. Interestingly, many people at that time did not regard letters as private. Some were highly literate and skilled essays, and delighted recipients would take them to salons or dinner parties to read aloud for general benefit and entertainment. A special favourite was a letter from someone in a faraway place who could tell in her own voice what was happening there. It was not unusual for one person to arrange publication of another person's letter without asking permission.

Hand-written, letters were not so quickly dashed off as are messages by people quick on the keyboard today. Carpal tunnel syndrome had not yet been identified, but we can certainly imagine people tiring from writing out these lengthy missives longhand. Rahel Varnhagen, a late eighteenth-century *salonnière* praised by Goethe for her impassioned and intellectual letters, sometimes complained of awkwardness and fatigue when a quill was not available and she had to write with an awkward stick of wood (Tewarson, 129). No doubt some people in the eighteenth century were emotionally dependent on their correspondence and correspondents. Some no doubt neglected family, nearby friends, work, and household matters in order to devote many hours to their letters and relationships conducted over a distance. Such people may have been addicted to their correspondence, the relationships it provided, and their own writing as an element within it. Even in a time of scarce quills, rough roads, and barely reliable stagecoaches, people poured their hearts out in letters. For some, letters compensated for intimacies and satisfactions that were missing in daily life. They were a source of intimacy and solace. If support from a distance was a problem in human life, it's not a problem restricted to our own times. It's just that e-mail makes it all very easy, contracts the time frame, and expands the range in space.

There is nothing wrong, in principle, in having a relationship with a far-away someone with whom you exchange deep thoughts and feelings and who compensates in certain ways for things you're missing in daily life in your "real" home. Such relationships between human beings have existed when-ever human needs and relationships, travel and the ability to write, have made them possible. If some are addicted to distance relationships, the addiction does not arise from e-mail technology. It could happen with long-distance relationships conducted by ordinary correspondence. In extreme cases (and I hope my relationship with JV is not one of these), we might say a person has become addicted to a long- distance relationship and the writ-ing that sustains it. It's certainly possible. But to say that such relationships, through e-mail, are actually addictive would be to make a further claim. It would mean that e-mail and the relationships it sustains have qualities that tend to make us want more and more, to become preoccupied with the cor-respondence, and give it an inappropriately prominent role in our lives. Could that be true? Is such writing addictive? If so, would it be more addic-tive through e-mail than in non-electronic letters? The differences between physical and electronic correspondence are differences of degree, not princi-ple or kind. The degrees lie in speed and in ease. But those degrees add up to a lot. When you can send a message in seconds and receive a reply in min-utes, the possibilities for compulsiveness are surely greater. Effortlessness and speed, and the global reach, hold out risks as well as possibilities.

In his recent book *The Ingenuity Gap*, Thomas Homer-Dixon reprints a telling cartoon. It shows a man seated at his computer, looking at the screen and saying to himself, "I'm finally on line, connected, plugged in, hooked up on the Web. I'm surfin'. I'm part of the most sophisticated system ever devised for communicating with fellow human beings " (319). A child enters the room, waving a drawing and wanting attention. The chap scowls. "Now—if people would just shut up and leave me alone." Leave me alone (here) so I can communicate with my fellow human beings (far away). For few will it go so far as addiction, but to me, that's the risk—that distant con-nections may be built at cost to people close to home.

Works Cited

Bruford, W.H. 1998. *Germany in the Eighteenth Century*. Cambridge: Cambridge University Press.

Homer-Dixon, Thomas. 2000. *The Ingenuity Gap*. New York: Knopf.

Tewarson, Heidi Thomann and Rahel Levin Varnhagen. 1998. *The Life and Work of a German Jewish Intellectual*. Lincoln: University of Nebraska Press.

Section II

Perspectives

6

Writing and the Idea of Addiction

Kristjana Gunnars

Annie Dillard, the noted American essayist, has written many books on the act of writing. She talks about writing as a lifestyle rather than as an occupation or a career or any other such "misguided" idea. To her, writing is a fundamental, human principle, rather than a kind of "work." One image she uses to describe the writer stands out in her various essays on the subject. It is the image of the writer as a weasel, which occurs in her book *Teaching a Stone to Talk*. Dillard describes how a weasel will encounter a "target" and focus on it by jumping onto its prey and latching itself to it like a leech or a barnacle. The weasel will hang limply from its target, and go along wherever the prey goes. Then she says that is what the writer must do. Be like a weasel, and latch onto writing for dear life, hanging on wherever it takes you. She adds that "a weasel lives as he's meant to, yielding at every moment to the perfect freedom of single necessity." The "single necessity" for the writer would be writing itself. She explains that "I think it would be well, and proper, and obedient, and pure, to grasp your one necessity and not let it go, to dangle from it limp wherever it takes you" (16).

This image is striking for the way it describes the writer's sense of necessity and desperation about the writing act. There is also an illustration here of how the writer needs to give herself over to writing, hang on to it, and let it take her wherever it is going. The sense of not being in control, of somehow, quite violently even, hanging on to something that is much larger and more unpredictable than the writer, makes the whole issue of what writing is about rather animalistic, nearly biological. This is in contrast to the more common approach writers take when talking about their work, which is often linked to things spiritual and emotional. Dillard's more uncomfortable image of the leech-like weasel makes writing seem more akin to a kind of biological addiction.

Dillard's addiction to writing is a bit like the addiction of alcoholism, which is described by Tom Dardis in *The Thirsty Muse*, an exploration of the effects of alcohol on four major American writers, as a process which, once begun, becomes uncontrollable. The reason for the lack of control in alcoholism is that the body takes over the willpower itself and asserts its own cravings, brought about by the cellular and metabolic changes of drinking alcohol. In the same way, once begun, the writer's very involvement in writing makes the writer's spiritual body change so that only more writing will answer her needs.

One writer for whom Dillard's description seems to ring true is Bessie Head. Head grew up in South Africa, but ended up as a refugee in Botswana. She was unable to get citizenship in Botswana, and was a woman without a home for many years. Her "one necessity" was to write, and through writing she also became a citizen. Head describes her need to write in almost visceral terms, and writer's block as something akin to suffering withdrawal. In her autobiographical essays this perspective is prevalent. For example, in "Let Me Tell a Story Now...," published in her collection *A Woman Alone*, she confesses her inability to tell a story she really needs to tell. "I would like to write the story of the man and his wife who never took the train journey," she tells us,

> but I can't. When I think of writing any single thing I panic and go dead inside. Perhaps it's because I have my ear too keenly attuned to the political lumberjacks who are busy making capital on human lives. Perhaps I'm just having nightmares. Whatever my manifold disorders are, I hope to get them sorted out pretty soon, because I've just got to tell a story. (7–8)

Her description of her writing self is physical. She talks about "going dead inside," about what she is hearing, and about nightmares and other possible "disorders" which can be relieved only by the act of writing.

What these writers are talking about is not the wish to write or the desire to write, but the sheer necessity of it. Canadian poet and novelist Susan Musgrave makes similar assertions, but in her case they are made poignant by her own comparisons to her husband, writer Steven Reid. Reid has been addicted to heroin and cocaine, and has ended up in jail more than once. Musgrave comments in an interview in the fall of 2000 that she herself does not take drugs or drink or smoke. Instead, she writes. "Writing is where I go for help," Musgrave asserts, and here the act of writing has become her "one necessity" that keeps her going in spite of tremendous personal upsets. Bessie Head also talks about her own relationship to writing as if it were impossible to have life without also having writing. Some of her concerns probably come out of the political, social and racial situation in which she found herself, where she is a member of a group, and possibly a gender, that remains unheard and invisible. Therefore the need to speak up and speak freely is all the more urgent. But the need to write is the same for Musgrave and Head: a way of keeping going.

There is an almost alarming intensity to Bessie Head's anguish about writing. For example, when she is talking about the offensiveness of sentimentality, it is as if the softer emotions are a betrayal of the writer's real condition. She writes in "God and the Underdog," for example,

It has often amazed me how people substitute slushy emotions for such great words like friendship, compassion. You might feel soft and mushy about a little doggie. But between two living human beings there is always Truth and Truth is like that double-edged thing and is constantly expressing itself as Fireworks. (46)

What is inside the human being requires the best effort of intense, true expression. As to what is inside, in her case she explains herself as being made of "tricky material," and that "There is nothing neat and tidy about me, like a nice social revolution. With me goes a mad, passionate, insane, screaming world of ten thousand devils" (47). This "mad, passionate, insane, screaming world" latches on to writing as the only way to express itself, and not eat the writer up through a repression of speech.

What drives Bessie Head to write is, as she tells it, an awareness of evil. The conflict between good and evil is for her so central, that only by writing can she keep what she finds evil at bay. And the idea that evil is outside, in politics or economics or in society or in "bad" individuals, is too simple. Evil is also inside, and only writing can help save her in a manner of speaking:

I found myself in a situation where there was no guarantee against the possibility that I could be evil too. I found that one earns only a slight guarantee against the possibility of inflicting harm on others through an experience which completely destroys one's own ego or sense of self-esteem. This can be so devastating that one is not likely to survive it. (63)

Life can be so treacherous, she implies, that the very act of surviving intact is the very act of being destroyed. "These trends of thought have very much occupied my writing life," she explains (63). In this way, Head refines the meaning of Dillard's "one necessity" and makes the necessity of writing a moral and ethical issue, as well as an act of survival.

What lies underneath the writer's singular need to write is a broader need. This is specified rather starkly by British cultural commentator David Jones. Jones has written many essays on the subject of "man's" need for culture, above and beyond the practical. There will always be a need for the cultural, he argues. In his essay "Use and Sign," published in the collection entitled *The Dying Gaul and Other Writings*, Jones talks about the practical and the cultural as the "utile" and the "extra-utile." About the extra-utile he says that we endeavour towards the arts in the same way we strive towards the sacred, or the religious. He writes "We are concerned only with the addiction of man to certain practices which are commonly called 'religious,' but to which he is in fact equally addicted in secular or non-sacral contexts" (177). The secular-sacred, which he terms the extra-utile, is actually poetry. In his phrasing, "man is a creature which ... has consistently shown a duality of behaviour." This duality is both ingenious practicality and also a preoccupation with "activities which are far from having an obvious end" (177–78). If those other activities are not done for utilitarian reasons, they must be done "for a sign" (178).

In short, "man" is addicted to the sign, according to Jones. He also argues that while there is distinct progress in human technology, there appears to be little if any progress in the arts. "Michelangelo is no 'better' than ... the paleolithic masters" (178), he writes. If anything, there appears to be a decline in artistic accomplishments at the same time that technological achievements continue to grow. The relatively static nature of "man" the artist discerns only proves to him that the need for art is continuous, and *poiesis* is something we cannot live without. It is an ironic reality that as technology progresses, the artistic "roots" that allow us to go on become less and less alive. In Jones's colourful prose, "as the lengthening light of our technocracy illumines and conditions us all, so the strengthening chill of the utile shrivels roots in us all, the shoots of which have helped us to tolerate our mortal state and to yield blossoms in our most lachrymal valley" (178–79). It is here we find the explanation for writers like Bessie Head, for whom life has had its intolerable sides. Writing for Head is the very thing that makes the unbearable part of life tolerable. There is no need for "progress" in the arts, because they represent the human being's continuous addiction to sign-making.

Another paradox Jones notes, after the irony that technological progress increases the need for artistic expression while at the same time it decreases our ability to engage in the world poetically, is the notion that artists, poets, and writers also become increasingly anachronistic as the world becomes more technically oriented. In Jones's words, those "who serve the extra-utile [people we call artists and poets] are ... scarcely less anachronistic than the priest" (182). Here is the dilemma for writers who wish to engage in the basically human activity of "signage" without, as Barry Callaghan has said, feeling "the need to please," which would be a utilitarian act. The poet's activities are deemed useless by a technologically and market driven world; at the same time the poet has a greater need to write. What is important here is the opportunity to live symbolically, in signs, as well as practically. "The nature of man demands the sacramental," Jones writes. "If he's denied the deep and the real, he'll fall for the trivial, even for the ersatz; but have it he will" (182). There is widespread consensus that we are, in fact, falling for the trivial, and that we are therefore dumbing down. This is happening, presumably, because the need for the sacramental remains the same, regardless of our ability to create it and sustain it in a real and profound way. But there is less and less of the sacramental around, which does not eliminate the need.

We can, as Jones does, talk about *poiesis* as an addiction in the sense that we need the poetic in some form or other, and will have it no matter what we have to sacrifice in the bargain. Jones explains that

> It is not because it affords him ["man"] some consolation [as Susan Musgrave describes her need to write]. Still less is his addiction to the extra-utile that of the drug or drink addict. His incurable thirst is best expressed by the Psalmist: "Like as the hart desireth the water-brook." (182)

It is as natural for human beings to turn to the symbolic, to sign-making, as it is for the hart to go to the water. Here we are back to the animal imagery we began with in bringing up Annie Dillard's weasel, for whom clinging to its prey and letting it take him where it is necessary to go is a similar phenomenon. Jones goes so far as to maintain that without the "significatory" in our lives, there would, in fact, be no "us" and we would be a whole other genus or species. Not, in other words, even human (184).

While Annie Dillard talks about writing as something that presents itself to the writer in the form of a "single necessity," and Bessie Head speaks of writing as the only thing that will keep her going in a hostile and racist world, there is a paradox built into the writing act which they do not mention. David Jones has argued that we are "addicted" to poetry the way the hart is drawn to water, and this echoes what writers themselves often claim to have experienced. But it is also often pointed out by writers that putting words to paper is a difficult and ironic act, which takes you places you may actually be trying to avoid. In effect, writing is an exercise that forces the writer to face the very things that make life difficult. Perhaps that is the source of the attraction in the first place. It could be simply the power of "truth" in that truth is something we dare face.

French theoretician Hélène Cixous has been one of the most vocal writers on the subject of the dark side of that necessity. In her essay "Writing Blind," for example, Cixous talks about the writer as being herself the "one necessity" of writing. The subject is writing, the object is the writer, to whom writing calls from the depths of some kind of darkness or purgatory. In her way of speaking, it is not the writer who chooses to write because he is "addicted" to the process and where it leads. Instead, writing somehow exists before the writer enters, and writing latches itself onto the writer, or is "addicted" to the writer, in order to be alive (144). In another essay titled "Unmasked," Cixous tries a more feminist angle to the idea that writing, text, exists before the writer herself enters, and somehow claims the writer for itself. She likens writing to the traditional aspects of women's lives that have been determined by various cultures to be "unclean." At the same time, the writing act is unavoidable and, echoing Dillard, bordering on biological necessity.

Cixous explains how she ties up the need to write with the journey to a kind of underworld on the one hand, and the necessity of loving on the other. We are "addicted" to writing because, she argues, we are in need of loving others. Writing takes you out of yourself, the way acting does, and makes you look at others with empathy. To get to that place of empathy, the writer needs to go through painful self-examination and acknowledge what is otherwise rejected about oneself. "That writing suffers in fact the fate of birds, women, the unclean," she says, "Because it runs the risks of its truths." There is nothing safe or comfortable about this journey, she insists. This is the archetypal Dante-esque path through the underworld, and its uncovering of falsehood and hypocrisy, in order to get to the flower of God in the end. Cixous writes that the writing act "makes its way into places where danger grows—there are few people there—it is joyfully received only by 'people whose souls are already shaped'" ("Unmasked," 132).

The whole idea of the "unclean" has very little to do with what is repulsive in some way, and everything to do with the idea of joy. Cixous's argument is that we equate cleanliness with purity, and the joy of digging into our roots, metaphorically speaking, is finding the way in which things are mixed. In "Unmasked" she explains herself in this way:

> But what does not-clean mean?—none of these mixed dishes, undisguised, unprepared, not transformed in appearance so as to become edible. Certain things, creatures, actions have remained raw, alive, ever since the moment of creation. "They have continued to be the root," divines Clarice Lispector. The root is twisted, doubled up, entangled, it digs with all its force into the ground, evil and good happily mingled, before the tree with two separate halves, it is humble [humilis] for it knows that nothing is simple, that it is itself not simple, thought is a struggle with itself, one cannot reach, but one can stretch, from the two forces together springs forth the moment. And this energy is joy. (132–33)

Discovering the "raw" state of things, the honest way in which creation presents itself, is a prerequisite for real writing. Non-writing, the thing that society and culture draws us to by its commercial economy, is actually "prepared" for us, is "disguised" from its true nature, and transformed for us so that we no longer recognize the origins of things. It is this process of "acculturating" us to a social economy that prohibits joy, which is what writing acts against. As she puts it, "it is joy that is prohibited—the thing that escapes all economies" (133).

At the heart of the "addiction" to writing which writers so frequently talk about, both in formal treatises and in casual conversation, lies the whole notion of joyful energy which Cixous points to. It is, almost literally, the question posed in Judaeo-Christianity that if the salt loses its flavour, how is life to be salted? Art, *poiesis*, as David Jones would say, is the salt without which life cannot be bearable. The argument Jones makes about when people are robbed of the "real" thing, true and deep art, they will go for the artificial version, popular culture, simply because "man" needs something, is a very serious comment. Cixous is saying something very similar when she posits that the social economy in which we live is designed to "prohibit" joy in favour of what can be commercialized, and joy is something the writer retrieves by writing. Cixous equates such joylessness with misogyny. "I do not understand that insidious joyless thing called misogyny" (133), she writes, and it is here she makes her connection between writing (roots) and woman (that joy which is rejected).

True writing, the kind that follows the twisted roots that take you to the "happy mingling" of both good and evil, is the act by which we "escape all economies" and establish ourselves. It is interesting in this regard to note the many times Bessie Head talks about the concept of evil in her various essays, all in relation to her own life as a writing life. In talking about Boris Pasternak, for example, she speaks of "the man's heart which he keeps such a secret, as though he is conducting a silent conspiracy of his own against all those things which are not truth but evil" (59). She is clear in her mind that "evil" is "rubbish," the things we need to continually weed out of our lives (59). Furthermore, as mentioned above, she acknowledges that "there was no guarantee against the possibility that I could be evil too." It is the act of writing that enables her to look at evil and acknowledge her own participation in the question, which takes her out of the way in which social problems are popularly conceptualized. That kind of acknowledgement is also more freeing. In the paradigm presented by so many writers and artists, in fact, it is only the artist-writer who can say such a thing and live with it.

For Hélène Cixous, the cause of women and the cause of love are, in the matter of texts, the same. Lovers and writers fight against the same thing, she argues, which is the force of hatred and also of selfishness. "'Me, me, me, me me me,' says hatred," she complains, "so how could it ever get in a 'you?'" It is the search for the "you," the "two different yet equal beings," that is the writer's search, as well as the lover's and also the actor's ("Unmasked," 134). The essay in fact ends up discussing the theatre and how the theatre is the last place left where there is no misogyny, because in there everyone is engaged in the attempt to empathize with someone other than herself. The writer is involved in the empathetic project because the writer belongs in the theatre, the writer belongs with the lovers who have been thrown out of Scripture ("Bible-outcasts" like Tristan and Isolde, Romeo and Juliet, Paolo and Francesca).

Thinking itself is an attempt at love, and at getting out of "all economies." In Cixous's words, "All those who love and who think, who think and who think about loving, know that there exist during every period a few clandestine beings, born to watch over the little double flame, that it doesn't go out" ("Unmasked," 134). The small group of people who share this experience are, somehow, real writers, real readers, real people of the theatre. And these people are also, somehow, dangerous. It is, she writes, the "most dangerous cause there is: to love the other, even before being loved. Without waiting, without counting. The cause of 'you'" ("Unmasked," 134). Uniting her argument with David Jones's comments, Cixous makes the confident assertion that

> *No, poets—real poets—do not hate the other, it's impossible, how*
> *could they give up half their language, why would they want to*
> *cut their tongue in two and spit out one half? Those philosophic*
> *lovers who live in the forest of languages cannot be in favor of*
> *closing the borders and ejecting one word out of every two.*
> ("Unmasked," 134)

In this way she aligns the act of finding words and creating texts with the act of love and empathy.

Literary theoreticians have, since the shift in thinking about writing that has occurred with the works of Julia Kristeva, Jacques Derrida, and Roland Barthes, found a lot to say about the relationship between writing and desire. Desire is, in and of itself, a force that propels the writer forward. Desire is a good term for the need to write, if not the addiction to writing, because desire appears to be outside of a person's control as well as something he reaches towards of free will.[1]

On a less academic level, Canadian writer and ironic theorist Robert Kroetsch has commented extensively on desire. In an essay he calls "Why I Went Up North and What I Found When He Got There," published in *A Likely Story*, his collection of essays on writing, Kroetsch posits the figure of a young and naïve writer who is following his call to write. Quite naturally, this leads him into the Canadian high North. That is one of Kroetsch's ironies, but also a good metaphor for what he wishes to say. The desire to write takes the writer into the most difficult terrain, and all props and helpful hints are, or have to be, removed from him first, before he can begin to write. Even language must be taken away. This denuding of stimuli sharpens the writer to what is really present, which is desire. Yet writing does not fulfill desire, which is why the writer has to keep going, much like the young traveller who never reaches a destination. Kroetsch says, wryly, "To write is to step or stumble over the edge of the known into that category of desire that defines itself, always, just a hair's breadth short of fulfillment" (14).

In his essay "I Wanted to Write a Manifesto," Kroetsch makes a case reminiscent of Hélène Cixous in "Writing Blind," which is that language comes before writing. The writer is drawn into the act of textual practice by the force of language, and cannot not do so. This is another way of framing the notion of "addiction" to writing. Repeatedly in the nine essays that comprise *A Likely Story*, Kroetsch positions the writer as somehow powerless before his task. And writing is, in and of itself, not just putting words on paper. Writing is desire, loss and grief. In "The Cow in the Quicksand and How I(t) got Out: Responding to Stegner's *Wolf Willow*," Kroetsch writes that "Language comes after; language is an announcement of deathly consequence. To begin to write is, already, to accept loss" (69). The loss he is speaking of is that which slips between the reach and the achievement, the desire and the fulfillment. The accomplishment never can be reached, which is what makes writing a hopeless grief. He explains what he means in terms of writing on the prairies. He could, he recalls, not really say what he wanted to say. Therefore he became a writer. It seemed inevitable. In "The Cow in the Quicksand," he explains:

> *Mysticism, as I feel the word in my bones, has something to do with whatever it is that can't be fully articulated. As a prairie writer I've committed myself to speaking the unspeakable, and unspeakable here is a pun. My Aunt Mary told me not to say what I was saying. My critics ask me what it is I'm trying to say.*

---

1. It is beyond the scope of this essay to go back into the philosophical, linguistic, and psychosocial aggregates of the idea of desire in writing. See Julia Kristeva's *Revolution in Poetic Language*, her *Desire in Language: A Semiotic Approach to Literature and Art*, and Judith Butler's *Subjects of Desire: Hegelian Reflections in Twentieth-Century France*.

I'm talking about our very unwillingness as well as our inability
to speak the name of all that we are. I'm reminded of the claim
that, during the Dirty Thirties, farmers stopped naming their
farms—because the names made the farms too easy for money
collectors to find. (72)

So the writer perfects a strategy of avoidance, which is what keeps her
"hooked" on writing, because it is always necessary to give it another try.
Another approximation.

The notion of evasion as central to writing, both paradoxical and necessary, is connected with Kroetsch's way of conceptualizing the North. The
North cannot be named, and is forever eluding our grasp. "Our strategies,"
he confesses, "even when we claim to tell the God's own truth, are strategies of evasion. We are so often trying to slip out of the grip of someone or
something" (72). (He calls it a "metonymic slithering of the world.") In
"Playing Dead in Rudy Wiebe's *Playing Dead: A Reader's Marginalia*,"
Kroetsch tries to create an architectural model for the writer's need to
evade. After noting that Wiebe's essay is all about space, Kroetsch describes
how he discovered the marginal nature of writing by looking at an already
printed text and finding that he should be writing on the margins of that
text, not in the centre. Here is the picture of the writer struggling towards
the centre without ever being able to actually occupy it, because it is already
written by others. This is so even when there is no text on the (blank) page:

Perhaps the generative moment of my young writer's life came
when I realized I had not two pages to write upon but rather two
margins to write in. I could write alongside, with and against,
the blackly printed page of our inheritance. I could write along-
side, with and against, the unspeakable white glare of what I
call, metonymically, North. (96)

The only strategy left for the writer is to do like the North itself, and make
the margin so large that it threatens to overwhelm the center, spatially. The
writer is also, like Bessie Head has said, in need of telling a story. There is an
endless succession of stories that need to be told, never exhausted, and they
are all, as Kroetsch admits, lies (100).

To go back to David Jones, who argues in "Use and Sign," as well as else-
where, that we as human beings are, while technological and utilitarian in
nature, so much in need of "signage" as well, which is *poiesis*, and "extra-
utile," that we would cease to be ourselves, or human, if we did not obey this
"addiction," as he terms it. Robert Kroetsch echoes those arguments in *A*
Likely Story in various ways, but much more ironically. He describes himself,
the boy and the young man and the aging writer, as quite useless in overt
ways. But he knows, and the reader knows, that his function in society is
essential, for it is the writer who is called upon to "create worlds," as
Kroetsch terms it, or to mythologize our existence. Kroetsch makes one of
his rare non-ironic statements in his essay responding to Margaret Laurence,
"Sitting Down to Write: Margaret Laurence and the Discourse of Mourning,"

when he notes quite seriously that "The writer is part of an apparatus that produces the texts that society and culture require in order to be society and culture" (151).

This statement is not paradoxical, and can be read literally, as David Jones might do. And the writer is called to do this from within. As the hart is drawn to water, and as the weasel in Annie Dillard's strange metaphoric description, the writer does latch on to that "one necessity" for "dear life." Perhaps this sense of calling is to be seen as an addiction in its own way. Not, perhaps, quite as Susan Musgrave does, where writing is a substitution for drugs; a comfort. But writing is seen by so many practitioners as something deeper than that. A deeper addiction which, as David Jones has noted, is an echo of the priest who obeys the call to the priesthood. Quite useless and quite necessary at once for others, and essentially life-granting for the writer herself. What the writer is reaching for but cannot quite achieve, and what is so compelling that it could be called an addiction on many levels, are essentials like freedom (from all economies), understanding (also of one's own complicities), joy (the rejected), honesty, wisdom, love[2] and an ability to face death. That is why Robert Kroetsch calls writing "a god-game" (150). Life without the possibility of these would, as the above writers amply testify, not be worth living. The writer goes towards those depths through writing. Language and *poiesis*, the understanding is, will take you in the direction of those essentials if you let it.

Works Cited

Cixous, Hélène. 1998. "Unmasked." Pp. 131–38 in *Stigmata, Escaping Texts*, translated by Keith Cohen. London: Routledge.

Cixous, Hélène. 1998. "Writing Blind." Pp. 139–53 in *Stigmata, Escaping Texts*, translated by Eric Prenowitz. First published as «Écrire aveugle,» in *TriQuarterly* 97 (1996): 7–20.

Dardis, Tom. 1998. *The Thirsty Muse; Alcohol and the American Writer*. New York: Ticknor & Fields.

Dillard, Annie. 1982. "Living Like Weasels." Pp. 11–16 in *Teaching a Stone to Talk*. New York: Harper & Row.

Head, Bessie. 1990. *A Woman Alone; Autobiographical Writings*, selected and edited by Craig MacKenzie. London: Heinemann.

Jones, David. 1978. "Use and Sign." Pp. 177–85 in *The Dying Gaul and Other Writings*. London: Faber and Faber.

Kroetsch, Robert. 1995. *A Likely Story; The Writing Life*. Red Deer: Red Deer College Press.

2. Combining wisdom and love, Kroetsch posits in "Playing Dead" that "To care for this landscape [the landscape of the North and of writing] is indeed to be in love—and love is a state of knowing everything and knowing nothing" (95).

7

Addiction and Authorship

Crispin Sartwell

Addiction and authorship is a good theme for me, since I'm both an addict and an author. I've decided that I've already done all the research that I need to do: now all I have to do is write. Writing and substance abuse are both things I have done compulsively. When I don't write for a while, a little voice goes off in my head that says "write, write, write." That voice is pretty similar to the voice that used to say "drink, drink, drink." I always tell people that I write not because I want to but because I have to. They look at me funny at that point. If they are untenured academics, they look at me maybe with envy, like they wish they had this particular compulsion, or they wish that this particular compulsion originated within themselves instead of coming from the tenure and promotion committee. There's a similar kind of puzzlement, though usually not envy, when addicts tell non-addicts what it's like. Usually the first thing that an addict will say is that she can't not do whatever it is that she's addicted to. And this compulsion emerges from something in herself, so that when in the recovery parlance she admits she's powerless, she's admitting to powerlessness not only over what she's addicted to, but over her addiction itself. That is, what addicts are powerless over is, finally, themselves. But most people live in the belief or illusion that they're free, and in some sense most people are free over the very things to which others are addicted. They're free in at least the Humean manner: if they decide not to drink, they don't drink. But alcoholics know what it's like to decide not to drink and then to drink anyway, to decide to stop and then continue, to decide to quit and then go on a binge. Non-addicts still want to make this a sheer matter of choice; they can't or don't want to understand compulsion, can't or won't understand the experience of acting under almost total constraint, where that constraint originates internally.

1.

I personally do not believe in precisely the same way. I desperately wanted to quit alcohol and drugs for many years. And I could continue to want to quit even as I was lifting the pipe to my mouth. What is going on inside someone who is having that experience is very hard to describe to people who don't have that experience, but if you take me seriously, I suppose it will be obvious to you that the self is divided or perhaps fragmented in that experience. Something is trying to make something else in the self stop; something is trying to make something else keep going; you're in an explicit "inner conflict," a notion which could only possibly make sense given a multiple self. Actually, putting it that way is not at all satisfactory because it makes it sound as though there is some unitary self that has been sledgehammered like glass, whereas I am going to agree with the fashionable or formerly fashionable folk who hold that the coherent self, insofar as it is not just a delusion, or even insofar as it is a delusion, is an achievement reflecting a certain social/linguistic positionality. I have never experienced a free or univocal self. There was no self prior to or external to my addiction. I experienced a variety of proto-addictive internal divisions from the times of my earliest memories. I don't think that I had a free self and that that self was enchained by addiction; I think I had an addicted self that eventually found something to which to be addicted. Compulsion was my destiny and before I had it I was groping toward it. Nor do I think that I could have lived without becoming addicted; the cycle of addiction and of recovery was as it were bundled up inside me from the beginning and simply unfolded.

This experience I have been describing in addiction, this explicit experience of self-division in which you can actually sometimes feel yourself being torn apart (as when you resolve not to drink as your arm is actually raising the bottle to your lips), is seen even more elaborately in the experience of what is called in the world of recovering addicts "denial." This phenomenon is familiar to almost everybody: someone who is shooting up every day thinks or at least says he can stop at any time. Or someone is drinking all the time and saying there's no problem, and perhaps other people are saying there's no problem too: they are caught up in the system by which an addiction tries to conceal itself from itself. In some forms of denial you're just an idiot who doesn't know what you're doing, who misses the obvious. But in others you're playing this incredibly elaborate game with yourself in which part of you is hiding from another part, in which you don't know over here what you know over there or where, as we say, the left hand doesn't know what the right hand is doing. Sometimes it almost seems that you don't know that you are, say, drinking, which would be an amazing piece of epistemic legerdemain. Or more likely you know what you are doing in the most direct literal sense but you don't know what that means, or you don't want to reveal what it means to yourself, etc. There is a whole range of possible distributions of delusion, a whole range of tiny or huge self-delusions, or tiny self-delusions that amount to one huge self-delusion and so on. Each of these would correspond to some specific form of self-division, because something is hiding from something else and it's all taking place in the inner terrain: the patterns by which a self could be mapped or in which the bits of a self could be arranged are indefinitely large.

Now here's a start on developing my basic thesis: these forms of self-division or fragmentation make the self explicitly, or obviously, a place where power is transacted. This is something that, for example, Nietzsche saw: that the self is an arena of power. I don't see how this could be true if the self were singular, if there was only one of me, even only one of me at a given time. Think of such locutions as "control yourself," for example, which is the kind of thing people say to assholes and addicts, two groups between which there is considerable overlap. And notice, this notion of "controlling your-self" is a fundamental strategy for training children in how to behave. But when we train children that way, we are not only teaching them, say, "impulse control," we are also teaching them an ontology of the human self; we are showing them who they are, or rather we are making them into selves we recognize as human, by inculcating the particular sorts of configurations of the self that we recognize as comprehensible, as opposed, for example, to animal or machine selves. Now when you tell me to control myself, what is supposed to be controlling what? I guess part of me is supposed to be con-trolling another part of me, right? Well, I'm trying to make you see that this would make no sense at all for a Cartesian subject. And so one thing I am saying is that the common-sense self that we make our kids into by yelling sentences like "control yourself," the common-sense selves that we conceive ourselves also to be, are not much like Cartesian coherent or singular selves. Our common-sense notion of the self is a notion of something multiple, in which some parts are or ought to be empowered over other parts.

And we do have ways of talking about bits of the self that would allow us to make sense of the self as a site of power-transaction: consider the word "will," for example. Maybe when you tell me, as I dance around and scream or start barking like a poodle to "get a hold of myself" or something, you mean something like this: my will should get a hold of my body: I should be telling myself what to do: there's some kind of inner voice that should be hectoring my dancing legs or shutting my screaming mouth. This picture, which I admit I don't know how to evaluate, would of course also entail that there is a corresponding capacity in my legs or in my mouth to listen to what this hectoring voice is saying and respond. The will is conceived as the dic-tator or the police of the self: it's supposed to seize the unruly populace of impulses and transform or execute them. Without this vision of the self, Western culture would be unrecognizable politically and psychologically. But the vision is optional in the sense that there are cultures who get along with-out it and the disciplines of the self that it engenders. One might say that power as it operates within the self and power as it operates in the public sphere are mutually simultaneously caused; the culture comes out of peo-ple's heads and returns there. And in that sense, addiction is a culture as well as a self, as is freedom from addiction. We in the West imagine a free self, and we construe freedom as the perfect subordination to will. That is indeed one of the fundamental attractions of addictive substances: one loses the hectoring will in one's head and yields to one's impulses more easily: intoxi-cation in that sense is a liberation of subordinated aspects of the self, and it is in part this liberation that the addict seeks again and again in what finally becomes a slavery to one's own impulse.

This conflict embodies as it were the history of metaphysics and ethics, in which reason is meant to govern will which is meant to govern impulses and the body. You can see this picture at its most elaborate development even in Plato, who also draws the analogy between political arrangements and arrangements of the self. Plato repudiates a bottom-up sort of slavery/ liberation in which the body governs the will or the people the ruler, and develops a model of liberation/slavery in which reason subordinates the body and the philosopher the people. What I am suggesting is that this conception of the self as a hierarchy is much closer to our current common-sense notions of self than is the picture we get, for example, in Descartes.

So we might think initially of the common-sense self as a hierarchy of power among impulses and will or "reason." And just to make it even more complicated, I think that probably there are supposed to be many acts of will going on simultaneously and that all parts of your body are supposed to be listening, that the notion of self-mastery presupposes a wonderfully lush and wacky ontology of a committee of wills or selves issuing orders to a commit- tee of impulses and body parts. Sometimes these body parts listen to this committee, but sometimes they don't: your body can be recalcitrant to your will. Maybe they end up in a kind of negotiation, where the committee will allow your head to sleep as soon as you finish reading the chapter or some- thing. Now it gets even funkier. Think about the role of desire here. I guess maybe desire, some of it anyway, comes from the body. It articulates the will but it is involuntary. I have no control, literally none, over what I desire. If I want some kind of kinky sex with the wrong partner or something, I can't make myself not want that: indeed, if I try to make myself not want that, I convert the desire into an obsession and myself into an addict. So then the will sifts these desires and I guess prescribes a series of bodily actions or inac- tions to realize or fail to realize these desires. For that is also certainly what it means to "control yourself": your will should be doing a better or more emphatic job of sifting your desires and "holding you back." So maybe we get a feedback loop: bodily desires or impulses get sifted by the will which moves the body which produces desire out of its particular situation.

I am not endorsing this psychology, but I am saying that this is a recon- struction of a kind of common-sense Western notion of the self. And I am saying that this is wild, bizarre, really interesting, because it turns out that a common-sense understanding of the self makes the self into a profuse mul- tiplicity of faculties and functions, one that is hierarchically organized, that is constantly articulated and reconfigured in internal transactions of power.

Now let me focus on one part of this: the will. "Get control of yourself," I think, means something like this: tell yourself what to do, and listen. Leave aside for the moment that we don't understand how this could literally be the case; it corresponds roughly, anyway, to the way we think about these things. The will in this little structure is conceived to be linguistic: the little Napoleon in your skull makes you do things by issuing orders in a language; the body is supposed to become a mirror or reflection of those orders. It is like the *Tractatus* in reverse: the body is a representation, a reflection, of the will: the body assumes the form prescribed in the propositions formed in the will. Then we can as it were read off your identity from your body, we can infer from your bodily actions what your self is, how it is arranged, which parts are privileged and which subordinated. And then we perform a moral assessment on your self from that point of view. If you are criminal or reprehensible that is an inference we draw from what your behaviour shows about yourself: you fail to manifest certain prescribed forms of self-control. Or like the po-mo folks say: the body is a site of inscription.

What I am saying would of course have to be supplemented by a Foucault-type disciplinary analysis, because the will does not operate in a vacuum and these little propositions of which it makes the body a mirror are developed in the public language and themselves arise or are articulated within institutional power-contexts. The will is trying to impose a comprehensible form on the body, trying to convert the body from a random or meaningless set of gesticulations into a story or into some appropriate repertoire of behaviours, appropriate by the standards of, say, a university, a prison, a coffee shop, a marriage. And really our individual histories are like this. Babies start off twitching randomly and more or less incomprehensibly; with great struggle we teach them to twitch meaningfully; we subject them to language and incorporate them into institutions—the family, the daycare centre, whatever—until their twitchings are semiotic and their bodies are subject to their wills. The will is itself a reflection of the institution and vice versa, which is absolutely as it must be, when it is conceived to be fundamentally linguistic.

Now it is actually a hopeful thing, I guess, that the body cannot always be effectively inscribed. Sometimes you still twitch incomprehensibly. Sometimes you act on your desires even when your little will is telling you not to. Sometimes you can't bring your body into the appropriate configuration: it resists, like when you're dieting or something and your will is trying explicitly to reconfigure your body and perhaps is unable to do so. Or when you're engaging compulsively in any behaviour. Here, in a way, what we think of as the "appropriate" power relation of will and body are reversed. This apparently chthonic, prelinguistic animal thing is resisting the blandishments of its trainer: it's like the lion devouring the lion-tamer. In fact, you might notice that it's possible for the will to get rearticulated by the bodily compulsion in such cases: that's what I did, so that must be what I want. Compulsion is a useful, at times liberating, experience because it reverses the power relations within the self or makes them dialectical, which is exactly why compulsive behavior is also aberrant, scary, in need of treatment, and so on. We conceive of it as the invasion of the animal into the pristine world of the pure linguistic self and its perfectly efficacious syntax.

2.

All of this brings us to the notion of authorship. It's often pointed out that authorship is a position of power: that the words "authorship" and "authority" are related. I'd feel a lot more powerful myself if anyone ever read my books, but I guess this is basically right. I guess I am an authority on whatever my books have been about, although right now I can't remember what my books are about. But actually the point is that the position of authorship is a claim to authority: that to present yourself as an author is to assert a kind of power, just in virtue of the nature of the voice in authorship. Now even though I think that is fundamentally true, let me point out what is obvious: that there are indefinitely many ways to take up this position, each of which has a somewhat different relation to power. You can, for example, present yourself as an author in a total expropriation or erasure of your own subjectivity, as you are expected to do in a scientific paper, for example, or maybe in philosophy too or in some forms of omniscient fictional narration. That is a very authoritative kind of authorship. Then again, there are all kinds of partial or perspectival or personal authorships and every place in between. There are authorships, like mine maybe, that are continually trying to undercut their own authority, but maybe that is also a way of trying, disarmingly, to demonstrate or claim precisely the authority that is disavowed. So there are a lot of ways of authorship, and personally I prefer the absolute bludgeon, like Nietzsche, say, where we're just going to kick your ass, where the power is as desperate and explicit as possible.

In my view, power in contemporary western culture is fundamentally linguistic (though of course there is still the occasional jackboot). It used to be that the power that was exercised through language was fundamentally bound up with a semantics: we deployed a set of concepts in order to articulate an ontology or to organize or produce a world that could be controlled through comprehension. Call that "modernity." But that is not the way power operates with relation to language anymore, or rather, a new systematics of language/power is now overlaid on the conceptual scheme or taxonomic scientific representation. Language operating as power now mutates toward a pure syntax where in a way the idea is just to keep mumbling or blabbering or scribbling in the appropriate way and really the shit means nothing at all. Think of politics in the US, which now consists almost wholly of empty cant phrases: "Let me be clear. We must educate every child for the global economy of the twenty-first century." In a way you might just as well say "blah blah blah yackety smackety"; the point is certainly not whatever this might mean; the point is simply to allow yourself to be borne aloft into power by muttering the correct phrases. This is what Baudrillard might call a hyperreal politics, a politics that is all syntax or that is a pure play of signifiers. It would be like cool and hip if it wasn't so incredibly boring. It's also a lot like, say, the uses of the cant phrases of Marxism in pre-fall-of-the-Wall Eastern Europe; the point is just to let yourself be borne aloft by ideology, where ideology finally becomes a pure syntax. The media are like this too: basically pseudo-semiotics. The point is to have a voice going, to have the television on, to be listening to a CD: the point is a quasi-human noise. It's not the sign/signified relation that's essential but rather a kind of basic syntactical arc: the construction of a news story about a crime, for example, or a weather report, or a sitcom. The point is the shape of the noise, the smiling face that has nothing to do with the content, the comforting presence that allows you to stop thinking and simply immerse yourself in the sea of pseudo-signs. And if it sounds like I despise this, I don't. I do it myself and I think that thinking is a terrible burden of which I would usually like to be relieved.

The power of authorship, however, is a rather odd power, and authorship finally melts or dissipates to a single extensionless point. One might say that the power of authorship is a power exercised through language. In this sense, and maybe you have seen this coming, the author is a will. The will reconfigures the body linguistically into the inscription of the will's proposition, or rather the will *sentences* the body—delivers a verdict on the body to the body—then punishes or rewards it or rearranges it, manacles it etc. And authorship has at least this in common with the will: its power is linguistic. But now here is something to think about: authorship, at least in its best, most thorough, most compelling moments, is not conceived as a power in language, but a power over language. The master prose stylist is not out here reconstructing the world to match some sentence; she's empowered over sentences, is a master of the language. Now this is a very odd and fundamental craft, where the materials are not things over which we have power in virtue of knowledge, but in which the materials are the very stuff of power itself, the fabric of power in our culture, the materials constituent of the will. The author is making a pseudo-semiotics out of these materials, as it were producing a will. Of course these materials are the bits of the public language. I am not asserting that the author is creating power or administering power *ex nihilo*; what I am asserting is that the author is conceived as being empowered over the instruments of power and for that reason as transcending or preceding the work of language itself. It is as if the author is working from the will to will, or as if the author is simultaneously subject to the language and also creating or inventing a language.

We authors, in part, simply allow ourselves to be borne aloft by language; every writer knows that language is a recalcitrant medium that imposes its own demands, to which you must conform your will. Nevertheless, the relation of an author to language is not exactly the same as that of an American politician or East European *apparatchik*. Because here the craft isn't governing, or whatever you might want to use language to accomplish, as if language were ever a mere instrument, but rather the craft is language itself. Perhaps the author creates a pure syntax, perhaps even a syntaxless semantics, or whatever; but the author's medium is itself the language, which seems to bespeak an empowerment over or previous to the language itself. One possible function of the author in this sense would be to invent the syntax that bears others aloft, or to deflect or reconfigure such syntaxes. Someone, I suppose, coined phrases like "information economy," "not a single child can be left behind," "putting people first." And whoever did this coining has a somewhat different relation to cant/ideology than do the poor chumps who hear it coming out of their television sets. To its hearers, these phrases are, again, a pure syntax, are merely noise organized in a familiar way. But to their authors, they are, as it were, conjurations: they are nonsense syllables, but with an incantatory force. The degree to which they succeed in bringing power to their utterers is a measure of the magical power of their authors. The people standing behind the politicians and making their mouths utter the correct incantations are still the priests or Rasputins that stand in a shadowy way behind the mannequin and authorize it to speak and to rule. The phrases they put into the mouth of the rulers could not merely be any old slice of syntax; certain phrases have a kind of efficacy in bringing power to their utterers. Their meaning, however, is not obvious, for if one really bothered to contemplate or analyze what might pass for their content, one would find it trivial or ridiculous. And part of their magical force is precisely that they slide by without anyone trying to figure out what they mean. And yet they have the effect of lending their speakers an identity, of invoking some spirit of politics that now inhabits the suit before you. The phrases "sound presidential" or whatever, and to know which phrases can bring this identity or spirit to inhabit a suit is the art and authority of the speechwriter.

This Rasputin figure in the political body corresponds to some equally mysterious entity in the self. Language is not only something that is imposed on persons by an external force; it is something we invented and it is something that operates internally as well as to which we are subjected. Each of us is an inventor of language as well as its slave; each of us cooperates in his oppression and oppresses himself; each of us partly invents the ideology to which we are subjected and partly subjects ourselves to it. The author function in the culture corresponds to whatever in the person would be the inventor or the channeler of will. When someone says, "you should get some willpower here," what in the world does the word "you" refer to? It refers, I guess, to something that could compose a script for the will, something that invents a syntax for the will, an author in the body. Maybe this thing is prelinguistic or maybe it is language itself. Maybe it is a Cartesian ego or maybe it is a cyborg/sadist/strumpet/stone/slave/seed. Maybe there is no such thing.

Power, even or particularly power as it operates within a single self, is always dialectical. Will is never perfectly and instantly obeyed. The will orders the body forward, or reconfigures it, but except in cases of deep insanity, the possibilities of what can be willed are articulated within the bounds of bodily possibility. I'm not out here willing myself to jump over the moon; in a way I'm not able to will that except in a moment of deep aberration. When I empower myself over you, say in bed as we have sadomasochistic sex, my desire for you informs my will which informs my action which reconfigures your body. But unless I have mutated from friendly sadist to dangerous crazy person, the possible reconfigurations of your body I consider or impose are constrained by the reconfigurations your body can possibly assume. Power in this sense is never transparent and is never originary: power and its object are mutually simultaneously constituted. Do you see that? Power works with, and not only against, the stuff over which it is empowered, or it is at best completely irresponsible or at worst utterly delusory and demented.

The power over language that we might find in authorship is like that too. Language is itself an opaque medium. It cannot be reconfigured at perfect whim, not at all; power over language is as dialectical as any other power. And yet it has got to be a very fundamental power because it operates with and over the materials of will. The speechwriter must work in and on the public language, and at most achieves a kind of deflection of the already-existing syntax; her power is precisely this deflection, or at any rate is embodied in its possibility. On the background of the possibility of this deflection, even the choice merely to have the mouthpiece emit existing cant phrases appears as a kind of empowerment.

3.

Now let me say this: I hate my will. My will is extremely powerful and I experience myself as its slave. Isn't this some crazy shit we've got going? I experience my self not as the will that linguistically articulates my body, but at least also as the body that resists that articulation and delineates the limits of its possible forms. Addiction is often conceived of as a failure of will. Now if that were so—and perhaps in one mode or moment it is so—addiction would be an act of revolution, an act of liberation whereby the body frees itself, in at least one mode or moment, from its linguistic articulation. But in fact, and not necessarily incompatibly, addicts often suffer from an excess of will. Ask yourself what it takes to pour vodka down your throat until you puke or pass out. Ask yourself what it takes to do that, say, every day. I'll tell you what it takes: it takes will-power. You have absolutely got to stop listening to your body; you've got to overcome a thousand bodily recalcitrances and make yourself keep pouring. Ask yourself what it takes to keep doing this even while everyone around you is telling you that you need to stop, and so on. It takes a masterful will. But in my opinion, what is sought through this intensification of will, finally, is a place where the will is annihilated. One seeks through a kind of absolute self- command, a perfect discipline of ingestion, to bring body and will into the sort of flawless alignment which collapses them into identity. One seeks to make correspondence of will and body perfect, to create a body that is perfectly inscribed or which cannot be inscribed, wherein the dialectic of will and body is annihilated because the will finally conforms to the body instead of vice versa: a reversed semiotic in which the reality effects an inscription, in which body writes will, in which the inscription is composed by its object. What this amounts to, finally, is a complete erasure of inscription, or a collapse of the self out of the linguistic order. The desire for the end that is the desire to be seduced, to tumble into the abyss of pure desire or even the erasure of desire, an Edenic dream of man before or outside of language, where I escape finally into and from my will, a dream of nondifferentiation where I desire whatever I get, or desire nothing at all, a masochistic letting go into a will that is not mine or a perfect masochistic seduction where there is no will operational, just a door into absence from myself, a relief from myself, a place where all the chattering stops, where I let go finally, completely. And then this dream too would be a return to a kind of perfect authorship reduced to inanimacy, a perfect empowerment over the language which could not itself be linguistic, a pure vanishing point of questionless crushing power where one is nothing and everything, a religious ecstasy that turns one to stone.

So here is my thesis for the moment: addicts suffer from an excess of will, and through a deep prolonged intensification of will they seek an annihilation of the distance between will and body: they seek to collapse into a single thing or to find a non-fragmented or non-differentiated or non-alienated identity.

Or perhaps we should conceive this as an animal identity, or a machine identity, or an identity of stone: an identity that can no longer be conceived fundamentally in terms of language and self-division, an identity that is no longer a "self," because the "self" as we conceive it is always a site of power. Understand: obviously it takes willpower to inject heroin into your bloodstream. But where you get when you do this is a place at which the will is less importunate: at which you experience a surcease or extinguishment of will, which for a person suffering from an excess of will is the deepest relief and release, the only real vacation. To be in a heroin nod is to finally feel cured of the self, defragmented. What lurks out there as the end of the high, the end of highs, is the extinction of consciousness, the extinction of the self: death as a feathery sifting back to presence.

Authorship in this sense could be conceived as an addiction, or as the addiction, or as a kind of meta or mega addiction. And I have literally been addicted to authorship in my own opinion, in a deeply self-destructive, that is, deeply self-creative way. Certainly I have written compulsively. All my writing, and I think this is true of a lot of people, has been aimed primarily at treating myself; I am always telling myself what I think I need to hear, am always writing the books I think I need to read. My books are attempts to reconfigure my self or to manufacture a new self. They have not been entirely unsuccessful in this regard and so to that extent they are worthwhile even if they don't really ever gain much of an audience. They always have a pretty wide audience in my head. But now this makes it sound like my authorship is just more willpower: just more linguistic refiguring of the self in which the self is simultaneously empowered and stripped of power, in which I "seize command" of myself. But that's not the way I experience it.

The power of authorship is a power, dialectical to be sure, over the public language. Authorship uses the public language or sometimes rips it apart, not as a whole or not in an utter expungement or obliteration, obviously, but in inflection or deflection. In this sense my authorship feels like my tethered escape from the public order of signification, that is from the contexts of institutional power through inscription. It is also, simultaneously of course, my entry into precisely those institutions in the most concrete ways: through like tenure or through university presses. Maybe my authorship is where I try to participate in the ever-ongoing work of inscribing you in the service of these institutions. But it is also the point at which I seem to have some control over these inscriptions or even to resist them. I have no idea what I mean by "I" in this context. It is not exactly the inscribed body, the object of will, though that is there. It is not exactly the will itself either, because the will is language in my head. It is what engages dialectically with the will and with the public language to make the language of the will; it is a participation in my own inscription, it is an incantatory power that is myself, if that makes any sense.

Yet it has to appear to come from outside myself because it comes from outside the transaction of desire/will/scripted body which is the fundamental loop, spinning in which I find myself. And it has to appear to come from outside myself because it is a craft the materials of which are found in the public language. A potter will say: the pot makes itself with my hands, or the pot takes form in my hands but I don't, e.g., force it into form. And an author will say, or will if she's any good: the sentence or the book or the story or the characters, take shape in my hands, or write themselves using my hands or whatever. This is what I mean when I say authorship is a disappearing point, a point where finally literally there is nothing.

Thus, authorship is a self-assertion and also a disappearance, a place where the desire/will/body loop collapses and the "self" is lost or is perfectly present, which finally are exactly the same thing. The human self as all these po-mo folks have been insisting for all these years, is a sad delusion; we're fragmented, incoherent, etc. Of course we are, and there's no easier way to see this than to actually draw out some of the implications of a "common sense" view of the self, as I have been doing. But then these fragments might also be imploding in an authorship or in an addiction, do you see? They might be collapsing into the ideal presence of an animal or an inanimate object, into a full-bore objectivity, a pure block or plenum that is surface all the way down, infinite or indivisible; or it might be imploding into an extensionless authorship in which there is not even any surface or in which a surface is inconceivable, in which there's just language making language, a will being used by a language and a language being used by a will, in which the will is itself a patchwork of linguistic bits.

A lover of mine once told me that my vision of the ideal sage was a vision of an inanimate object. I told her that was false but even as I said that I knew it was true: I yearn for the perfect presence of a boulder; or: I want to die. Even as all these power relations are established within the self, even as all these various self-divisions are conceived and imposed and even as they gain leverage over the self and splinter it into a thousand pieces they are also collapsing or revealing themselves as delusions or insane intimations of immortality and disembodiment. Even as we are dividing ourselves against ourselves we are resisting the blandishments of will and collapsing into a perfect incomprehensible presence.

8

Confessing Addiction:
A Response to Crispin Sartwell's "Addiction and Authorship"

Alan Bewell

In responding to Crispin Sartwell's suggestive paper, with a view to fostering further discussion, I would like to place the confession with which he opens his talk—"I'm both an addict and an author"—within a discursive context.

The "confession of the addict" is a very modern genre. In some ways, it is the prototype for all modern confessions, from Dostoevsky to Nabokov to perhaps Jerry Springer, in which the author speaks of a compulsion that both defines and divides his or her identity. This discourse emerged during the Romantic period, most explicitly with Thomas De Quincey's *Confessions of an English Opium Eater*, and, of course, with the social and cultural mythologies that developed around his friend Samuel Taylor Coleridge. The "confession *of* the addict" constitutes a certain way of framing questions of human subjectivity. Since the beginning of the nineteenth century, the "addict" has represented a special kind of subject, produced primarily in philosophical, medical, and literary discourse. It is not a discourse that exists on its own, however, for the "confession of the addict" is part of a larger "discourse on addiction." Where confessions had previously functioned within a juridical or theological context, the confession of the addict promises to tell us things about ourselves that maybe we did not know, maybe we have always known, yet which we normally choose to deny.

Addicts confess to non-addicts. The authority to speak comes from the addiction. As Crispin Sartwell remarks: "I've decided that I've already done all the research that I need to do: now all I have to do is write." The truth that is revealed by the addict is a truth that has been gained through addiction. Yet since the promise of the author-addict (whatever the addiction might be) is that what will be brought to light in the confession is not a private or individual experience, but a truth about the human condition that the non-addict would otherwise remain unaware of, the confession of the addict makes larger claims about human nature and volition. For Sartwell, addiction is at least one place where the delusion of freedom melts away. Why are non-addicts fascinated by such confessions? Why is the reading about compulsion so addictive? Why do literary addicts of all kinds—from drug addicts to food addicts, from alcoholics to workaholics—continue to find an audience for the confession of their compulsions?

Michel Foucault argues in his *History of Sexuality* that what defines the modern period is that it can't stop talking about sex. Perhaps this is only part of the story. Maybe to be modern is to be unable to stop talking about one's addictions. Thus, the musician Robert Palmer's "Might as well face it, you're addicted to love" may contribute less to the history of sexuality than to the discourse of addiction. Deep down all non-addicts know that they too are addicts, in the same way that an alcoholic who no longer drinks knows that he is still an alcoholic. We know that we too could become addicted to a drug, a passion, an idea, and we too could follow this addiction to its end. The "confession of the addict" therefore can be said to produce a special kind of subjectivity that calls into question conventional rationalistic or moralistic representations of the self. For the confession to work its magic, it cannot simply produce an addict; it must also construct an audience of non-addicts, and this latter group must see in this confession the enactment of some kind of deep truth otherwise denied to them. Every confessing addict seems to say to his auditors: "Might as well face it, you're addicted to _____." (Here you are to fill in the blank.)

From its beginnings, the discourse of addiction, of which the confession of the addict is one component, has been one in which notions of identity have been contested. Questions about human desire, willpower, the body and the mind are continually raised by any attempt to sort out who is controlling whom in the world of the addict. Sartwell nicely points out the manner in which the addict's fractured and contradictory being seems to confirm the "common-sense Western notion of the self" as a self-divided being. The word "addict" comes from the Latin word "addictus," meaning "given over." It referred to slaves, as in "one being given over to another." But who does the giving, and who is given over when this process takes place within the body and mind of the "addict"? Who speaks when the addict speaks? Is it the drug talking?

De Quincey seemed to suggest this possibility when he said of his *Confessions* that, "Not the opium-eater, but the opium, is the true hero of the tale" (114). Perhaps what speaks is the "enslaved" self, the self possessed by, or "under the influence" of, something else, the "addicted" self "given over" to somebody or something else. Perhaps, the addict is a "truer," more authentic self, whose compulsions are not an exterior control, but the expression of a purer being, a deeper self, that has been occluded or managed by society and language. Since the Romantic period, the discourse on addiction has served as a dark mirror in which questions of human identity have been scrutinized. In it, traditional hierarchies of body, soul, and mind have been either anxiously affirmed or radically destabilized. Sartwell's paper contributes to this latter tradition of destabilizing confessions.

The focus of Sartwell's paper is on the internal conflict that shapes the identity of the addict. One might note, however, that the identity of the addict is also shaped by a contestation of discourses that take place within society itself. There is not just one kind of addict, but many, as the subjectivity that constitutes the "addict" changes depending upon what discourse he or she appears in. It is worth recognizing that Crispin Sartwell does not address the subjectivity of the addict through medical discourse, where that subjectivity is seen as an expression of pathology. Issues of public health and of the impact of an addictive lifestyle upon the health of the addict are nowhere present in his paper. His addict is not understood within a context of sickness and its treatment, nor is it linked to powerful public discourse on the link between addiction and AIDS. Sartwell's "addict" is primarily a subjectivity shaped within the context of philosophical discourse. His "confession" addresses philosophical questions about the nature of human identity, as the addict questions notions of will and social convention. Being an "addict" does not appear to be all that bad a condition, but then again we live in a society where, as Eve Sedgwick has suggested, addiction seems epidemic. Ultimately, in such a context, the term may not mean much.

Sartwell adopts the position that the addict engages in a willfulness that takes him beyond the will. Addiction is not "enslavement," but an attempt to abolish hierarchies. I find this argument, oddly, fairly conventional, and here I guess I am indicating some disappointment with the deep truth that this contemporary confession brings to light. Adopting a fairly traditional idea that the will is fundamentally linked to language and institutions, while "desire" and the body stand "outside of language," Sartwell sees addiction, like authorship, as a kind of enfranchisement, which uses the very means of self-control to go beyond it; it is a means of going beyond a hierarchical and contradictory self structured by language and power.

What is this "pure desire" that stands outside of language? When he says, "I have no control, literally none over what I desire," the "I" that he is referring to sounds much more centred, much less self-divided than the contradictory "I" of the addict, with which he begins his paper. Replace pure mind with pure desire, and it sounds like the "thinking subject" has now been replaced by the "desiring one." Also, what is this state of peace that comes through the journey into addiction? The drug that destroys may seem to promise some kind of deeper truth—that of oblivion, objectivity, or in Sartwell's words, the "collapsing into the ideal presence of an animal or an inanimate object, into a full-bore objectivity a pure block or plenum that is surface all the way down, infinite or indivisible." The promise of a kind of earthly paradise, either Coleridge's Xanadu or Sartwell's pure objectivity, is, indeed, inseparable from the discourse of addiction. Yet I wonder whether this description is fully expressive of the contradictions that have traditionally shaped the discourse of the addict, contradictions that I sense are deeply part of Sartwell's own viewpoint, but are not, at least in this context, stated as directly as they might be.

In considering Sartwell's comments on the relationship between addiction and authorship, it might be worthwhile considering two other author-addicts. Take for instance Coleridge's latter years when, as a public laudanum addict, he held court to the major literary, medical, and philosophical figures of his day. Coleridge at this time was not famous for what he wrote, but for his extraordinary powers as a talker. Here is Keats's description of his one encounter with Coleridge:

> I walked with him at his alderman-after-dinner pace for near
> two miles I suppose. In those two Miles he broached a thousand
> things—let me see if I can give you a list—Nightingales,
> Poetry—on Poetrical Sensation—Metaphysics—Different genera
> and species of Dreams—Nightmare—a dream accompanied by a
> sense of touch—single and double touch—A dream related—First
> and second consciousness—the difference explained between will
> and Volition—so many metaphysicians from a want of smoking
> the second consciousness—Monsters—the Kraken—Mermaids—
> Southey believes in them—Southey's belief too much diluted—A
> Ghost story—Good morning—I heard his voice as it came
> towards me—I heard it as he moved away—I had heard it all
> the interval—if it may be called so. (Armour and Howes, 277)

Keats nicely captures the obsessive qualities of Coleridge's talk, and the weird experience that his contemporaries felt as they encountered a person who seemed unable to stop talking, whose identity was reducible to a ghostly stream of language: in De Quincey's words, an "eternal stream of talk" (197). Wordsworth described his non-stop talking as being akin to a

> majestic river, the sound or sight of whose course you caught at
> intervals, which was sometimes concealed by forests, sometimes
> lost in sand, then came flashing out broad and distinct, then
> again took a turn which your eye could not follow, yet you knew
> and felt that it was the same river: so there was always a train,
> a stream, in Coleridge's discourse, always a connection between
> its parts in his mind, though one not always perceptible to the
> minds of others. (380)

When at another time, having devoted hours listening and nodding his head in agreement to another Coleridgean talkathon, Wordsworth was asked by a puzzled auditor if he had understood what Coleridge was getting at, Wordsworth was more blunt: "Not a word of it."

Coleridge's fame as a talker emerged at the same time as his fame as an addict, and the variety of opinions concerning the relationship between the two suggests the perplexity with which Coleridge's auditors listened to his extraordinary talk. Some thought that talking was a substitute for writing: strong authors write, weak ones talk. Many saw this talk as the expression of a diseased will. Dorothy Wordsworth blamed opium: "The principle effect of opium on Coleridge," she writes, "was to bring up his weaknesses abreast of his strength, to nourish that dreamy self-indulgence and that habit of endless talk which he had even when a child" (373).

Others saw the compulsion to talk as itself an addiction. Others quoted from the "Rime of the Ancient Mariner," noting Coleridge's "strange powers of speech" (134). Like the Wedding Guests, Coleridge's auditors were often rapt by this talk. Needless to say, they noted that Coleridge's "glittering eye" was not only similar to that of the Ancient Mariner, but also, as Harriet Martineau notes, "common among opium eaters" (297). This is an extraordinary kind of authority in which the power of the words does not lie in the ability of the auditors to understand them, but instead in the obsessive stream of language itself, the possession of words, of a will that has become almost entirely caught up and addicted by words. Nobody knew what to make of Coleridge's strange and wondrous inability to make normal conversation, his incapacity for dialogue. Some called it genius, others sickness, others addiction. Nevertheless, Coleridge's contemporaries couldn't get enough of his talk. Crispin Sartwell is not unlike Coleridge in his ability to produce a similar state of uncertainty.

In contrast to Sartwell's essentially dualistic view of the power struggles that shape the self, one might place De Quincey's more geological view of the self as a palimpsestic site of contestatory powers. Rather than seeing the self as being structured by a power relationship between a linguistically constructed will and a nonlinguistic desire, De Quincey sees the self as a palimpsest in which no writing—either of will or desire—is ever lost, in which opium discloses the many layers that underlie the construction of a being. For De Quincey, opium does not enfranchise; it gives knowledge of the contradictory, and often tragic depths of one's being. There is no peace at the end of the opium-eater's journey, only guilt and pain raised to an even more apocalyptic pitch. It does not lead to a place beyond language, but instead uncovers layer after layer of inscriptions, as one layer has replaced another not by erasing it, but by writing over it.

In De Quincey's *Confessions*, there is no place outside of language, or no inside of desire, "no erasure of inscription," as Sartwell argues, to which opium takes the addict. The journey is instead downward and inward into more fantastic and more horrific levels of impassioned power and fatalistic impotence. The self that emerges in De Quincey's *Confessions* is structured by a play of power and contradiction on all levels of his being. Against his description of what addiction means to the addict, *Trainspotting* is a very slight production, indeed. Perhaps this is a sign that the relationship between the powers that shape the modern subject, most powerfully articulated in the conflict between addiction and will, have lost much of their sublimity. Maybe, to use Wordsworth's words, in the contemporary understanding of the self the truths that once powerfully resided in the discourse of the addict have faded "into the light of common day."

Works Cited

Armour, Richard W. and Raymond F. Howes (eds.). 1940. *Coleridge the Talker, A Series of Contemporary Descriptions and Comments*. Ithaca, NY: Cornell University Press.

De Quincey, Thomas. 1971. *Confessions of an English Opium Eater*, edited by Alethea Hayter. Harmondsworth, England: Penguin.

Foucault, Michel. 1978. *The History of Sexuality*. New York: Pantheon Books.

Sedgewick, Eve Kosofsky. 1993. *Tendencies*. Durham: Duke University Press.

9

In Vino Veritas?

Anthony Cunningham

> *The wine urges me on, the bewitching wine, which sets even a*
> *wise man to singing and to laughing gently and rouses him*
> *to dance and brings forth words which were better unspoken.*
> *Homer,* The Odyssey

> *Give strong drink unto him that is ready to perish, and wine*
> *unto those that be of heavy hearts. Let him drink, and forget*
> *his poverty, and remember his misery no more.*
> Proverbs

Human motivations are notoriously difficult to track. The roots of the desires, inclinations, and passions that ostensibly move us often lie deep in psychological labyrinths, and these roots can be difficult to recognize even after their offshoots culminate in some action or other. Quite frankly, sometimes we have precious little idea why we do what we do, much less a clear picture of why others do what they do. Perhaps because the prey is so slippery and elusive, many of us find the enterprise of trying to capture and understand human motivations fascinating, particularly when the stakes are high and the mysteries deep. In this vein, I should like to try my hand at saying something about why so many illustrious (and thoroughly ordinary) writers have faced life with a pen in one hand and a bottle in the other. Faulkner, Hemingway, Fitzgerald, Melville, Sinclair Lewis, Steinbeck, Hart Crane, Dylan Thomas, Edgar Allen Poe, Eugene O'Neill—all these writers and many more have lived with drink somewhere close to the centre of their lives. In some of these cases, alcohol played a pivotal part in a premature demise, so the stakes were high where their drinking was concerned. Moreover, the question whether there might be some significant connection between literary creativity and alcohol must have some allure for anyone who truly appreciates beautiful literature and poetry. Quite simply, it would be very interesting to know if alcohol and literary creativity are allies of some sort. My philosophical speculations are meant as nothing more than reflective observations, but hopefully they can contribute something meaningful to an understanding of why so many writers have found a friend of sorts in drink.

Speculation in this territory is daunting. When it comes to charting human motivations, cause-and-effect relationships can be particularly complex. For every straightforward case where the path to action is clear and distinct, there are many others where numerous elements join forces to produce an eventual action. In some of these cases, trying to discern degrees of responsibility for the contributing elements is a bit like trying to separate different pigments once they are mixed: you just can't do it and there is little sense in trying. When it comes to a possible link between creative writing and alcohol, my guess is that any such link is not straightforward in the sense of there being one dominant cause common to most cases. In other words, I doubt that the same exact things drive all writers to drink in the same exact way. If I am right, then no one simple story will suffice for laying bare some grand connection between writing and alcohol.

Fortunately, I am not after anything like a comprehensive picture that spells out all the relevant causes and connections in fine detail. Indeed, I am less interested in certain sorts of explanations, however true and important they may be in the overall picture. Let me briefly mention some explanations that do not concern me here. For instance, some observers have noted that the writer's life is ultimately a solitary one and that writers left to themselves are often their own worst critics. The idea is that left alone as they must be to toil obsessively over their own work and fearful that their work may never be what it might be, some writers turn to the bottle for comfort, sometimes as a way of filling up the space between the periods when the words come and sometimes for solace when the words don't come as they should. Likewise, some observers have noted that the depiction of the literary life as a hard-drinking one may well function as a self-fulfilling prophecy: So long as drinking is seen as part and parcel of the craft, then aspiring writers are likely to drink dutifully, and as we all know, duty often has a way of evolving into habit, whether for good or ill. And particularly if some people are hard-wired psychologically with predilections for alcoholism, then we should not be surprised if those who feel duty-bound by their craft to drink are likely to populate the alcoholic ranks far out of proportion to their numbers in the general population. In this case, the result will simply look like one of the inevitable hazards of the profession.

Interesting as these speculations are, they and others like them do not interest me here so long as they make no claims about any connections between alcohol and the intrinsic content of the writing or writing process. What interests me is not whether the drinking life tends to intersect incidentally with a writing lifestyle or personality. Instead, I wonder whether there might be something about a drinking life that bears some deeper connection to creative writing itself. On closer inspection, it may even turn out that explanations like those above actually play a less incidental role when placed in the context of a bigger picture. We shall have to see. Part of what moves me to frame the issue in these terms is the fact that creative writers have a well-deserved drinking reputation that is not paralleled by other people who spend a fair part of their lives engaged in serious writing. No doubt there are philosophers, historians, classicists, and English literature scholars who regularly drink to great excess. But either these writers tend to drink far less than creative writers on average or else they have done an extraordinary job of concealing their habits, thereby heading off the hard-drinking reputation they may actually deserve. Moreover, even if the average philosopher drinks just as much or more than the average poet or novelist, I feel safe in saying that most people would be surprised by a philosopher insisting that drunkenness is a vital element of the philosophical method. Sure enough, many confused and frustrated undergraduates have no doubt warned their philosophy professors about Immanuel Kant driving them to drink but few of them have honestly concluded that the key to understanding the *Critique of Pure Reason* might be found at the bottom of a whiskey glass. Perhaps hard-drinking creative writers should not be taken at their word, but many have insisted that drinking somehow plays an important part in their creativity. Of course, alcoholics often insist that they need alcohol just to function and the sad fact is that the claim is true for those in the throes of addiction: for those who are hooked, drink is a prerequisite not just for writing, but more basically, for getting through everyday life. For the writer addicted to alcohol there may truly be no good words without drink. Nevertheless, the possibility that alcohol plays a deeper role in writing than simply staving off withdrawal or providing some respite should be taken seriously. Thus, I wish to consider the speculation that booze might sometimes play the role of genuine muse for creative writers.

One clear way in which alcohol could conceivably play this role would be as a mind-altering agent that fundamentally affects the writer's perception of the world in some important way. In *The Doors of Perception*, Aldous Huxley recounts his controlled experiments with mescalin, a drug that dramatically altered his perceptions:

> In the mescalin experience the implied questions to which the eye responds are of another order. Place and distance cease to be of much interest. The mind does its perceiving in terms of intensity of existence, profundity of significance, relationships within a pattern. I saw the books, but was not at all concerned with their positions in space. What I noticed, what impressed itself upon my mind was the fact that all of them glowed with living light and that in some the glory was more manifest than in others. In this context position and the three dimensions were beside the point. Not, of course, that the category of space had been abolished. When I got up and walked about, I could do so quite normally, without misjudging the whereabouts of objects. Space was still there; but it had lost its predominance. (20)

He continues:

> *"This is how one ought to see," I kept saying as I looked down at*
> *my trousers, or glanced at the jeweled books in the shelves, at the*
> *legs of my infinitely more than Van-Goghian chair. "This is how*
> *one ought to see, how things really are."* (34)

As Huxley describes his experience, his perceptions under the influence of mescalin are not only very different, but somehow deeper and more profound. Huxley and many others who have experimented with psychotropic drugs often tell tales of seeing into the nature and meaning of things with a clarity and perspective unavailable to the unaltered mind. Just how such an experience might affect a writer and how an altered perspective might affect writing itself would presumably vary depending upon the details of the experience and the psychological idiosyncrasies of the writer. However, it would be hard to imagine such experiences not having some significant effects of one kind or another. If such experiences genuinely open a window to another world then we should expect the experience to be very influential. If alcohol can alter experience in this manner then perhaps it serves writers as a kind of portal to a different way of seeing the world.

Alcohol may well serve as a kind of portal, but if so, not the same kind of portal afforded by mescalin in Huxley's example. Though alcohol certainly affects perceptions of the physical world, the alterations do not tend toward anything like fundamental reconstructions of the very way we see it. We have little trouble conjuring up images of people under the effects of psychotropic drugs contemplating birds, trees, or flowers and, at least by their own lights, unlocking some deep mystery of the universe. But such images do not ring true when it comes to those under the influence of alcohol. And even if alcohol can sometimes fundamentally reorder perceptions in this way and to this degree, then the alteration usually is not something that can be brought back from the experience. In other words, people who drink enough to effect radical changes in physical perceptions are usually so far gone that the experience and its purported insights will be lost to them when they return to sobriety.

Yet before writing off psychotropic drug experiences as unhelpful for understanding how alcohol might influence the way writers see the world, reconsider the differences in the subtle details of the reports on these experiences. A great many such reports centre on dramatic alterations in perceptions of time, space, colour, and the like. Again, these seem unhelpful as guides for thinking about experiences with alcohol. But some reports make various sorts of claims of another kind. For instance, consider someone who attests to something like appreciating the "unity of all things" while under the influence of a psychotropic drug. In such a case, the purported insight or truth cannot be a straightforward instance of physically seeing something, as we might see birds, trees, or flowers in their dramatically altered states. It is worth noting that such claims usually are not fleshed out in terms of a two-part process of cognitive apprehension (seeing the unity of all things) and affective reaction (concluding that this fact matters). Rather, seeing and feeling are usually experienced as inseparable: seeing the unity of all things (or any other purported insight in this vein) is a matter of somehow feeling the interconnectedness of everything and everybody. Thus, insight does not so much lead to feeling as it fundamentally consists in feeling.

Whether such phenomena are genuine insights that track anything beyond the psychological states of the person doing the seeing is a worthy question in its own right, but one that does not concern me here. Instead, I am concerned with the possibility that emotions might likewise play a key role in an understanding of an interesting link between alcohol and creative writing. Indeed, I think the twists and turns of human emotions have a major role to play in any revealing explanation of why alcohol should find such a welcome home in many a writer's life.

To tease out this explanation, consider the role of emotions in literature and poetry where readers are concerned. In this vein, first consider the ancient Greek tragedies. The tragedies were not performed for idle entertainment. Rather, they were meant to give communal voice to the deepest human aspirations, fears, longings, sorrows, and joys. The idea of catharsis speaks to the intended effects on an audience: the tragedies were meant to call forth powerful emotions in response to the events and characters portrayed on stage. Catharsis goes beyond simply ridding pent-up emotions, the way a cathartic agent might rid and cleanse the body. The best understanding of catharsis includes the sense in which emotions are called forth as an expression and education of our very humanity. In other words, the tragedies were meant to provide an opportunity to feel the right emotions, toward the right things, to the right degree, in the right way. Thus, the tragedies were designed both to manifest and mould the character of their audiences. By taking their audiences away from everyday distractions and preoccupations, and by highlighting tragic elements of human life and character, the tragedies called special attention to what should matter most in well-lived lives and to how even the best lives are always fragile.

The best literature inevitably aims to capture, express, and evoke powerful emotions in this same sense. Literature can do other things too, but insofar as they fail in this respect, they almost always fail, pure and simple. The stakes in literature need not always be as high as those in the tragedies, but there must be something that captivates us and resonates with our lived experience. Without the same, literature loses its power except as idle entertainment. Idle entertainment amuses but seldom moves us deeply. On the other hand, great literary works that truly move us can often be very hard and even disturbing work for readers. For instance, a work like Toni Morrison's Nobel Prize-winning *Beloved* can leave an attentive reader emotionally spent. One cannot sympathetically follow the life of Sethe, an escaped slave who makes her way from Kentucky to free Ohio, only to be forced by tragic circumstances to take the life of one of her children, without experiencing a painful catharsis. When we read Sethe's desperate attempts to explain her actions to her dead child returned in the form of a beautiful young woman, Beloved, we cannot help but be moved by this kind of pathos:

> *Yet she knew that Sethe's greatest fear was the same one Denver*
> *had in the beginning—that Beloved might leave. That before*
> *Sethe could make her understand what it meant—what it took to*
> *drag the teeth of that saw under the little chin; to feel the baby*
> *blood pump like oil in her hands; to hold her face so her head*
> *would stay on; to squeeze her so she could absorb, still, the death*
> *spasms that shot through that adored body, plump and sweet*
> *with life—Beloved might leave. (251)*

For a reader sympathetically immersed in the details of Sethe's desperate quest for understanding and forgiveness, herein lies the power and glory of this novel. Great literature does not simply work on readers in ways that give vent to emotions that are fully formed and ready to go; rather, it artfully calls forth and even educates the emotions. Attentive, engaged readers can emerge from a novel like *Beloved* with a heightened sense of what things really matter in life.

If the greatness of literature resides in its power to capture, express, and evoke the deepest human aspirations, fears, longings, joys, and sorrows, consider the role of emotions in the writer as opposed to the written word. Writers must surely be able to feel and understand emotions to capture, express, and evoke them. Experience, either real or imaginary, is absolutely vital in this vein. To capture the emotional lives of human beings and to portray lives and moments in ways that call forth emotional responses in readers, writers must be emotionally engaged. Of course, a writer can be emotionally engaged and still be a bad writer; such engagement is necessary but not sufficient for good literature. Yet, notice that where other forms of writing are concerned, it is not so clear that emotional engagement plays the same critical role, or at least not to the same degree. Actually, my guess is that the writings of philosophers, classicists, historians, and the like suffer, and sometimes suffer quite badly, for the lack of passion, both in terms of their own detachment and the detachment of the writing. Nevertheless, the opportunities for detached, clinical writing that is still good work are far greater in these quarters. If my aim is to take readers through Descartes's *Meditations*, the rise and fall of the Roman Empire, or the Industrial Revolution, I may be able to go a fair distance in these directions without being emotionally engaged and without emotionally engaging readers. The same is not so for literature.

Emotional engagement may sound simple and straightforward enough when it comes to writing: consult lived and imaginary experience to give voice to a range of human emotions in stories and words that will in turn give rise to significant emotional responses in a reader. However, this is far easier said than done. Surely it is no accident that novelists so often speak of having to work long and hard to discover the final forms of their characters. Properly speaking, this may be invention rather than literal discovery, but if so, it isn't *ex nihilo* and it isn't easy. Conjuring characters and images that faithfully track and capture human experience is a subtle, daunting business in more ways than one. For one thing, writers must see, feel, and understand what they aim to capture. This is more than a matter of simply feeling things like fear, anger, loneliness, despair, grief, resentment, love, or joy and then using these experiences as the raw material for a literary imagination. People vary greatly in their ability to recognize and understand their own emotional states. Experiencing these states and having an appreciation of them are certainly not identical. Fine awareness, reflection, and self-knowledge are essential elements of any such appreciation, especially where more powerful, intense emotions are concerned. Understanding one's own emotional experiences often requires diligent struggle. No doubt this is clearest in the case of traumatic experience. War veterans, rape survivors, victims of incest, and torture victims often testify to the difficulty of giving voice to the complex, painful emotions that sometimes haunt them. And without some such voice, these unresolved, unarticulated emotions can easily lay waste to a life. Of course, there are important differences of degree and kind between traumatic experiences and everyday ones. Nevertheless, what they share so far as my point here is concerned is that their attendant emotions are not automatically transparent even to the person who experiences them. Having emotions and knowing emotions are two different things. If writers are to capture emotions they must first understand them, and this is no small feat.

In order to understand our own emotions we must be able to put them into words, at least to some degree. I am not suggesting that a person must have a concept of an emotion in order to feel that emotion. Certainly small children can experience certain emotions long before they have the ability to give voice to them or articulate them in terms of well-defined concepts. Likewise, there are plenty of historical examples of people having what sound like certain emotions without having concepts that clearly define the borders of these same emotions. For instance, Icelandic sagas seldom spell out the emotional states of their heroes in anything other than purely physical terms. "Reddening" is the most frequent somatic indication of emotion in these sagas and readers must infer the likely emotional state from the narrative context. Obviously, reddening alone cannot distinguish between emotions like shame, embarrassment, or anger. But an attentive reader can usually have a fair guess at what a character is feeling based upon the details of the situation. Writers, readers, and saga heroes alike surely can experience many emotions without anything like a rich, complex vocabulary to describe these emotions.

Nevertheless, if one is to understand emotions in order to capture them and not simply feel them, then words matter, and particularly where complicated emotions are concerned. Some primal emotions may need little by way of language to experience and understand them. Anyone chased by lions, tigers, or bears doesn't need much in the way of sophisticated concepts to be afraid and to be painfully aware of the fear as fear. But notice two important points here. In many cases, self-consciousness may actually make a difference so far as the nature of the emotion is concerned. Thus, there can be differences between instances of sadness and loneliness that are not recognized as such and the same seen for what they are. The same can be said for other complex emotions. And self-consciousness so far as one's own emotional states are concerned can often require some subtle and sophisticated distinctions. For instance, envy and resentment can certainly be experienced without the requisite concepts to give voice to the differences between them. But if a writer means to understand and capture these emotions then they must be conceptually distinguished on some level in ways that go beyond their superficial manifestations. After all, not only can these very different emotions bear striking similarities so far as their outward expressions are concerned, but since most people are loath to admit to envy and much more inclined to acknowledge resentment, the differences between these emotions must be charted by way of some fairly subtle and sophisticated words.

Notice that being able to give voice to one's own emotional states and experiences in ways that clarify them for oneself isn't necessarily the same thing as providing a similar voice for others. In other words, writers must not only understand emotions; they must be able to convey them. Finding words and images that can do justice to the emotional twists and turns of life is most often a struggle. Indeed, if literature is to be any good, it must usually function as a kind of crystallizing filter for everyday life. What I mean by this is not that literature need go above or beyond everyday experience. Rather, what good literature must do is distill out what is emotionally salient about our experiences. When literature hits the mark, it most often leaves us with a sense that something we only dimly or incompletely saw has been brought into clearer focus. Literature resonates when it clarifies our own vision and experience in this sense. The fact is that we are often too distracted, confused, exhausted, listless, or indifferent to notice all sorts of things that matter in our everyday orbits. Good literature makes us stop and notice things that warrant noticing. This is a difficult feat to pull off because not just any words will do.

Given these facts, were all writers and poets all-knowing sages, their task would still be difficult enough. But of course writers are first and foremost people and this obvious fact complicates matters. When they struggle to give voice to the emotional complexities of human life they most often must draw from and deal with their own personal struggles of one kind or another. Obviously, this depends upon the particular writer and the particular literary target. Not every piece of writing forces a writer to confront personal demons of one kind or another. But many do, and when they do, the task of finding the right words or images to give voice to the literary or poetic experience is also an exercise in coming to grips with one's own life. In this respect, writing can be painful, even traumatic. Understanding oneself and one's own life needn't be automatic nor a piece of cake. Opening or reopening old wounds is seldom easy. Even when the writing isn't autobiographical in some strict sense, as in the case of a work like Eugene O'Neill's *Long Day's Journey Into Night*, a work that forced O'Neill to wrestle with his own family's flaws and tragic disappointments, just dealing with the same emotions carries the potential for pain and suffering. The writing process is scarcely an impregnable shield for writers who journey down emotionally dangerous paths.

This potential for emotional pain and suffering suggests that writing cannot be completely divorced from the writer's life. Writing forces writers to confront their own lives in one way or another, to one degree or another. An interesting corollary to consider here is that the emotional intensity of writing can sometimes overshadow the rest of life. When writers struggle to give voice to what really matters most, everyday life may pale in comparison. Almost any kind of work can become life itself under the right circumstances, but perhaps a writer's life is particularly vulnerable in this respect. Many kinds of work have clear delineations between the work and the rest of life, but not so with writing. For a writer, each and every experience is a possible subject. At first glance, this might seem like a fortuitous integration of life and work: writers can live their everyday lives with an omnipresent attunement to the elements of their experiences that warrant closer inspection and ultimately, the honour of being written. Yet there is a thin, perilous line here. It is one thing to live and write as a part of that life. It is another thing to live on behalf of writing. Captivated by the practice of weaving a world of words, writers can fall prey to seeing life as nothing but a potential subject for writing. Indeed, the very emotional intensity of the writing life can make the rest of life seem flat and uninteresting by comparison.

If we draw together these considerations, a plausible link between alcohol and the creative writing process emerges. Alcohol can play preparatory, cathartic, and palliative roles with respect to powerful emotions for writers. So far as preparatory aspects are concerned, alcohol can sometimes help writers by steeling them for the confrontation with emotionally difficult terrain. Alcohol can sometimes help a writer face the life task of giving voice to stories or images that are either directly or indirectly unsettling and fearsome. In many cases the link between the content of the writing and the fear and anxiety will be direct: capturing pain, suffering, loss, despair, loneliness, betrayal, abandonment, terror, cruelty, death, horror, and tragedy can call for grappling with personal demons or for immersion in a dark imaginary world that may seem all too real once a writer is fully immersed. Writers are hardly the only people prone to feeling a need for a stiff drink when faced with the fearsome task of regularly confronting their own painful emotions, but when writers must do so there is often a categorical quality to the command. The writer simply must travel this difficult path, come what may; life as the writer knows it cannot go on until the right words are found to give voice to the experience. On the other hand, sometimes this link between fear and anxiety and the content of the writing may be less direct: the sheer aspiration to capture meaningful things in an artful way carries with it the potential burden of falling short, and for a writer bent on getting it right, the spectre of failure can be terrifying. Of course, the prospect of failure is hardly comforting for anyone regardless of the pursuit so long as the pursuit matters. But not having the words to give voice to what one feels deeply can be excruciatingly painful, especially for those who define themselves by their ability to do so. Even writers who regularly find their voice must live with the possibility that they may not always be able to find it or that the voice they find may not do complete justice to what they feel.

The sheer fact that a writer is psychologically prepared to confront and experience powerful emotions in the sense of being willing to do so as part of the writing process does not mean that access to emotions is automatic. At first glance, one might be tempted to think that will and memory are enough to guarantee access to one's own emotions. Were this so, a writer's agenda would be relatively simple and straightforward: merely recall the emotions one has experienced in life and extrapolate from them as necessary to create words and images capable of capturing, expressing, and evoking these emotions. Yet emotions must not only be recalled but felt (or re-felt) to do them justice in this vein, whether the task is feeling them in order to capture them or feeling them so as to write from the standpoint of someone gripped by the requisite emotions. The fact of the matter is that emotions can seldom be felt at will, and often there are involuntary barriers to feeling them. This is where alcohol can play a cathartic role for writers.

Down through the ages many writers have waxed poetic about the inspirational powers of alcohol, but to be honest, I see no reason to believe that alcohol adds any substantive element of its own to human vision. In other words, whatever truth there may be in wine is a truth or insight that is theoretically there to be had irrespective of the wine. But alcoholic spirits can indeed play an important part in inspiration by drawing out and heightening emotions, desires, and inclinations, and by silencing or tempering others, thereby shaping our vision and action in significant ways. In some cases, the emotions, desires, and inclinations that are drawn out and heightened may be so dormant, contained, or dominated under ordinary circumstances as to effect a dramatic alteration in vision once emancipated. Likewise, tempering or silencing others may eliminate an affective stranglehold that effectively awakens a very different person. Most of us have witnessed this in everyday life to one degree or another. For instance, under the influence of alcohol, perhaps perfect equanimity gives way to frank, intense expressions of grief, loneliness, despair, envy, fear and the like in a moment of honest clarity. Or perhaps the shackles of caution and convention are thrown off in favour of heartfelt confessions of love, confident reproaches of the powerful, rapier-like instances of brash wit, or other risky feats of unexpected daring. Sometimes these instances may be little more than isolated cases, but there are plenty of people who reliably become different people under the influence of alcohol. Whether the person they become is the "real" person is not my concern here. My point is simply that in many cases alcohol clearly has the power to effect major changes in what we might think of as a person's affective orbit. And such changes inevitably induce fundamental changes in the way that a person sees the world, whether the changes are only changes in focus, clarity, and emphasis, or more pervasive alterations in a view of what matters.

Of course, alcohol is not alone in its ability to effect changes in a person's emotional landscape. After all, factors like music, place, memory, relationships, faith, work, and sex can all deeply and spontaneously affect our emotions. However, alcohol is a particularly powerful and reliable portal to one's own emotions. Alcohol cannot create or import feelings that were not already present in some shape or form, but alcohol can often filter and distill emotions into a more concentrated, purer form. Note that I do not mean to suggest that writers turn to alcohol to enhance the emotions of choice in some self-conscious, deliberative way. No doubt what writers feel the need for perhaps more than anything is powerful, passionate feeling. Indeed, the need for strong, deep feelings is something close to a way of life for most serious writers. Some writers may be able to access the necessary feelings with little trouble or trauma. Others may find that alcohol greases the wheels of feeling in a useful way, even if alcohol is hardly a prerequisite for feeling. Still others may find it difficult to feel deeply or to handle these feelings without the cathartic powers of alcohol, especially when alcohol assumes a well-entrenched place in the pattern of a writing life. Of course, many such writers may avoid writing under the direct influence of alcohol. But they may depend on alcohol to frame thought and feeling in their life. Like any other aid, alcohol can be difficult to forsake once practice becomes habit.

Perhaps this cathartic element has little or nothing to do with some writers addicted to alcohol. Even so, the connections between writing and the emotions must be taken seriously. Those who root about in the realm of human emotions, trying desperately to give voice to them and doing so as a fundamental pattern of their lives, inevitably tread in a difficult, volatile realm. Even those who are successful and who may not need alcohol to access emotions may find a friend in drink as a comfort or respite from their efforts. When all is said and done, serious writing is emotionally draining work and comfort can be hard to come by. Of course, just how effective alcohol may be as a palliative agent in the aftermath of struggling with powerful emotions in the service of the written word is an open question. Some scientists believe that long-term alcohol abuse may actually alter brain-cell function in ways that extinguish or at least diminish the physical capacity for a sense of well-being without alcohol. If this is so, then writers who rely heavily on alcohol may unwittingly condemn themselves to drink. In serious writers the urge to write is akin to the need to breathe, and the ability to feel a broad range of emotions and feel them deeply is just part and parcel of serving that need. If alcohol invites deep feeling but also destroys or hampers the ability to feel deeply in its absence, then alcohol assumes a role as an irresistible portal in the life of writers who drink liberally enough for long enough, whether for comfort or inspiration. Looking at the self-destructive drinking of a writer like Ernest Hemingway, it is hard to avoid the conclusion that life, writing, and drinking were so thoroughly entwined in his case that there could have been little hope of disentangling them.

In such cases, the temptation may always be to wonder what the writing might have been like without the drink. And of course in the case of writers whose lives were cut terribly short or whose work deteriorated badly in the face of drinking that rendered them insensible, the answer will be that the work surely suffered for drink. But if what I have suggested here about the connections between writing, drinking, and the emotions is true, it may also be so that many fine works of literature and poetry would not have been so fine without alcohol. Some superb writers with a story or poem to tell may have no need of drink as a muse, but for many reasons, other equally wonderful writers may not be able to give voice to what they have to say without the help and comfort of alcohol. If this is so then maybe the writing life for such writers may be deeply tragic in a fundamental sense: life without writing may not be worth living, but what it takes to write may condemn a writer to extreme suffering. Whether this price is worth paying is a question that probably depends upon perspective for an answer. For readers, the world would surely be worse for the loss of great works "lost" to sobriety. But for writers the answer may be more complicated. No doubt many a writer who lost a life to alcohol might well have forsaken writing if the price had been known at the start of a writing life. But once embroiled in such a life, retreat is an entirely different matter. Ultimately our attachments and commitments literally define who we are, and in many cases, laying down the pen would be tantamount to suicide.

Works Cited

Huxley, Aldous. 1954. *The Doors of Perception*. New York: Harper & Brothers.

Section III

Critiques

10

Tender is the Waltz or Save Me the Night: Scott and Zelda Fitzgerald and Alcoholism

Ellen Lansky

> *Sometimes ... I don't know whether Zelda and I are*
> *real or whether we are characters in one of my novels.*
> (Cowley, "Introduction," xii)

> *Fitzgerald's heroines were audacious and ingenuous*
> *and his heroes were fabulous strangers from lands of*
> *uncharted promise.*
> (Zelda Fitzgerald, 440)

Almost every biographical account of the Fitzgeralds includes a scene in which Scott, enraged over Zelda's novel *Save Me the Waltz*, delivers lines that he could have cribbed from Petruchio's "I say it is the moon that shines so bright" speech in Shakespeare's *The Taming of the Shrew* (5.5.1–25). In a meeting mediated by Zelda's psychiatrist, Dr. Rennie, Scott—a bullying Petruchio—declares, "I want you to do what I say... . I want my own way. I earned the right to my own way" (Bruccoli, 349, 353). Zelda, a sharp-tongued Kate, responds: "It is impossible to live with you. I would rather be in an insane asylum where you would like to put me" (351). In their roles as husbands, Scott and Petruchio both insist on defining the terms of the world for wives from whom they demand complete subordination. In Shakespeare's comedy, Kate submits and she and Petruchio are ultimately reconciled, but Zelda won't and Scott and Zelda are not. Consequently, the Fitzgeralds' married life was a domestic catastrophic melodrama—an alcoholic version of *The Taming of the Shrew* in which there are two Petruchios and no Kates. The curtain drops on them when the alcoholic wife dies in a psychiatric hospital and the alcoholic husband drops dead in Hollywood.

The competitive alcoholic spouses were never reconciled, and their conflicts were never resolved—but not for lack of trying. In *Invented Lives*, James Mellow notes that the Fitzgeralds chose fiction writing as their primary method for interpersonal communication and their main problem-solving strategy (xvii). Writing fiction about themselves provided a way for the Fitzgeralds to communicate, to examine their relationship to each other, to writing, to drinking. Mellow comments on "the transactional nature of Scott's and Zelda's writing, the private dialogue of exoneration and blame, image and counterimage, evasion and fact, that they resorted to in their otherwise fictional enterprises" (397). Though this kind of transaction could be interpreted as healthy (*Orlando*, for example, enabled Virginia Woolf to explore her relationship with Vita Sackville West), many Fitzgerald scholars find it to be confusing and detrimental to the novels. For example, Mellow contends that "the problem with *Tender is the Night* is that Fitzgerald tried to solve in literary terms the problems he could not resolve in private life" (422). Certainly, one problem with *Save Me the Waltz* and *Tender is the Night* is that the Fitzgeralds involve their reader in their insoluble "real life" and "fictional" marriage problems; the authors configure the reader as a fixer, a problem-solver, a rescuer whose task is impossible. An intertextual reading of *Save Me the Waltz* and *Tender is the Night* produces a triangular relationship that involves the two authors, their novels, and their readers. Read together, the novels create a public record of alcoholism in the *École Fitzgerald*.

Tender is the Night and *Save Me the Waltz* are novels whose central inscription is a marriage complicated by alcoholism and whose readers are constructed as participants. Both alcoholic authors take a Petruchio-like "I say it is the moon" position vis-à-vis the reader. The Fitzgeralds construct the reader and tell the reader how to read the book. Through careful handling of narrative point of view and other rhetorical strategies, the author positions the participant reader to champion his or her autobiographical character. Scott instructs his readers to side with him and the fantasy Scott character, the dedicated husband who devotes his life to curing his wife's schizophrenia. Zelda instructs her readers to favour her and the fantasy Zelda character, the wife who achieves a measure of success as a professional artist and as a conventional wife.

Also, both novels map out and publicize fantasies that the authors were unable to realize in their lives. In Scott's autobiographical novel, the alcoholic husband saves and cures his schizophrenic wife—which was something that he was unable to do in his life. Furthermore, as Judith Fetterley points out, Scott suggests that the wife's sanity comes at the husband's expense and sacrifice ("Who Killed Dick Diver?"). In Zelda's novel, Alabama Beggs shares with Zelda Fitzgerald a southern belle upbringing, a handsome and successful artist husband, a New York City celebrity honeymoon, an unmanageable household in the suburbs, a charming daughter, a trip to France, a romance with a dashing French aviator, dance lessons, a hasty return to the United States for the father's death. Unlike Zelda, she doesn't fail to become a professional dancer, and she doesn't suffer a debilitating nervous breakdown complicated by alcoholism. These authorial fantasies are intrusive and disruptive to the novels. Both authors leave the reader to resolve the discrepancies, ruptures, unfinished business and disagreements between the authors and their autobiographical characters.

— • —

Alcoholism and schizophrenia are both complicated by culturally constructed gender assignments: alcoholism as a male condition and schizophrenia as a female condition. In *The Female Malady*, Elaine Showalter notes that "Some feminist critics have maintained that schizophrenia is the perfect literary metaphor for the female condition, expressive of women's lack of confidence, dependency on external, often masculine definitions of the self, split between the body as sexual object and the mind as subject, and vulnerability to conflicting social messages about femininity and maturity" (213). This assignment of gender to schizophrenia and alcoholism is a problem for a number of reasons. Among them is the fact that theorists such as Judith Butler (*Gender Trouble*) and transgender activists such as Kate Bornstein ("Gender Outlaw") and Leslie Feinberg ("Transgender Liberation" and "Transgender Warriors") have shown that gender categories aren't so impermeable after all. Bodies transgress the overdetermined boundaries. To claim that a disease or a condition has a gender assignment, then, is an especially specious move because it denies the reality of, for example, schizophrenic men and alcoholic women. Mental illnesses including schizophrenia are not gender-bound; neither is alcoholism.

Alcoholism and insanity are not mutually exclusive categories of disease either. The testimonies and observations in Alcoholics Anonymous indicate that alcoholics, especially when drunk, frequently exhibit insane behavior and feel crazy. However, until recently, the medical profession has regarded psychiatric disorders and addiction disorders as discrete and impermeable categories. In a recent *Psychiatric Annals* editorial entitled "Comorbidity, Dual Diagnosis and Addictions—We Can't Ignore Them," Jan Fawcett, M.D. notes that "Historically, concepts of treatment of psychiatric disorders have developed separately from concepts of addiction and its treatment ... [and] the results of these differing perspectives combined with a high degree of overlap or comorbidity has left us with a limitation in our collective ability to diagnose and effectively treat psychiatric patients with addictive comorbidity and patients manifesting addictive behaviors who have significant psychiatric illnesses" (397). Unfortunately, this revisionist approach to the gendering, diagnosis, and treatment of addiction disorders and psychiatric disorders came too late for the Fitzgeralds.

— • —

An autobiographical novel necessarily diminishes aesthetic distance between fiction and life, and it invites the reader to make connections between the characters and events in the fiction and the people and events in the author's life. *Tender is the Night* and *Save Me the Waltz* are frequently described as "autobiographical." Fetterley remarks that *Tender is the Night* is "profoundly autobiographical in its central impulses" ("Who Killed Dick Diver?," 127). Mary Wood calls *Save Me the Waltz* an "autobiographical novel" and Nancy Milford deems it "intensely, even naïvely autobiographical" (217). Mizener notes that Fitzgerald "always ... wrote about himself or about people and things with which he was intimate. As a consequence his life is inextricably bound up with his work" (xvii). The same could be said of Zelda and her work. Their autobiographical novels necessitate a reader who is willing to become "inextricably bound up" with the novels and their authors. Thus, the reader becomes a participant, a component of the Fitzgeralds' addiction complex.

Zelda's participant reader is charged with several fixing, rescuing, and saving tasks. The reader's job is to affirm the autobiographical character's reform from waywardness and to confirm the author's competence as a sane woman and a professional writer. This confirmation would then save the author from being relegated to "amateur" status as a writer and rescue her from her husband's and her doctor's contentions about her insanity and her shortcomings as a wife.

In *Tender is the Night*, Scott's construction of Dick Diver as tragic hero also requires a participant reader. The reader's role is to minimize the negative consequences of Dick Diver's addiction to alcohol while maximizing the dramatic sacrifices he makes as Nicole's personal saviour. At the same time, Fitzgerald's ambivalence about his hero complicates his novel and confuses the reader. In *Some Sort of Epic Grandeur*, Matthew Bruccoli observes that "Dick Diver is of course the man who plunges from great promise to great failure; but the name also has the slang meaning 'cocksucker'" (341). Given Fitzgerald's homophobic representations of Dunfrey and Campion in the novel, this is clearly not an affectionate use of queer slang. Also, in the early versions of *Tender*, Fitzgerald called the protagonist Francis Melarkey; the author links his own first name to an Irish-sounding last name that, as Scott Donaldson notes in "A Short History of *Tender is the Night*," indicates "both a degree of discomfort with the material and a measure of authorial self-disgust" (182). Bruccoli notes that "the characterization of Diver is complex because Fitzgerald brought to it both self-pity and self-contempt" (341). Still, Fitzgerald puts the narrative emphasis on Dick's heroic sacrifices of his career, his self-esteem, and his health in the service of Nicole's recovery from schizophrenia. As Fetterley notes, Fitzgerald offers the reader the figure of the funicular as an interpretive tool: "The cable car image determines the trajectory of the text and as Nicole rises, Dick goes down" ("Who Killed Dick Diver?," 127).

Both authors control their participant readers in several ways. First, both Fitzgeralds use the third person limited omniscient narrative point of view in order to situate the reader in a particular character's consciousness. The reader, then, identifies and sympathizes with this character. The author is also able to encourage the reader to "protect" or "defend" the central character. Second, the central characters' drinking and drinking problems seem to come out of nowhere, leaving the reader to either ignore the drinking or to connect it to something in herself. Furthermore, the way in which they both represent drinking and alcoholism in their novels is distinctly *École Fitzgerald*. In "Milk of Wonder," Marty Roth notes that drinking and alcoholism are "invisible" in Scott's work—"the drinking is there but nobody sees it, or, if it is there to be seen, it is not connected to anything else" (4). This phenomenon is also evident in Zelda's novel. I will suggest that the characters' drinking is connected to their authors' drinking. Finally, the married authors' ulterior motives—namely, using their novels to broach real life problems and to testify to the authors' sanity (Zelda) and righteousness (Scott)— results in narrative lines that drift off, leaving the reader to fix the novels.

F. Scott Fitzgerald controls the reader's response to Dick Diver by filtering the reader's perception of him through the character Rosemary Hoyt. Fitzgerald attributes to the reader the responses of a late adolescent heterosexual young woman to a handsome, composed older man. Dick Diver is the consummate nice guy. Fitzgerald first describes him as "a fine man in a jockey cap and red-striped tights" (6), and the reader has no reason to think that Dick Diver is anything but fine. To Rosemary, whose perspective the reader takes, he "seemed kind and charming—his voice promised that he would take care of her, and that a little later he would open up new worlds for her, unroll an endless succession of magnificent possibilities" (16). One could swoon. He invites her to his dinner party, flatters her by telling her she looks "like something blooming" (22). When Rosemary tells her mother she's "desperately in love with him" (22), the reader empathizes.

Fitzgerald's use of the third person limited omniscient point of view also manipulates the reader's initial response to Nicole. Fitzgerald's method positions the reader so that it is practically impossible to identify or sympathize with or even to like Nicole Diver. At first, on the Riviera, Nicole appears to Rosemary as a series of body parts and accessories. Rosemary notices only Nicole's "back, a ruddy orange brown, set off by a string of pearls" (6). The pearls dominate the image, and her back is turned to the beach conversation as well as to Rosemary and the reader. Dick gives "a quiet little performance for the group," which provokes "a burst of laughter" (6). Tellingly, "the only person on the beach not caught up in it was the young woman with the string of pearls" (6). Fitzgerald's portrait of Nicole culminates in a psychotic episode in the final paragraphs of Book One. At Dick's dinner party, Nicole "was still as still" (33). Her silence only heightens the mystery, secrecy, hints of shame and confusion that result when Violet McKisco comes upon her babbling incoherently in the bathroom. The bathroom in itself encodes private mysteries, secret activities, sickness. Nicole's incoherent babbling in the bathroom, then, is "sick" speech: madness.

Fitzgerald also uses Rosemary to ease the reader into a drinking relationship with Dick Diver. In Book One, the only reference to Dick's drinking occurs when Rosemary has her first drink. She takes a drink because "she felt some necessity for it. Dick drank, not too much, but he drank, and perhaps it would bring her closer to him" (61). The reader, too, can get closer to this wonderful Dick by drinking with him. By introducing Dick through Rosemary's point of view, and by presenting Nicole as mysterious, silent, even crazy, Fitzgerald assures the reader that everything about Dick is fine and that it's safe to drink with him.

Zelda Fitzgerald's third person limited omniscient point of view enables her to manipulate the reader's response to Alabama Beggs and David Knight. The reader is situated in Alabama's consciousness and has the experience of "growing up" with her. As a child, Alabama "wants life to be easy and full of pleasant reminiscences" (13). She slides down bannisters, gets into her sister's makeup, tells her mother that she wants "to go to New York ... to be [her] own boss" (20). As an adolescent, she's "the wildest one of the Beggs," and everyone indulges her. Having planted the reader in the consciousness of this irresistible character, Zelda introduces David Knight as a handsome but utterly arrogant man. His idea of a romantic flourish is to carve a doorpost with this legend: "David, David, Knight, Knight, Knight, and Miss Alabama Nobody" (39). This nasty gesture makes way for other nasty gestures, such as asking Alabama, referring to her dancing, "'Are you under the illusion that you'll ever be any good at that stuff?'" (119), and saying, "'Yes, this is both the Knights'" (96) when he answers the phone. He's not only frequently arrogant and nasty; he's also frequently arrogant, nasty, and drunk.

Zelda minimizes her heroine's drinking through shifts in narrative point of view. Having established a third person limited omniscient point of view, from which the reader can both observe and identify with the rebellious and high spirited Alabama, Zelda makes some pronoun shifts that turn the reader's attention away from Alabama's drinking. Rather than attributing drinking and drunkenness to Alabama, Zelda makes vague references to a drinking culture through a shift to a second person "you." But Zelda's "you" doesn't mean "you, the reader"; her "you" signals a third person: "Almost everybody had theories: that Longacre Pharmacies carried the best gin in town; that anchovies sobered you up; that you could tell wood alcohol by the smell" (48). It's not Alabama that's drinking the gin, eating the anchovies, or smelling the wood alcohol; it's "you." Then Zelda shifts to an even more remote third person point of view—putting the drinking farther from her protagonist: "There were people in automobiles all along the Boston Post Road thinking everything was going to be all right while they got drunk and ran into fireplugs" (54); in Paris, "All of them drank" (99).

In the same way that he would "sneak" drinks in his life (see Dardis, 125), Scott "sneaks" Dick's alcoholism into his text, as if the reader won't notice or comment. After Nicole's schizophrenic episode at the carnival, Dick tells his colleague Franz that he wants to go away from the clinic for a while. Franz's response is, "'You wish a real leave of abstinence'" (194). Fitzgerald would have understood "leave of abstinence" as a combination diction error/Freudian slip, and the reader is expected to recognize and deny its significance. Then in Munich, Tommy Barban observes that Dick doesn't look "so jaunty as [he] used to, so spruce" (197). The "leave of abstinence" juxtaposed against Tommy Barban's comment suggests that drinking is at the bottom of Dick's retreat. But a problem the reader faces is that Fitzgerald hasn't rendered Dick's drinking. Instead, he encourages the reader to think that "Dick had come away for his soul's sake ... [that] he had lost himself ... [that] he had been swallowed up like a gigolo and somehow had permitted his arsenal to be locked up in the Warren safety deposit vaults" (201). Dick's decline is ostensibly Nicole's fault—or so the reader is led to think.

Book Two ends with a scene which depicts the kind of catastrophic melodrama that was common in the life of the alcoholic author, but inconsistent for the character and confusing for the reader who is not familiar with the author's lifestory. In this scene, Dick Diver gets disgracefully drunk, behaves abominably in a night club, picks a fight with Italian taxi drivers and police, and endures a severe beating—which he instigates by taking a swing at a plainclothes detective. The alcoholic author himself had an almost identical experience. Jeffrey Meyers observes that "Fitzgerald called this degrading experience 'just about the rottenest thing that ever happened to me in my life'" (119–20). Furthermore, in his article "Dick Diver's Plunge into the Roman Void," Robert Roulston contends that "the section devoted to Dick's ordeal in the Eternal City assumes an importance utterly disproportionate to its length" (97). Certainly, as Roulston notes, "Rome, the mightiest of religious metaphors, is an apt setting for Dick's mightiest betrayal" (91), and Fitzgerald was aware of Rome's religious resonances. Nevertheless, to this point in the novel, Dick Diver has not shown himself to be interested in instigating this kind of scene. Alcoholic catastrophic melodrama has been heretofore ascribed to other characters: McKisco in the drunken duel, for example, or Abe North's alcoholic antics in Paris.

The Roman beating scene is crucial in the novel because at this point the alcoholic author's life story intrudes on the story of Dick Diver. The author's alcoholism interferes with the characterization of Dick Diver, and this interference problematizes the novel for readers. At this point, there is too much Fitzgerald in Diver. Fitzgerald engaged in bar brawls frequently, but Dick Diver doesn't. To this point in the novel, Dick hasn't even been drunk. Furthermore, this dive into lowlife behaviours completely violates the reader's class expectations of Dick. Drunken brawls are not for gentlemen physicians. The image of the author begins to bleed through the portrait of Dick Diver, and Scott Fitzgerald becomes increasingly visible.

There are similar moments when Zelda sneaks alcoholism into the text. Before Alabama and David leave for Europe, in a hand mirror she regards the spots on her face and says to David, "One more party … and I'd have to see Viollet-le-Duc about my face" (58). Those marks on her face signal the presence of alcoholic toxins in her body—probably from drinking bad gin. The toxins rupture both Alabama's face and Zelda Fitzgerald's efforts to repress her female protagonist's drinking. Since the drinking in the novel has, to this point, been vaguely ascribed to others, the marks on Alabama's face seem as inexplicable as the Roman beating scene in *Tender is the Night*. Neither author has prepared the reader for these scenes.

In another example, when David urges Alabama to drink with him, she begs off—insisting that "I get so sick when I drink. I'll have to have morphine if I do, like last time" (119). The first part of Alabama's statement indicates the kind of response to drinking that a person who is not addicted to alcohol can have; she understands that drinking produces adverse consequences, and the prospect of sickness overrides any compulsion to drink. But the next sentence reveals a problem after all. A great gap exists between a hangover that requires a hair-of- the-dog restorative and a hangover that requires a morphine shot. Alabama does not exhibit the kind of alcoholic drinking that necessitates morphine shots, but the author certainly did. Nancy Milford notes that in France, "after a considerable amount of drinking, Zelda went so completely out of emotional control that a doctor was sent for and she was given a shot of morphine to calm her" (125). Another authorial intrusion is marked by a noticeably awkward pronoun shift. A remarkably ungrammatical sentence describes Americans in Paris, and the pronouns shift from third person to first person plural: "There were Americans at night and day Americans, and we all had Americans in the bank to buy things with" (98). In this shift, Zelda suddenly and inexplicably appears as part of the first person plural pronoun.

At the ends of the novels, the authors' aim to enlist affirmations, justification, or pity from their readers supersedes their attention to the construction of their novels. Consequently, the authors' fantasy characters lack integrity and consistency, and the narrative lines lack resolution and closure. Scott Donaldson makes this observation about the reception of *Tender is the Night*: "At the time the book came out, a number of reviewers thought Diver's decline and his rapid acceptance of it unconvincing. That was not precisely the problem: The problem is that one does not know how to respond to Diver" (*Fool*, 190). Zelda's novel evinces the same problems insofar as Alabama's renunciation of her dancing career and her rapid acceptance of her role as subordinate wife seem as unconvincing as Dick's.

The taming of Alabama seems like a mistake in characterization until one considers the novel as evidence of the author's sanity and rehabilitation. Milford notes that "part of [Dr.] Forel's cure had been a somewhat mysterious 'reeducation' of Zelda in terms of her role as wife to Scott" (201), and Zelda offers *Save Me* as a testimony to having learned her lesson. Alabama sets goals for herself, works hard and makes huge sacrifices to attain them, then renounces them with surprisingly little remorse. Alabama channels all her attention and energy into her dancing—despite entreaties from her husband and daughter to act in more wifely and motherly ways. She surrenders her privileges and lifestyle to take a position with a ballet company in Naples. In Naples, she rehearses all day and at night she drinks beer in the Galleria with her dark Russian girlfriend (158–59). Lifting the beer glass in public without the legitimizing company of a man signals Alabama's declaration of independence from the subordinate role she is supposed to occupy as David's wife. However, it's not long before Alabama's "work" produces blood poisoning; her toe shoes—like a dirty needle or bad alcohol—infect her foot. It's punishment. Alabama cannot establish herself as a dancer and remain in the artist's power position. She recognizes this fact and she resigns herself to this turn of events. Though "the bottom fell out of her stomach" when she learns that her dancing career is over, and though she tells herself that "This was a stone that would need a good deal of salt and pepper"

(181), she swallows it. She goes home with her husband to sit at her father's deathbed. When she catches herself thinking about ballet, she thinks to herself that "she'd spend the rest of her life composing like that, fitting one thing into another and everything into the rules" (193). This behaviour seems utterly unlikely for the Alabama who was "the wildest one of the Beggs," but the author's own agenda has supplanted her attention to character development.

The structural problems in *Tender* also seem like mistakes until one considers the novel as testimony to Scott's supreme sacrifices for Zelda. In Book Three, for example, Scott seems to have abandoned his attention to narrative point of view. Books One and Two generally adhere to third person limited omniscient (Rosemary and Dick, respectively). Book Three skips from third person omniscient in chapter one to Dick's consciousness in chapters two, three, and four, to Nicole's consciousness in chapters five through nine, back to Dick in chapter ten, and then to an oddly detached editorial third person in the final chapters, eleven through thirteen. These shifts are especially confusing when the reader sees Dick through Nicole's perspective. In chapter twelve, for example, Nicole listens with growing intolerance as Dick blathers to Rosemary about the necessity for actresses to "'go all out of character... [then] slide into character again'" (288). Nicole, whose perspective the reader takes, watches Dick slide all out of character. She stands up and declares that she's "'going to take the car home'" (289). This is a confident assertion of independence, sanity, and self-control. In fact, "she had a sense of being cured and in a new way" (289). Since the reader has been heretofore positioned to regard Nicole as a major drag on Dick's life, work, and personal integrity, it is difficult to abandon Dick and summon sympathy for Nicole at this late point in the novel—but that is what Fitzgerald asks the reader to do. He invokes the logic of the funicular: she rises; therefore he sinks.

The logic of the funicular proves to be spurious and detrimental to the novel's structural integrity but serviceable for the author's aims. Embedded in the faulty funicular logic is Fitzgerald's fantasy that the husband can cure the wife, that the wife's cure necessitates the husband's decline, and that the process of curing the wife produces the husband's alcoholism. Dick Diver treats his wife so successfully that she is not only cured, she is better than ever. Unlike Zelda who "was not pretty any more" (Milford, 269) and not cured either after her treatments at Prangins and Phipps, Nicole retains her beauty, and "the only physical disparity between Nicole at present and the Nicole of five years before was simply that she was no longer a young girl" (291). Her schizophrenia seems to have actually enhanced her life, which is utterly illogical—in fiction or in life.

While Nicole experiences a sort of "fantasy schizophrenia"[1] that bears

---

1. My notion of Zelda's "fantasy schizophrenia" was enabled by Bruccoli's biography *Some Sort of Epic Grandeur*. Bruccoli notes that "in achieving Zelda's impossible cure in fiction Fitzgerald may have been trying to absolve himself of whatever guilt he felt for his wife's madness—as well as to punish himself for his self-indulgence and self-betrayal" (341).

little resemblance to Zelda's (or anyone's) experience with the disease, Fitzgerald's rendering of Dick Diver's alcoholism is a feat in verisimilitude. The problem is that the author asks the reader to interpret alcoholism as something that Dick "catches" in the course of his funicular descent, but before the reader can pity the doctor whose wife has driven him to drink, Fitzgerald shifts the narrative point of view so the reader regards Dick with a jaundiced eye. Fitzgerald skews the funicular's action: she rises too high too fast and he sinks too low too fast. Her schizophrenia is too fantastic; his alcoholism is all-too-real. This mixing of fantasy and verisimilitude, fiction and autobiography, underpins the novel's convoluted structure and inexplicable characterizations. Apparently, the novelist's concern with structure and characterization were subordinated to his primary aim: to cast the wife as the efficient cause of the husband's alcoholic decline, thus garnering the reader's support, sympathy, exoneration, and understanding for the husband, himself.

Both novels pass out in their final scenes, leaving readers to tie up the dangling narrative lines. The Knights give a cocktail party that becomes an afternoon of the living dead. The guests rise "to leave the pleasant place"—as if it were a cemetery—and give farewells which leave David and Alabama in a fog of morbidity:

> *"We've talked you to death."*
>
> *"You must be dead with packing."*
>
> *"It's death to a party to stay till digestion sets in."*
>
> *"I'm dead, my dear. It's been wonderful."* (196)

David and Alabama sit "in the pleasant gloom of late afternoon, staring at each other through the remains of the party" (196). The repetition of "pleasant" calls up the cemetery ambience that pervades the place; the "remains" of the party invokes the corpse of the father and the dead guests that have just exited. Alabama finds the atmosphere in their rented house to be stuffy as a coffin—dank with a post-party miasma of cigarette butts and dead cocktails; she says she's going to "air the room" (196). In the story's last moment, David and Alabama Knight "sat together watching the twilight flow through the calm living room that they were leaving like the clear cold current of a trout stream" (196). This "trout stream" image links Zelda's novel to Hemingway's *The Sun Also Rises*—another novel whose alcoholic characters are drunk and unable to solve their problems and whose author and characters invite the reader to participate in the novel's scene of addiction.[2] The difference is that at the end of Hemingway's novels, Brett and Jake acknowledge the essentially insoluble nature of their troubles. "'Isn't it pretty to think so?'" comes with its own answer, and the novel closes. In Zelda's novel, the reader is left to clean up the mess of the party and to determine the

---

2. For a further elaboration of this addiction complex, see my essay "The Barnes Complex: Ernest Hemingway, Djuna Barnes, *The Sun Also Rises*, and *Nightwood*." Pp. 205–24 in *The Languages of Addiction*, edited by Jane Lilienfeld and Jeffrey Oxford (Boston: Bedford St. Martins, 1999).

destination for the two characters; the author has only indicated that they are leaving.

Scott's novel also passes out in its last pages. Before leaving the Riviera, Dick Diver gets roaring drunk. Then he wafts out of the novel. Nicole, now as sane as can be, loses track of her ex-husband. Their children fade, and Nicole's new husband, Tommy Barban, seems to have given up his career as a mercenary soldier. Scott, who seems tired of the novel and his characters at this point, reduces Dick to an alcoholic fume floating around upstate New York "in one town or another" (315)—leaving the reader to find him and finish his story, to clean up the mess that the addict has left.

Both novels have been received as weak and flawed in terms of such basic aspects of fiction writing as plot structure and character development. Scott identified "problems of construction" (Turnbull, 206) as a major weakness in Zelda's writing, even though he participated in the editing and revision of *Save Me the Waltz*. His book was also initially received as "a flawed novel." The flaws were found in plot—"the focus of the plot shifts, the story rambles," and characterizations—"it failed in its handling of the central relationships" (Mellow, 416). This alleged failure to handle the central relationships suggests that Scott was unable to resolve the impasse at which Dick and Nicole arrive in the same way that Zelda (with Scott's help) was unable to resolve David's and Alabama's impasse. Reading the novels intertextually indicates that Scott's inability to handle his novel's plot and relationships and Zelda's inability to handle her novel's construction and relationships is not necessarily a flaw but rather a logical consequence. They both wrote about what they knew, and neither one knew how to resolve or dismantle or extricate himself or herself from an alcohol-and-insanity-ridden relationship. Thus, he was unable to "fix" *Save Me the Waltz* and she was unable to "resolve" *Tender is the Night*. That job is left to the reader, whose role in the *École Fitzgerald* addiction complex is to fix the flawed novels and/or to cover up for the shortcomings of the author by blaming the spouse.

— • —

The Fitzgeralds' biographers inevitably deal with the figure of the respective spouse, whom they tend to construct as an opponent, an antagonist. Mizener, Turnbull, and Donaldson produce a talented Scott tormented and hobbled by both alcohol and mad Zelda. Meyers positively loathes Zelda and heaps her with blame and derision. Nancy Milford's biography of Zelda and Judith Fetterley's revisionist sketch of their relationship tend to construct Scott as the alcoholic oppressor who was crazy himself and Zelda as the oppressed wife, driven mad by her drunken raging husband. James Mellow presents a worst case Scott-and-Zelda, with Zelda slightly more troublesome and disreputable than Scott. These biographers (excluding Fetterley, whose article is more critical than biographical), who generally adhere to gendered notions of alcoholism and madness, also exhibit a tendency to construct him as the alcoholic and her as the madwoman; him as the professional writer, her as the amateur. There has yet to be a definitive critical biography that comprehends the influence of alcohol and the effects of addiction on both Scott and Zelda Fitzgerald and their work.

Scott is the "known" alcoholic in the *École Fitzgerald*, but Zelda's relationship to alcohol was also a problem. Zelda began drinking when she was a teenager in Montgomery, Alabama—before she met F. Scott Fitzgerald. Milford notes that "she smoked, and she drank gin, if there was any, or corn liquor cut with Coke, if there wasn't" (16). In *Fool for Love*, Scott Donaldson writes that Scott "knew that [Zelda] drank more than other girls" (62). Donaldson also comments on a letter that Fitzgerald wrote to Zelda's sister Marjorie in December, 1938: "[Zelda] was so drunk the first time [Scott] met her at the country club that her partners were carrying her around in their arms" (63). Though Donaldson contends that "Probably Fitzgerald exaggerated here in the course of arguing against the Sayres' conviction that he'd driven Zelda insane" (63), he does not dispute the record of Zelda's early drinking.

Zelda's alcoholism was complicated and obfuscated by the nervous breakdowns that she experienced intermittently from the late 1920s until her death in 1948. Zelda's biographers and others have attributed her breakdowns to a number of probable causes. One is that Zelda's family had a history of mental illness. Nancy Milford notes that "Although [Mrs. Sayre] was upset by her daughter's breakdown, her reaction was one of resignation. She had gone through similar periods with her oldest daughter, Marjorie, and with the Judge" (164). Another probable cause is that Zelda had a number of "perfectly simple operations" in Europe; Donaldson notes that Zelda's sister Rosalind asked, "'Do you think Zelda's abortions could have anything to do with her illness?'" (*Fool*, 69). Scott tried to blame her breakdown (and his drinking) on her dancing. Apparently, Scott was able to make a convincing case for dancing as a primary cause for Zelda's breakdown; for example, Mellow notes that "the doctor and her husband had decided that her obsession with dancing had been a cause of her breakdown" (365).

Zelda's drinking was also a precipitating factor. Turnbull reports that when Zelda had her first breakdown that landed her at Malmaison on April 23, 1930, "she was slightly tipsy on her arrival and according to recent reports had drunk a great deal" (192). In the early fall of 1930, when Zelda was institutionalized for schizophrenia, Scott wrote to Max Perkins from Switzerland, "'Zelda is almost well. The doctor says she can never drink again (not that drink in any way contributed to her collapse)'" (Milford, 170). And later, Milford reports that on the way home from a foreshortened vacation in Florida, "Zelda found a flask in [Scott's] suitcase and drank everything in it. She woke Scott at 5 am and told him that dark things were being done to her secretly" (208). A few weeks later, she entered the Phipps Clinic—approximately two years after she had arrived drunk at Malmaison. Her doctors and husband determined a link between Zelda's drinking and her madness, but they did not consider alcoholism as either a contributing factor in Zelda's mental health or as a problem in itself.

Tom Dardis and other biographers have thoroughly documented Scott's progressive alcoholism, but most have circumvented the insanity he exhibited under the influence of alcohol. Dardis notes that by the early 1930s, "drinking had become the central point of Fitzgerald's existence, the one thing around which everything else revolved, including the constant problem of Zelda's instability and his sudden difficulties in selling his stories. By 1933 his daily drinking had begun to affect him so severely that home remedies no longer sufficed to sober him up" (120). His addiction to alcohol also affected his behaviour and his general social comportment. Many of the particularly revealing accounts of Fitzgerald's maladaptive behaviour involve acute intoxication, and his drunken antics are well known to those who have read the biographical material. To rehearse a few of the more notable, more scandalous episodes: He was drunk when he threw a leg of lamb at Zelda and her dinner guests. He was drunk when he stared at a couple "so persistently that the couple called for the head waiter" (Mellow, 268). He was drunk when he deliberately broke Sara Murphy's special Venetian glasses and when he dropped a ripe fig down a princess's decolletage (Meyers, 114). He was drunk when he took Thornton Wilder up to the attic at Ellerslie, where he stumbled "over a gun, picked it up, waved it around, and accidentally shot it off; the bullet lodged into the wall perilously close to Wilder" (Mellow, 310). Later, as his alcoholism was progressing and his life was terminating, Fitzgerald's behaviour became even more insane when he was drunk. In *Beloved Infidel*, Sheilah Graham recalls several examples of Fitzgerald's drunken insanity. He got drunk in Chicago and embarrassed her in front of a radio producer. One night, drunk, he struck her and then, in Graham's recollection, "he began hopping around like a frenzied Rumpelstiltskin, chanting Lily Shiel, Lily Shiel, Lily Shiel" (296). Fitzgerald followed up the Rumpelstiltskin act with death threats, inappropriate calls to Graham's colleagues and employers, phone harassment, break-ins, and stalking. Even James Mellow, who so often in *Invented Lives* dismisses Fitzgerald's bizarre and completely inappropriate behaviour as "sophomoric" or "ebullient," admits that "there were occasions when Fitzgerald's drunken activities verged on a frightening kind of madness" (186–87).

That Scott was "mad" seems indisputable—even to himself. After all, this is the man who wrote a series of essays called "The Crack-up"—in which he lies about his alcoholism while admitting—in confessional tones—that he "had been mortgaging [himself] physically and spiritually up to the hilt" and as a result had "cracked like an old plate" (72). He prefers to couch his condition as a "nervous breakdown" rather than attributing it to his alcoholism— in the same way that he preferred to locate the source of Zelda's madness in her dancing. What's telling, and what has to be said even to those who may disdain the feminist approach to the Fitzgeralds, is that Scott—the husband—could deny his alcoholism and publicize his crack-up and continue to live his life with a certain amount of freedom while Zelda—the wife, like it or not— also indisputably mad and alcoholic, was institutionalized and silenced.

As writers, they were competitive and antagonistic, and part of this acrimony derives from Zelda's desire to transcend her role as F. Scott

Fitzgerald's wife and the model for his female characters. Though Turnbull notes that even before they were married, "he often read her things he was working on and profited from her advice" (87), that harmonious working relationship was short-lived. She began to write and publish in the late 1920s, when Scott was drinking and floundering with *Tender is the Night*. Milford notes that by 1929, Scott "was astonished by her productivity and even resented it in comparison to his own vexing inability to move forward on his novel" (152).

As noted in the essay's opening, a particularly vituperative clash occurred when Zelda positioned herself as novelist and began to write *Save Me the Waltz*. The Fitzgeralds' biographers all note that she finished writing the novel while she was an in-patient at the Phipps Clinic, and it is also widely remarked that Scott was enraged when Zelda mailed her manuscript directly to Max Perkins, Scott's editor at Scribner's. He accused her of plagiarism, insisting that "literally one whole section of her novel is an imitation of [his manuscript], of its rhythm, materials" (Milford, 216).

Scott and some of his biographers regard Zelda's ability to finish a novel in a psychiatric ward as a dirty trick—an indicator of her wifely insubordination and "shrewishness." James Mellow notes that "her hospitalization had provided her with a safe retreat, a sanctuary in which to complete her book within a month's time" (401). Mellow justifies Scott's rage about Zelda's stay at Phipps and her finished novel; he claims that "Instinctively, Fitzgerald too may have sensed that Zelda's retreat from the problems of reality had been a bit too opportune; at least that would explain his anger at having to cope with the burdens of a household and a child while Zelda had the luxury of painting and writing at his expense" (401). Meyers claims that Scott "felt she had ... stolen the clinical material and European locales of the novel he had been working on for seven years" (222).

While some of Scott's biographers decry Zelda's theft as a sort of feminine wile, Zelda and some of her biographers regard Scott's intervention on Zelda's novel as an oppressive exercise of patriarchal power. In her article "Who Killed Dick Diver?," Judith Fetterley reminds us that as a sane man and a professional writer in a heteropatriarchal culture, Scott occupied the power position, and he used his power to control Zelda's creative process as well as to determine ownership of shared experiences. Mary Gordon remarks that "Our conventions dictate that the woman take on the man's name; this would suggest that we consider a subsuming of the female identity in the male a seemly one" (xvii). Scott Fitzgerald certainly found it a seemly convention. Consequently, he felt justified in claiming that he "owned" the experiences from their lives which they used in their autobiographical fiction; she was the wife, and she belonged to him.

When Scott's initial dismay and rage about Zelda's novel dissipated, he positioned himself as Zelda's writing master—orchestrating the revisions and editing of *Save Me the Waltz*. He went so far as to revise the characterization of David Knight, the fictional husband, so that he is more sympathetic. Mizener notes that Zelda's novel's "central section was an attack on

Fitzgerald. Perkins and Fitzgerald worked together to get her to make the revision of this section which was published" (240). Scott also did everything he could to shore up his power position as husband and professional writer. Fetterley notes that Scott engineered Zelda's book contract so that it "contained a clause 'that stipulated that one-half the royalties earned would be retained by Scribner's to be credited against the indebtedness of F. Scott Fitzgerald'" ("Who Killed Dick Diver?," 113). He dictated the terms and conditions of her novel.

After "treating" Zelda's novel, he still managed to appropriate and commodify her life experiences in his fiction. Her breakdown and treatment enabled him to revise his work in progress so that *The Boy Who Killed His Mother* evolved into *The Drunkard's Holiday* and eventually *Tender is the Night*: a story about alcoholism and schizophrenia which appeared two years after the publication of *Save Me the Waltz*. He incorporated her letters in his novel with the certainty that doing so was his prerogative as professional writer and husband. Like Petruchio, and like a bullying alcoholic, he claims the right to define the universe—for himself and his wife—as he sees fit.

— • —

The lives of Scott and Zelda Fitzgerald ended as their novels end: vague, fading, unresolved. Toward the end of Scott's life, he maintained a large geographic distance from Zelda, and he spent the last four years of his life with Sheilah Graham. This was not unlike Nicole Diver's move from Dick Diver to Tommy Barban: not entirely liberating nor rehabilitating, but less disastrous. There are some big differences between Sheilah and Zelda. Sheilah did not drink and Zelda did; Sheilah was not schizophrenic and Zelda was. Sheilah Graham had a strong sense of herself as an accomplished and independent journalist; she had a career, and Zelda did not. Graham's book *Beloved Infidel* indicates that she herself suffered from the low self-esteem that often debilitates partners of alcoholics, and she put up with some outrageously abusive behaviours from Scott Fitzgerald. Nevertheless, Sheilah Graham was able to say to Scott Fitzgerald (rather melodramatically), "Shoot yourself, you son of a bitch. I didn't raise myself from the gutter to waste my life on a drunk like you" (Dardis, 141); she knew who she was and what she was. She could not rescue Scott, but she could save herself. Neither Scott nor Zelda had this kind of knowledge. When Scott died, he left an unfinished novel and an unfinished relationship with Zelda. Zelda did not attend Scott's funeral, a decision that, like Nicole Diver's continuing correspondence with the vanishing Dick, indicates her inability to terminate or close an already defunct partnership. Unlike Sheilah Graham, Zelda did not have a strong sense of herself apart from Scott, which must have made the last few years of her life even more sad and lonely and miserable. She died in a mental hospital fire, on a locked ward that offered no exit: not even a fire escape.

Perhaps it is the unhappy lack of resolution that marks the ends of their novels and the final years of the Fitzgerald partnership that leads their participant readers and biographers to lash out at Scott for oppressing and dominating Zelda or to excoriate Zelda for nagging and ruining Scott. Blaming Zelda and/or Zelda's schizophrenia erases Scott's alcoholism, which made an important contribution to the ruin—physical, emotional, and financial. Similarly, blaming Scott for Zelda's schizophrenia erases her own participation in their various enterprises, including alcoholism. Scott himself declared that "We ruined ourselves—I have never honestly thought that we ruined each other" (Mellow, 135). Perhaps it is this unhappy lack of closure hanging over the lives and novels of the Fitzgeralds that spurs their readers, biographers and other writers to go to great lengths to try to rescue or save them. Scott lamented to Max Perkins that he "'would give anything if [he] hadn't had to write part III of *Tender is the Night* entirely on stimulant. If [he] had one more crack at it cold sober [he believed] it might have made a great difference'" (Dardis, 123). Malcolm Cowley tried to take a crack at it after Scott's death, but his reshuffled version did not rescue the novel either. Cowley's action illustrates perfectly a participant's response to a mess an addict has made; he tries to fix it, and his efforts are futile. Finally, no one was able to rescue or fix either Scott or Zelda or their novels, and they were unable to save themselves.

Works Cited

Alcoholics Anonymous. 1976. 3rd ed. New York: Alcoholics Anonymous World Services.

Bruccoli, Matthew. 1991. *Some Sort of Epic Grandeur: The Life of F. Scott Fitzgerald*. New York: HBJ.

Bruccoli, Matthed (ed.). 1991. *Save Me the Waltz. Zelda Fitzgerald: The Collected Writings*. New York: Collier/Macmillan.

Comley, Nancy R. 1998. "Madwomen on the Riviera: The Fitzgeralds, Hemingway, and the Matter of Modernism." Pp. 277–96 in *French Connections: Hemingway and Fitzgerald Abroad*, edited by J. Gerald Kennedy and Jackson R. Bryer. New York: St. Martins.

Cowley, Malcolm. 1964. *Exile's Return*. New York: Viking.

——. 1951. "Introduction." Pp. vii–xxv in *The Stories of F. Scott Fitzgerald*, edited by Malcolm Cowley. New York: Scribner's.

Dardis, Tom. 1989. *The Thirsty Muse: Alcohol and the American Writer*. New York: Ticknor and Fields.

Davis, Simone Weil. 1995. "Effort and Desire in Zelda Fitzgerald's *Save Me The Waltz*." *Modern Language Quarterly* 56, no. 3 (September): 325–41.

Donaldson, Scott. *Fool For Love: F. Scott Fitzgerald*. New York: Congdon and Weed, 1983.

——. 1990. "A Short History of *Tender is the Night*." Pp. 177–208 in *Writing the American Classics*, edited by James Barbour and Tom Quirk. Chapel Hill: University of North Carolina Press.

——. 1996. "A Death in Hollywood: F. Scott Fitzgerald Remembered." *Iowa Review* 26, no. 1 (Spring): 105–12.

Eble, Kenneth. 1982. "Touches of Disaster: Alcoholism and Mental Illness in Fitzgerald's Short Stories." In *The Short Stories of F. Scott Fitzgerald*, edited by Jackson Bryer. Madison: University of Wisconsin Press.

Fawcett, Jan, M.D. 1994. "Comorbidity, Dual Diagnosis and Addictions—We Can't Ignore Them." *Psychiatric Annals* 24, no. 8 (August): 397–98.

Fetterley, Judith. 1978. *The Resisting Reader: A Feminist Approach to American Fiction*. Bloomington: Indiana University Press.

——. 1984. "Who Killed Dick Diver? The Sexual Politics of *Tender is the Night*." *Mosaic* 17, no. 1 (Winter): 111–28.

Fitzgerald, F. Scott. 1945. "The Crack-up." Pp. 69–84 in *The Crack-up and Other Essays*, edited by Edmund Wilson. New York: New Directions.

———. 1934. *Tender is the Night*. New York: Scribners.

Fitzgerald, Zelda. 1991. *Save Me the Waltz*. Pp. *1–196* in *Zelda Fitzgerald: The Collected Writings*, edited by Matthew Bruccoli. New York: Collier/Macmillan.

Gordon, Mary. 1991. "Introduction." Pp. xv–xxvii in *Zelda Fitzgerald: The Collected Writings*, edited by Matthew Bruccoli. New York: Collier Macmillan.

Graham, Sheilah and Gerold Frank. 1958. *Beloved Infidel*. New York: Henry Holt.

Higgins, Brian and Hershel Parker. 1975. "Sober Second Thoughts: Fitzgerald's Final Version of *Tender is the Night*." *Proof* 4: 129–52.

Mellow, James. 1984. *Invented Lives. F. Scott and Zelda Fitzgerald*. Boston: Houghton Mifflin.

Meyers, Jeffrey. 1994. *Scott Fitzgerald: A Biography*. New York: Harper Collins.

Milford, Nancy. 1970. *Zelda*. New York: Harper and Row.

Mizener, Arthur. 1959. *The Far Side of Paradise: A Biography of F. Scott Fitzgerald*. New York: Vintage.

Rivinus, Timothy. 1992. "Euphoria and Despair: Youthful Addiction in *This Side of Paradise* and *Novel With Cocaine*." *Dionysos* 4, no. 2 (Fall): 15–29.

Roth, Marty. 1990. "'The Milk of Wonder:' Fitzgerald, Alcoholism, and *The Great Gatsby*." *Dionysos* 2, no. 2 (Fall): 3–10.

Roulston, Robert. 1978. "Dick Diver's Plunge into the Roman Void." *South Atlantic Quarterly* 77, no. 1 (Winter): 85–97.

Showalter, Elaine. 1987. *The Female Malady: Women, Madness, and Culture in England, 1830–1980*. New York: Penguin.

Sontag, Susan. 1979. *Illness as Metaphor*. New York: Vintage.

Sournia, Jean-Charles. 1990. *A History of Alcoholism*. Cambridge, MA: B. Blackwell.

Tavernier-Courbin, Jacqueline. 1998. "The Influence of France on Nicole Diver's Recovery in *Tender is the Night*." Pp. 215–32 in *French Connections: Hemingway and Fitzgerald Abroad*, edited by J. Gerald Kennedy and Jackson R. Bryer. New York: St. Martins.

Turnbull, Andrew. 1962. *Scott Fitzgerald*. New York: Scribners.

Wagner, Linda. 1982. "*Save Me The Waltz*: An Assessment in Craft." *Journal of Narrative Technique* 12, no. 3 (Fall): 201–09.

Williams, Tennessee. 1986. *Clothes for a Summer Hotel*. New York: Dramatists Play Service.

Wood, Mary. 1992. "A Wizard Cultivator: Zelda Fitzgerald's *Save Me The Waltz* as Asylum Autobiography." *Tulsa Studies in Women's Literature* 11, no. 2 (Fall): 247–64.

11

The Script of Death:
Writing as Addiction in William Styron's
Darkness Visible

Andrew Stubbs

In the summer of 1985—shortly after his sixtieth birthday—William Styron began experiencing symptoms of clinical depression that culminated in his hospitalization in December of that year. *Darkness Visible: A Memoir of Madness* (1990) is a narrative probe of this fraught six-month period in his life. In fact it is only one, though the longest, of several accounts of his encounter with his mental illness written following his "recovery." The complex process of constructing a language of (self-)destruction got underway in December 1988 with an article in *The New York Times* on Auschwitz survivor Primo Levi, who committed suicide the previous April. Here, as his biographer tells us, Styron advances his general theme of depression as "a disease, not a failure of character" (West, 452). Speaking engagements followed at Johns Hopkins and before the American Suicide Foundation, where he met then *Vanity Fair* editor Tina Brown, who invited him to produce an extended account of his trauma. "Darkness Visible" appeared in *Vanity Fair* in December 1989. This is the basis of the eventual book-length memoir brought out the next year by Random House. (Styron, incidentally, was struck by a recurrence of the illness in Spring 1988.)

All this underscores the outward, public—rhetorical—elements of what was obviously an intensely, harrowingly, individual experience, suggesting in turn two major strains in Styron's argument. One has to do with the demands of creating a public document, an impersonal account of a lived experience, the other with personal involvement, as expressive needs put a counter-emphasis on literary and linguistic nuance. On the objective side, Styron cites contributing factors to his illness: his withdrawal from alcohol and growing reliance on prescription drugs (Ativan, Halcion, Inderal, Ludiomil). He is polemical, didactic: "until that day when a swiftly acting agent is developed, one's faith in a pharmacological cure must remain provisional" (*Darkness*, 55). He does not mince words in condemning Halcion, which he blames for his relapse, or the medical profession (represented by an iconic "Dr. Gold") that prescribed it. In Styron's pharmacy the cure is the disease: the one best equipped to alleviate suffering in practice perpetuates it. But *Darkness Visible* is also aware of the impact of other suicides (Levi, Randall Jarrell), some of whom were acquaintances (Romain Gary, Jean Seberg, Abbie Hoffman), on its author's mental state. At the very least, this raises the spectre of suicide as somehow endemic to the creative personality, which imparts to Styron's text a general tone of mourning not incommensurate with pastoral elegy. From the start we recognize that what Styron gives is not a clear, comprehensive, "scientific" exposition, but (also) a fiction—with the attendant volatility of dramatic narrative. We are compelled to wonder where the line is to be drawn between diagnosis and treatment, between cool, functional observation and a more effusive, volatile style of engagement. When do we cross from negative to positive, especially if suicide, as Styron almost succeeds in persuading himself, can appear as a logical response to a natural set of conditions?

This query is posed not to subtract from the validity of Styron's enterprise, but to indicate that the means he uses to arrive at the truth intersects with modes of awareness more typically associated with literary production. Nor is the overlap between fact and fiction a condition Styron is unaware of. As he points out, with some grimness, "Suicide has been a persistent theme in my books—three of my major characters killed themselves" (*Darkness*, 78). That the aetiology of mental illness can be traced through fictional presentations suggests that the generic distinction between case study and narrative is unstable, with curious consequences. Indeed, Styron, as author, conscientiously takes on the aspect of a character in his own drama, one who is writing his text as he lives/relives it, which creates an interesting double perspective. His subject matter is both mental illness and, reflexively, writing; the extent to which these two subjects permeate each other raises doubt as to whether absolute (dis)closure is really possible. We need to ask how much catharsis Styron really achieves here? Perhaps the degree of personal transformation arrived at through self-writing is measurable more in terms of what is left open, unsaid at the end: analysis is interminable.

In order to show the addictive aspect of Styron's suicidal drive, then, we need to articulate his writing motive from two points of view. One approach identifies the material conditions that impel the author towards death—again, his growing dependency on drugs and reliance on medical intervention. The other recognizes suicide as a cultural situation, influenced, say, by the self-destructive biographies of others, so that the destructive influences on Styron's actions now seem less accidental. More and more, self-destruction seems to carry the force of creative influence, of—more specifically—artistic necessity: it is a destiny that is prepared and waiting, as personal as a signature. Once we allow for this "scripted" (s/crypted) factor, the addictive pattern may be seen to attach not just to one moment among others in Styron's career but to the writing act itself. Styron does not simply move from disease to cure; rather, in producing multiple versions of the same experience, gets caught up obsessively in a (re)performance of death as text. In short, the key to reading *Darkness Visible* is to see how immersed it is in repetition, as if trapped between twin poles of affirmation and denial. Hence, any "ultimate" understanding it may reach of its author's predica- ment is instantly undermined by the compulsion to write more, to write again. *Darkness Visible* is a continuation of the author's addiction (figured as a simultaneous attraction to and repulsion from death), expressed as a need to observe clinically while being romanced by its subject. Running through Styron's essay is a narcissistic self-observation that tends to merge self and other, so that death and life become, equally, tropes of the writing act. Here is where personal catastrophe is elaborated, extended—in effect eroticized.

Under these conditions, the writing act posits a split subject. Styron's project is underlined by recurrence—his proneness to *re*-entering this "dark" terrain. The subject needs to be visited more than once: no account is full. At the same time, Styron seems obsessed by technique, with fashioning a rhetorical facade. *Darkness Visible* "is in part about language itself" (West, 452). Styron is painstakingly aware of the projective role that words play in providing not just a clinical portrait but, as we are saying, a dramatic re- enactment:

> When I was first aware that I had been laid low by the disease, I
> felt a need, among other things, to register a strong protest
> against the word "depression." Depression, most people know,
> used to be termed "melancholia," a word which appears in
> English as early as the year 1303 and crops up more than once
> in Chaucer, who in his usage seemed to be aware of its pathologi-
> cal nuances. "Melancholia" would still be a far more apt and
> evocative word for the blacker forms of the disorder, but it was
> usurped by a noun with a bland tonality and lacking any magis-
> terial presence, used indifferently to describe an economic decline
> or a rut in the ground, a true wimp of a word for such a major
> illness. (Darkness, 36–37)

On one hand, Styron seeks a language sufficiently "apt" to do justice to his subject. His motive is pragmatic, realistic. Language aims at alignment with a subject outside/other than itself. In this sense, the aim of writing is, indeed, to come to an ending, to place the author, finally, outside the sub- ject, and his angst. But *Darkness Visible*, we said, is intimately involved with its own process of composition. Opposites meet: pure exposition gives way to a more insistently ironic mode as words misfire, falling short (understate- ment) or shooting beyond (hyperbole) their target.

We note the risks that Styron takes in approaching his topic more than once, in feeling that continuous demand to re-explore. Repetition can be taken as a sign of failure—hence writerly guilt. To recall Freud in *Beyond the Pleasure Principle*, it verges on compulsion, marking depression, then, as a site of writing. Seeing writing as a performative (in Kenneth Burke's terms "dramatistic") act forces further questions. For example, is writing sickness or health? Does writing about mental illness deepen one's alienation or enable one to surmount it?

At first glance this diagnosis may conventionalize, over-simplify Styron's challenge in *Darkness Visible*. There is ample evidence that for Styron the problematic of mental strife is approachable only through the mediation of a creative process, that the two impulses—destruction and creation—mirror each other. So, Styron is probing writing's other side, the darker forces behind and within creative action. Writing, Faust-like, intrigues with the forces of nihilism to gain power. But this view can come to rest on a super-ficially therapeutic understanding of creational stress, which a ritual accept-ance of such tumult as this must manage to purge in order to arrive at (final) form. Its formula would be: *agon* leads to wisdom leads to publication of socially acceptable meaning. Under these conditions, literature moves safely out of the realm of fraud, is "justified" in humanistic terms. Take this one more step, though, and what Styron is investing in seems more threatening: a pathological reading of the entire enterprise of culture. Literature meets its doppelgänger. Against the visions of a range of literary critics from Arnold to Frye, the literary past becomes a taxonomy of destructive practices. Here is an indictment of all imaginative activity as death wish: not just a revelation of, but a lure towards annihilation. In *Darkness Visible* Styron generalizes his special case to a global theory of cultural production:

> *Since antiquity—in the tortured lament of Job, in the choruses of Sophocles and Aeschylus—chroniclers of the human spirit have been wrestling with a vocabulary that might give proper expres-sion to the desolation of melancholia. Through the course of litera-ture and art the theme of depression has run like a durable thread of woe—from Hamlet's soliloquy to the verses of Emily Dickinson and Gerard Manley Hopkins, from John Donne to Hawthorne and Dostoevsky and Poe, Camus and Conrad and Virginia Woolf. In many of Albrecht Durer's engravings there are harrowing depictions of his own melancholia; the manic wheeling stars of Van Gogh are the precursors of the artist's plunge into dementia and the extinction of self. It is a suffering that often tinges the music of Beethoven, of Schumann and Mahler, and permeates the darker cantatas of Bach.* (82)

Let us propose a clinical reading—or creative misreading—of this pas-sage, suspecting first a buried note of paranoia (the vision is apocalyptic). Do we not approach (Juvenalian) satire's general hermeneutics of corruption and futility as expressed through attributions of decadence (Styron's con-sciousness of Southern tradition)? Here is mental illness as heuristic: imagi-nation as a tragic formulation of despair. "Normally" one approaches a text as given, as an object, susceptible to interpretation. To approach a text as a symptom, as the basis of a case study, renders it a cover-up, a substitute for another text—one beyond the pale. But this other text is not just one we would prefer to reject—as bad news—or possibly try to rehabilitate. It is one whose "ultimate" meaning may repudiate the power of "mere" language—

Jacob wrestling with his angel. Culture as concealment renders culture as taboo, the sign of defilement, which makes every text a debauchery, a failure: it cannot say what it means. Hence Styron's interest in substitution in his retracing of the history of key terms. There is uncertainty about what words want, what their real (hidden) agendas might be. "Depression" as a metonym for melancholia aims to remove traces of the earlier signifier—so words are engaged in an ongoing state of war. And here again we see the possibility of addiction arising from the compulsive, verging on a carnivalesque struggle of language with itself.

This volatility of language captures the deficit situation that for Styron drives both public and professional miscommunication about affective disorders. But what if miscommunication is unavoidable? Still, stripping words of purpose does not result in a cessation of writing. It simply places the failure of words at the centre of imaginative experience. Thus arises the latent double message of language: speech and silence are forms of one another. The authorial drama as suicidal choice is, perhaps, an acting out of violence "always already" within language.

A symptom of this impossible position is awareness of the world as illusion, where the individual—as author—is paradoxically trapped by the infinite; this is the predicament of "radical thought" (radical thought as suicide, we are arguing) as denoted by Jean Baudrillard in *The Perfect Crime*:

> *Radical thought is a stranger to all resolving of the world in the direction of an objective reality and its deciphering. It does not decipher. It anagrammatises, it disperses concepts and ideas and, by its reversible sequencing, takes account both of meaning and of the fundamental illusoriness of meaning. Language takes account of the very illusion of language as definitive strategem and, through it, of the illusion of the world as infinite trap, as seduction of the mind, as spiriting away of all our mental faculties. While it is a vehicle of meaning, it is at the same time a superconductor of illusion and non-meaning. Language is merely the involuntary accomplice of communication—by its very form it appeals to the spiritual and material imagination of sounds and rhythm, to the dispersal of meaning in the event of language. The passion for artifice, for illusion, is the passion for undoing that too-beauteous constellation of meaning. And for letting the imposture show through, which is its enigmatic function, and the mystification of the world, which is its secret.* (104)

Let us note the proximity between Baudrillard's "fundamental illusoriness of meaning" and the aesthetics of the unspeakable, the politics of unreality, an intellectual position crucial to writers on the Holocaust such as George Steiner (cited at some length in *Sophie's Choice*) or Elie Weisel.

Moreover there is a link to be made between "illusion," "non-meaning," and "dispersal of meaning." This is encapsulated in Styron's fiction by a pattern that David Hadaller identifies as "gynocide": death of the feminine. If we follow Hadaller in associating the (repeated) violent absenting of the feminine with Bakhtin's heteroglossia, then fragmentation becomes a symptom of the excluded other. In fact it is attached to the polyphonic texture of Styron's work: in *Sophie's Choice* the unravelling of time, the ridiculing of desire through desire's binding to memory and death. As an extension of this process, the author as narrator in *Darkness Visible* does not simply contemplate death as an outsider, making death an object. Rather he unravels himself so as to enter death, to speak as death—an unmentionable subject—thereby showing intimacy with, even auditioning for approval by death through a network of textual gestures, protocols. He achieves this bond even as death escapes, i.e., remains, in the end, as other, as trickster—all of which gets back to the schizoid message his subject imparts to him. Self-destruction as fragmentation involves not just an unmediated alignment between truth and death but takes in Burke's notion of identification. Destruction entails a wished-for arrival at solidarity with some presence beyond the horizon. Fear, Freud informs us, is segmentation: "Paranoia decomposes just as hysteria condenses" (49).

Darkness Visible renders death feminine, with the feeling of artistic failure converging on the feeling of personal failure, so there is less and less divergence between art and life (twin lacks)—the very situation one faces once one takes the world as the imaginary construction of someone/something else—an enemy. One lives and writes inside the other, earlier creation, unable to surmount it, unwrite its laws. The feeling of limitation, of being reduced in the presence of a giant form with incalculable powers may appear as a failure of proportion, a forced conjunction of small and large, deficit and surplus, silence and loquacity, the trivial and grandiose. Obviously this can be seen as, also, a creative anxiety, a problem of authorship, of influence. The writer falls into a rhetorical void where exact comparison between here and there, word and world, good or bad (art), is frustrated; reality collapses to a façade, gets de-realized into "mere" art—which is also an image of the death camp.

Fact and fiction mix in Styron's work, as when actual historical events provide a familiarizing context or persons in real time (Nat Turner, Rudolf Höss) (re)appear as fictional characters. What, following J.L. Austin, we might call the "constative" drive in Styron might surface as documentary—an inclination not only to record, but to record exhaustively, minutely, finally. This suggests that the idea of order is attended by a non-rational compulsion, a need that cannot be fulfilled by order itself. (Michael Ondaatje in *Running in the Family*—which is a family history that takes in his father's self-destructiveness and paranoia—refers to his own writing motive as a wish to "get this book right" since he "can only write it once" [172].) But the drive to get something right has a hermeneutic significance as well. This is revealed in *Sophie's Choice*, in—again—parenthetical references to Steiner's *Language and Silence*, through which Stingo, the first-person narrator and budding author, tries to come to terms with the Holocaust, with the reality of the inhuman. Interestingly, Styron's "truth telling" is tied to what, seen from his authorial viewpoint, is the predicament of the outcast. He mounts an *iden-tification with* the other with a technical aim—to get the story told (with *The Confessions of Nat Turner* this was seen by some as appropriation of the other's voice). Gradually we come to see that *Darkness Visible* is a reitera-tion of a more general authorial dilemma, one Styron has encountered before.

This dilemma is about the propriety of fiction writing in light of its com-plicity with ideas of destruction, which suggests another connection between *Darkness Visible* and *Sophie's Choice*, not just their autobiographical dimen-sion but their addiction to language. *Sophie's Choice* is preoccupied with the complexities and proprieties of novel-writing in the person of Stingo. Since Stingo's biography overlaps with Styron's, we again become unsure where to separate outer (real) and inner (fictive) worlds, yet what remains (at least) to be said is that both works reflect on writing: what we read is the text's modelling of its own coming into existence. This places that narrative moment dangerously, yet miraculously, at the scene of its birth. Authorship itself gets positioned within the Oedipal dynamics of the primal scene, the key term being placement "within" (the text): authorship is voyeurism, as we see in the case of Stingo, who is mapped—as outsider and as intimate—into the love/war struggle of Nathan and Sophie.

The meta-textual dimension is paramount and ultimately a hinge on which turns the issue of propriety. This is the existential question facing writ-ers on the Holocaust: how does one "rationalize" writing in a world that con-tains such a monumental catastrophe? How does one write "after" (in Steiner's terms) the end of the world, a question *Sophie's Choice* shrinks—domesticates—by raising concerns about "great" and "bad" art? The creative/technical questions of what to write or how to write are over-writ-ten by the smaller (in Stingo's case), secondary, critical question of value. Here is where the rhetoricity of Stingo/Styron's project arises, because it forces one to ask the point of speaking, or living, as opposed to remaining silent. If bad art, kitsch, is the only possible means of expression in a post-Holocaust world, why not remain silent—possibly silence holds a greater power of correspondence with the real, with horror, than words? If we read literature from the viewpoint of one obsessed with destruction— private or public, individual or general—then "greatness" in art disappears. All art is junk, a possibility that presses on Stingo in an extravagantly personal way and lies behind the various critical pronouncements of the paranoid schizo-phrenic Nathan Landau. Madness, as we learn from Freud's *Schreber* (more on this to follow), makes claims of objectivity. It longs for reference to an outer world, can impersonate (quite convincingly) sanity.

What is at stake, we said, is the process of commentary on the scene of writing—on birth, the paradox being that it is precisely this device of inwardly turned or backwardly turned self-contemplation that leads neces-sarily to questions of non-existence. For a work that is in the process of being created is contingent: it might or might not exist. It is contemplation that carries the seeds of non-entity; the text as marked by its own, and by implication, its author's demise. Now we have commingled the topic of self-destruction and the topic of authorship—as if suicide is precisely the event that one approaches as an author, as the author of one's own end, as creative destroyer. What does this oxymoron reveal about Styron's perception of mental illness's inexhaustible threat? More to the point, and to return to our earlier question, does the need to repeat indicate something about the inability of language to *illuminate* the phenomenon of clinical depression?

A topos that surfaces repeatedly in *Darkness Visible* is light. Light, not darkness, supplies the iconography of madness, as in the opening paragraph:

> *In Paris on a chilly evening late in October of 1985 I first became fully aware that the struggle with the disorder in my mind—a struggle which had engulfed me for several months— might have a fatal outcome. The moment of revelation came as the car in which I was riding moved down a rain-slick street not far from the Champs-Elysees and slid past a dully glowing neon sign that read Hotel Washington.* (3)

Madness is blanketing illumination: "Neon sign"; "moment of revelation"; "I became fully aware."

Light seems to straddle two worlds. It marks the convergence of present and past (desire for a past condition) and therefore stands between outer perception and inner ("emotional") state. At various other moments when despair seems to be leading to a decisive climactic action, light attends. Light mixes, then, reality and desire—or, we might say, it is both natural phenomenon and figure of speech:

> *Doubtless depression had hovered near me for years, waiting to swoop down. Now I was in the first stage—premonitory, like a flicker of sheet lightning barely perceived—of depression's black tempest.* (43)

> *The fading evening light—akin to that famous "slant of light" of Emily Dickinson's, which spoke to her of death, of chill extinction—had none of its familiar autumnal loveliness, but ensnared me in a suffocating gloom.* (45)

> *Then I went to the kitchen and with gleaming clarity—the clarity of one who knows he is engaged in a solemn rite—I noted all the trademarked legends on the well-advertised articles...* (63–64)

Light is the meeting of actual and possible. By the same token, light is the problem of the text itself, since it seems to focus all of the text's ambivalences, its conflicts with itself about what to say/not say. Light, as a finite— final—moment in the text, is the text's power to reveal itself to itself. It provides a sound/ mirror to what has just been said, a kind of critical consciousness or authorial double, an awareness of metaphoricity.

Ironically, though, light is equally equitable not just with madness but with health. In his closing passage, Styron cites Dante:

> For those who have dwelt in depression's dark wood, and known
> its inexplicable agony, their return from the abyss is not unlike
> the ascent of the poet, trudging upward and upward out of hell's
> black depths and at last emerging into what he saw as "the shin-
> ing world." There, whoever has been restored to health has
> almost always been restored to the capacity for serenity and joy,
> and this may be indemnity enough for having endured the
> despair beyond despair. (84)

Nothing about its status as a textual icon reduces light's fundamental duplicity. It equally represents madness and the surmounting of madness.

That light performs twin duties in Styron's system makes it a point of
convergence between oppositions such as insanity-normality or destruction-
creation: above all what he pursues here is not the language of one or the
other but of both at once. Styron seeks a cultural order that includes both
terms, which suggests that his language of exhaustion is also a language of
plenitude. But we see this overlap already in his truncation ("inexplicable
agony") or qualification ("not unlike") of phrasing coupled with an ever-
replicating surplus ("upward and upward"; "despair beyond despair"). His
motive, ultimately, is less referential than dramatic (as we have been saying),
with the poles of choice clearly marked by negation—including the double
negative—and repetition. In the case of either, however, what he seeks is
participatory: an intimacy that allows the subject to be "visible" and invisible
("darkness") at the same time. More and more, in other words, his aim converges on the construction of a symbolic order that allows for reversal, as
when death becomes not termination but a symbolic investment—possibility. To speak of death in such terms, though, is to link it with desire, which
calls attention to the amorous and potentially revolutionary features of death
as just another trope. Baudrillard, dwelling on the distinction we are propos-
ing between exposition and dramatization, says:

> The rational, referential, historical and functional machines of
> consciousness correspond to industrial machines. The aleatory,
> non-referential, transferential, indeterminate and floating
> machines of the unconscious correspond to the aleatory machines
> of the code. But even the unconscious is reabsorbed by this opera-
> tion, and it has long since lost its own reality principle to become
> an operational simulacrum. At the precise point that its psychical
> reality principle merges into its psychoanalytic reality principle,
> the unconscious, like political economy, also becomes a model of
> simulation. (Symbolic, 3)

By its reversibility, light (like death) becomes a point of exchange and so
invested with value, something capable of being performed, capable of being
received or given away (a gift)—or substituted for something else. As both
real (or the real name of something real) and "simulation" it allows the real
to be positioned as something recollected, what Baudrillard calls "a phantom
reference, a puppet reference" (Symbolic, 3). The revolution that light as

death proposes is a revolution that reinstates old forms, a nostalgic wish for correspondence between signifier and signified. But this binding, moved by nostalgia, is already marked by excess and, so, is under the sign of a prohibition—it is a desire that can only be attained at exaggerated expense. Or, possibly (in the end), it cannot be purchased at all, so what one is left with is the hollow gesture, the mere wish, action that ends prematurely (before it becomes a real action). If light is the act that is a non-act (as death is a non-act that is an act), then it reaches (transitively) outward to a realm of absolution and inward to a zone of isolation, of purely psychologized action. But in this way all action takes place on, at the same time as it constructs, an inner stage that predetermines what action is appropriate. Does sensing the unreality, or simulated reality, of the inner stage offer a means of escape from the suicidal impulse—with its nostalgic longing for the real?

Styron relates going into the kitchen and preparing "with gleaming clarity" to dispose of a "notebook" he had been keeping for years—this he presents as his point of no return, an action without remainder. He has prepared in his mind, already, that loss of this book means his death is assured: "So as my illness worsened I rather queasily realized that if I once decided to get rid of the notebook that moment would necessarily coincide with my decision to put an end to myself" (*Darkness*, 59). From this point, he is caught up in a apparently necessary train of events, sacrificed control over his narrative of self-destruction, in effect reposing agency and meaning in outer events themselves, in (as Burke would say) the scene. In a curious way, this most personal of acts reaches its culmination in a sublime de-personalization, whose aim is to place the motive to death not in a decision of the author himself but in the force of circumstances outside. This outer condition is a narrative mechanism—and so an inner stage—that is put in place to contain, observe, and guarantee a specific performance.

Light, however expressive of a desire for resolution, for full meaning— hardly "light" subjects—nonetheless is concerned less with the ceremonious aspect of ending than with the trivial. Death rests on the same language of kitsch we have associated with "mere" rhetoric, vulgar commerce, making death a kind of junk form. As Styron prepares his death, "trademark legends on the well-advertised articles" call up the following list:

> *The new roll of Viva paper towels I opened to wrap up the book,*
> *the Scotch-brand tape I encircled it with, the empty Post Raisin*
> *Bran box I put the parcel into before taking it outside and stuff-*
> *ing it deep down within the garbage can, which would be emptied*
> *the next morning. Fire would have destroyed it faster, but in*
> *garbage there was an annihilation of self appropriate, as always,*
> *to melancholia's fecund self-humiliation. I felt my heart pounding*
> *wildly, like that of a man facing a firing squad, and I knew I*
> *had made an irreversible decision.* (64)

Curiously Styron speaks of an action that is "appropriate" to the scene, but his language speaks excess—fecundity—through a shrunken sense of particulars, in the self-effacement associated with "self-humiliation." He is fascinated with interiors, with the domestic (an ordinary evening in December), with events subject to routine. In creating the appearance of an external requirement, Styron authors his death as obligation.

In seeking an isomorphic correspondence between act and scene, Styron aims at an act of pure mimesis. It is the dependence of one system on another that generates the need to die, the occasion of dying. Suicide is a voluntary, irreversible participation in a public order of events. It is Faustian contract where one calls upon oneself, freely, to act out a drama of death with death as an absolute, an ideal, detached audience. Suicide, by its impersonation of the other as death, becomes the paradigmatic rhetorical act. It is already public, already show, even as the actor feels his isolation. The alignment of outer and inner must be perfectly timed: it must be the last moment. Timing (*kairos*) is crucial; a vague death wish, diffused over six months, does not itself produce dying. Rather, the death wish must be complemented by a decision to *act* it *out*, now.

The suicide's attribution, outward, of a structure of rationality is a pre-enactment of death intended to foreshadow physical annihilation. Now we see that the "other" (as an independent force) is called up as the prime mover to self-murder. Purpose, then, is assigned to death itself, not primarily to the actor. So, at any rate, the actor (Socratically) would have us believe. If, in the pseudo-organization imparted to material events, personal cause is effaced, then the motive to suicide must be other than a desire, by itself, to die. If desire is directed towards occasion, then suicide is a communal act. This would account for the element of travesty in the suicidal drama. One could, too, live one's life as a failed suicide (like Salieri at the end of Peter Shaffer's *Amadeus*). Failing at suicide is secondary failure—beyond the primary failure of suicide itself. But it involves others by calling others to watch. Death too is asked to attend, which points to the idea that the suicide accuses his audience of being failed suicides (or mediocrities). Again, there is an element of affectivity in suicide. A clue to this ulterior motive is the suicide's enlargement of personal crisis to a general philosophy of action. This is an act of paranoid distortion, an excess that falls back (and in) on nothingness. Here is another case of more leading to less. (Here is the mythic flight of Icarus, who went too high, and ended up falling below his prescribed position.)

If we examine certain cases of literary suffering, such as Job or Thomas Hardy's Jude, leading—actually or potentially—to suicide, we note an interesting factor. Suicidal longing is not directed simply to destroying the remainder of one's life. In fact it is directed towards cancelling the life/time leading up to now. Suicide makes it as if one was never born. In this event, self-destruction is retroactive, leading backwards to the moment of birth. If there is no life to begin with, if one's historical, bodily history has been revised out of existence, then the loss of self is in place from the start. If one was not born then one cannot die. And so suicide can be made to seem as if it did not happen: suicide effaces itself too. (Death, as in Donne, dies.) In a new set of hermeneutical conditions, authorship is defeated by authorship—a cosmic humiliation.

We start with the notion that suicide is an assault, belatedly, on the privileged moment of creation/birth, the concrete exemplar of which is the body of the mother, who gave the gift of birth/death. What lies below the self-destructive act would seem to be a profound (abyssal) misogyny. Styron is aware of course of the role of the past in controlling present conditions, abetting suicidal decisions. Think of the opening scene of *Darkness Visible*, Paris, where he has gone to receive the Prix Mondial Cino del Luca, where he passed valuable personal time in the spring of 1952. Present is layered on past, giving rise to sentimentality, expressed in double terms as a sense of completeness as well as incompleteness. He is aware of having "come fatally full circle" (4), yet later on, citing Howard I. Kushner's *Self-Destruction in the Promised Land*, he traces suicidal designs to "incomplete mourning" (80). One "has, in effect, been unable to achieve the catharsis of grief, and so carries within himself through later years an insufferable burden of which rage and guilt, and not only dammed-up sorrow, are a part, and become the potential seeds of self-destruction" (79–80). Kushner's reading of Abraham Lincoln's "hectic moods of melancholy" in light of Lincoln's "unexpressed grief" at his mother's death later holds attractions for Styron, whose own mother died when he was 14 under circumstances where he considered himself responsible. Now, the theme of failed mourning, coupled with death of the feminine ("gynocide") is in fact noted by Styron. As he tells us, reading himself, "I was stunned to perceive how accurately I had created the landscape of depression in the minds of these young women..." (79). Nostalgia, the feeling of guilt about one's origin, fuels a narrative longing, revealed as a psychological—indeed pathological—formation. This longing entails a prohibited identification with other. Styron writes, we have said, not only about, but from within, the experience of history's absentees. Pauline Styron, William's mother, died July 20, 1939 of cancer; a year earlier an episode occurred that sheds light on the residual guilt Styron felt at her death. This episode is crucial to the biography of Stingo, and so to the whole issue, as elaborated in *Sophie's Choice*, of authorship and its double: failed authorship.

On a winter day in 1938, Styron forgot to come home after school and start the fire—as he was expected to do—in the family living room, where his mother spent her days more-or-less immobilized (he went joy-riding with a friend). After her death, "he came to fear illogically that his forgetfulness ... somehow accelerated her sickness ands hastened her passing" (West, 41). Apart from the internal dynamics of unalleviated mourning, guilt (real or imagined) at the death of the mother represents, in terms of the mythology of the Freudian family romance, a reversal of the Oedipal relation. "Normally" in the Oedipal scene, the father is murdered, the mother is the beloved; the father is murdered by the son, who wishes to take the father's place, become his own father. In the reverse scene, the father, supposedly the object of the son's bloodlust, is the amorous object; the mother is the one who dies.

Coupled with the death of the mother as it is rendered—as part of

Stingo's past—in *Sophie's Choice* is another episode where Stingo is sharing a hotel room in New York with his father, who is visiting from their native Virginia. Aroused by the sound of a couple's lovemaking in the next room, Stingo fantasizes having sex with, among others, Sophie:

> *With a groan that was loud enough to jar my father from his tor-*
> *mented sleep—a groan that I'm sure sounded inconsolable—I*
> *embraced my phantom Sophie, came in an unstoppered deluge,*
> *and while coming called out her beloved name. In the shadows,*
> *then, my father stirred. I felt his hand reach out and touch me.*
> *"You all right, son?" he said in a troubled voice.* (364)

The episode condenses much of the novel's thematic material: the relations between past and present, fantasy and reality, desire and denial, eros and death, but the key facet of this scene is its acting out of sexual motif beside the sleeping father. Love of (nostalgia for) the father and death of the mother are acted in the same scene: the Freudian dynamic is obvious, here, but its key terms are reversed.

Freud reveals the possibilities of Oedipal reversal in his longer case studies—*Rat Man*, *Wolf Man*, *Little Hans*, and nowhere at greater length than in his *Schreber*, whenever the ramifications of gender choice are pursued. *Schreber*, which deals with a case of paranoid schizophrenia, is the basis for Lacan's *Psychoses*, which in turn stands behind Derrida's *Glas*. (To follow up, incidentally, on the *Glas* connection, note Stingo's rendering of the lovemaking in the next room: "It was sculpted sound, incredibly close, almost tactile [*Sophie*, 362]). Daniel Paul Schreber (Schreiber/writer) is a man who wants to be a woman, fears persecution by his doctor, dreams of the end of the world, transforms his fear of violence into love for the perpetrator of violence. For Freud: "His father's most dreaded threat, castration, actually provided the material for his wishful fantasy" (56); violation is naturalized, made "consonant with the Order of Things" (48).

The Oedipal moment normally symbolizes the son's selection of identification with the father, culminating in the desire to replace him in his mother's bed. The mirror/double of this is the son's identification with the mother, which leads to mother-killing—presumably to replace her as object of the father's affection. The flip side of the Oedipal contract is the Orestes tragedy, where son slays mother out of love for the slain father (murdered by the mother). It is not, however, the psychoanalytical applications of Freud's drama that primarily concern us here.

Rather, we need to approach the Oedipal relation as a rhetorical act—as providing a language for a certain type of textual performance. Endemic to rhetorical theory is an inventory of ratios, such as Burke's. Burke's ratios are pairings of elements selected from his pentad: act, scene, agent, agency, purpose. Thus we have an "act-scene" ratio, a "scene-agent" ratio, and so on. Ratios, then, are binaries designed to explain the "motive" of an action, or the text of an action. An important factor, as Burke tells us, is that any ratio can be reversed:

> *We originally said that the five terms allowed for ten ratios; but we also noted that the ratios could be reversed, as either a certain kind of scene may call for its corresponding kind of agent, or a certain kind of agent may call for its certain kind of scene. The list of possible combinations would therefore be expanded to twenty. And the members of each pair would then be related as potential to actual. Thus, a mode of thought in keeping with the scene-agent ratio would situate in the scene certain potentialities that were said to be actualized in the agent. And conversely, the agent-scene ratio would situate in the agent potentialities actualized in the scene. And so on with the other ratios.* (262)

Styron's descriptions of setting—the scene at his home where the suicidal choice is evidently made—invoke the scene-act ratio and/or its opposite. All is part of Styron's attempt, at pivotal moments, to make outer and inner worlds commensurate. Scene, we have noted, is an expression—or mask—for a psychological state. Patterns of feeling can be situated as "landscapes." The relationship of outer to inner is repeatedly negotiated in *Darkness Visible*. Stabilizing this relationship, we might conjecture, is a primary aim of Styron's narrative.

A further feature of Burke's ratios and of the special factor of their reversibility is that they supply a theory of reading, which is to say a theory of revision. Burke's *A Grammar of Motives* is saturated with doublets (such as matter and spirit) over and above the twenty technical ratios just mentioned. Burke tells us that "Marx reversed Hegel by treating material, or economic conditions, as formative of spirit (as against the Hegelian terminology that begins with spirit as source and ground)" (281). This invites us to join him in applying a ratio to the interval *between two texts*.

Burke is interested in capturing the way a later text aligns with—and departs from—an earlier one. A ratio thus spotlights a conjunction/disjunction between texts, not just within a specific text, and thus acts as a theory of reading. It functions, that is, as a theory of revision, and therefore of influence. Now, the revisionary feature—tied as this is with what is similar and what is different between two texts, with what is preserved and what is changed—with "permanence and change" Burke would say—gives access to the past of a text, its ancestral memory as it were. It locates a text in a tradition, so it is here that Burke's ratios intersect with Harold Bloom's "revisionary ratios" as set out in *The Anxiety of Influence*, where ratios are a means of talking about a later author's fraught, violent links to precursors. Note that Bloom's categories also entail reversal, with the belated writer (at his strongest) becoming an influence on the earlier. It is worth noticing that the "anxiety" of tradition is in the foreground of *Sophie's Choice*. It is a hot topic of discussion between Stingo and Nathan.

More to the point, *Darkness Visible* features Styron as a reader of the text of his own mental state: an "earlier" state of psychic abnormality must be both recorded (preserved) and overcome (changed). That Styron's memoir involves ancestral motifs suggests that *Darkness Visible* is a further stab by Styron at the traumatic origins of creation, with the "fall" into depression heralded by a lapse into a grotesquely loquacious rhetoricity. This taints his world with the same unreality Auschwitz brings to Sophie's, as in the description of Yetta Zimmerman's. (Stingo recalls: "When I first saw the place I was instantly reminded of the façade of some back-lot castle left over from the MGM movie version of *The Wizard of Oz*" [*Sophie*, 38].) This is a world of unreal people or, Freud's Schreber would say, "cursorily improvised men" (69), which we see in the cipher character, Jemand von Niemand, who forces Sophie to choose between her son and daughter.

If we take Freud's Oedipal drama, with its pairing of gender terms, as just another rhetorical ratio, we begin to see how *Darkness Visible* can be moved out of the regime of psychological explication—the hermeneutic mode—into narrative reflexivity. Narrative (scene) and author (agent) become one, which is a way of saying that narrative authors itself. Or, narrative is placed at the scene of its own (en)gendering, which sets up a double storyline: Styron/Stingo's unending story of his search for Sophie's story, which has an ending. Meanwhile, gender reversal as an account of the origin of writing, with the masculine component in femininity or the feminine component in masculinity co-emerging, is of course a recurring topos in Hélène Cixous. If authorship is crisis, caught between poles of desire and death, possibility and impossibility, then Styron, who seeks identity in the other, performs a kind of negative capability. Here is a phrase that takes on extra resonance in light of Styron's deployment of self-murder as a way of opening himself into story.

A further curious factor emerges with respect to the ratio, namely that, given its reversibility, the terms inside the ratio take each other's places: self, for example, adopts the position of other, other the position of self. Styron, continuously negotiating between being commentator as well as the subject of his discourse, remarks that depression calls up a double. His feeling is that he has gone outside, become a spectator, so he is no longer here but (also) over there, not on stage but in the "audience":

> *A phenomenon that a number of people have noted while in deep depression is the sense of being accompanied by a second self—a wraithlike observer who, not sharing the dementia of his double, is able to watch with dispassionate curiosity as his companion struggles against the oncoming disaster, or decides to embrace it. There is a theatrical quality about all this, and during the next several days, as I went about stolidly preparing for extinction, I couldn't shake off a sense of melodrama—a melodrama in which I, the victim-to-be of self-murder, was both the solitary actor and lone member of the audience.* (*Darkness*, 64–65)

Let us note the "theatrical" quality here, the feeling of unreality emerging through "melodrama," heightening our sense that illness is itself an image, though being a character in his drama gives Styron powers of prescience. In the economy of a ratio, opposed terms lose their specialized, denotative power and trade places (as when author becomes character); it is possible to see this exchange as appropriative. If identity involves mobility, speaking as the other cancels the other's more original voice.

The movement of terms into each other's spaces suggests the primary uncertainty about the will or desire (what we might call, after Burke, the rhetorical "motive") of words themselves. Note that while its terms are shifting, the ratio remains intact, a situation that implies two things at once, a perpetual revolution in meaning that is nonetheless accommodated within the static, conservative frame of the ratio. Two points need to be made here regarding this cross-over feature of terms bound in a rhetorical ratio as it touches Styron's predicament. First, as Styron comes to be aware, his illness is linked to unresolved feelings about his mother's death, however "illogical" or exaggerated or theatrical his culpability in that event may seem. Applying the notion of ratio, we might say that his feelings arise from a continuing re-identification, re-appropriation of the mother's position in suffering. Meanwhile, the conservative function of the ratio allows Styron to retain the moment of death as a memory: all narration circles back on this defining—begetting—moment.

The whole vicarious movement of fusion with the pain of the (m)other is actually, then, an attempt to put back something that has gone missing, to re-place a moment, affirm its independent (inescapable) authenticity. This gesture is intended to prevent the moment from disappearing altogether—thus monumentalizing birth/suffering, imparting to it permanent form. Styron, as author of his death, re-invents his mother's death (as history and as story) as a way of acting out his own birth/death under circumstances that he controls. The rhetorical motive behind the representation, the mimetic impulse itself, might be characterized along such lines, namely as a wish to put back, to restore to ground what was previously removed from it. This restoration is an alignment between inward memory and outward landscape not different from any sought symmetry between word and thing, word and act. What hides below this symmetry, however, is a repressed violence towards the psychological other, such as we encounter in Stingo's eroticism, his narrative compulsion.

The constative thrust in *Darkness Visible* is tantamount to Orestes's longing for balance, closure, to have accounts settled, order restored. It is not strange, when we think of Styron's situation in light of the "death of the author" syndrome, that the moment of an author's disappearance is a moment of precise mimesis. Derrida provides an instance in *Speech and Phenomena* where word and event are in perfect collaboration, showing how the alignment itself creates a demand for death. Derrida: "I say, 'I see a particular person by the window' while I really do see him" (92).

It is at this moment that the destructive agenda within language, the desire of words to annihilate the speaker, so as to stand alone, purged of intention, contingency—of rhetoricity—surfaces:

> It is radically requisite: the total absence of the subject and
> object of a statement—the death of the writer and/or the
> disappearance of the objects he was able to describe—does not

> *prevent a text from "meaning" something. On the contrary, this*
> *possibility gives birth to meaning as such, gives it out to be heard*
> *and read.* (93)

The birthing of meaning happens within the simultaneously destructive and creative moment of the ratio, which we now see as an instance of the origin, the point to which all nostalgia—tendentiously—aspires.

If death of the feminine is the other/outer story that Styron seeks as both fiction and history, and if this story is told backwards to a more and more original moment, then it is not surprising that *Sophie's Choice* unfolds retroactively—back to her past, to Auschwitz, to the moment of choice in the death camp. Sophie's "choice" at that time runs parallel to other choices she makes, choices that are always—fatally—wrong decisions about priority: they persistently address the question of which comes (or should come) first but they invariably place the first term as first. The entire narrative problematic (of how, or whether, Sophie's story—the story of her two deaths—can be told) is therefore expressed in Sophie's sequence of decisions: she chooses father over husband, first lover (Nathan) over second lover (Stingo), first born (son) over last born (daughter). The entire revisionary drama of precursor text to belated text unfolds as a drama of reinstatement, not change, and it is this defensive posture that drives Sophie's killing of her daughter and, inevitably, leads to her self murder—her second death. Sophie's "choices" (the plural indicates the recurring pattern) are passive: they unconsciously copy the "natural," forward movement of life in time, never challenge or reverse or overturn this momentum, never privilege the secondary term, which would be a radically revolutionary gesture.

A ratio, we have said, combines the luridly ambivalent with the rigidly structured, which is a way of saying that a ratio conceals its own psychosis, a psychosis that can now be recognized as endemic to narrative, to language itself. (Hence, possibly, rhetoric's reputation as both illegitimate and legitimate—it is capable of perfidious as well as sound argument.) We see this double edge in the mixture of involvement and detachment exhibited by the double, as Styron denotes him: Styron is at the scene but not in it, fascinated but aloof. The double is the intimate stranger, which is a way of saying that intimacy and estrangement, given the rule of interchangeability, are two sides of the same coin. We have seen that Sophie's choices are choices that alter, that threaten, nothing: they are choices of capitulation to an order of death that comes both before her (at Auschwitz) and after her (in America); but what, in the end, is Styron's choice?

If we focus on reversibility—which Sophie's choices do not allow for—a curious feature emerges from Styron's text: the author's consciousness of irony. The very forces that make Styron ill also save him; the very language in which he expresses illness is at the same time the language of salvation—the disease, in other words, is the cure, since light, hitherto expressive of mental disorder, is also associated with revelation, the return of sanity. Without claiming that either of these states is more or less rational than the other, we might note how his memory of his mother, a source of pain at a critical moment, gets exchanged for joy:

> *All this I realized was more than I could ever abandon, even as*
> *what I had set out so deliberately to do was more than I could*
> *inflict on those memories, and upon those, so close to me, with*
> *whom the memories were bound. And just as powerfully I real-*
> *ized I could not commit this desecration on myself. I drew upon*
> *some gleam of sanity to perceive the terrifying dimensions of the*
> *mortal predicament I had fallen into. I woke up my wife and*
> *soon telephone calls were made. The next day I was admitted to*
> *the hospital.* (*Darkness*, 67)

This revaluation is made possible by Styron's sense, as the abyss opens in front of him, of his mother's nearness. He hears the strains of Brahms's *Alto Rhapsody*:

> *my own avoidance of death may have been belated homage to my*
> *mother. I do know that in those last hours before I rescued*
> *myself, when I listened to the passage from the* Alto Rhapsody—
> *which I'd heard her sing—she had been very much on my mind.*
> (81)

Styron, who moments before had committed himself to an irreversible chain of events, now finds escape through "a gleam of sanity": light has switched poles, "gone over" from one condition to another, and takes the author along.

Burke tells us that a "[c]rime produces a kind of 'oneness with the universe' in leading to a sense of universal persecution whereby all that happens has direct reference to the criminal" (308). Here is what Freud would put forward as the narcissism of the anthropomorphic, though with a paranoid tinge: "Much of the world that would be otherwise neutral is charged with personal reference, thereby having much the quality that Aristotle asks of a dramatic plot" (308). In short, "for the criminal, the whole world is thus purposive, so that the experience of criminal guilt in a sense restores the teleological view lost by evolutionism" (308). We should pause here to emphasize that criminal action, whether Styron's guilt at his mother's death or his apparently compensatory plans for "self-murder," is expressed as an ordered event. The criminal plot, like the dramatic plot, uses violence in a "purposive" way, so the image of violence is not war but peace, not chaos but form—in effect a potently primitive longing to restore an earlier state of being (which Freud associates with instinctual life). Given Styron's supposition of strong underlying affinities between his descent into despair and themes in his fiction, a revealing connection emerges. He says that he found inspiration for *The Confessions of Nat Turner* in Albert Camus's *L'Étranger* (*Darkness*, 21), a book, we note, concerned with a causeless crime. But the lack of a cause is intolerable, so in the course of events Meursault's crime gets "rationalized" as, of all things, an assault upon the mother. Violence, we might conjecture, whether directed outward to others or in/back on oneself—in light of Burke's claim that it demands an ordered universe—suggests that at the centre of violence is an architectonic force, which reveals violence as, essentially, space. In this sense, Stingo's "sculpted sound," the whole sense of the tactile aspect of noise, is the psychosis of pure form surfacing in the quotidian, the domestic (interior) world we inhabit in order to subject reality to routine. What we need, to consolidate this notion, is an image of structure that carries the heaviness of a solid object while belonging to the register of dream. Such a structural motif (like Yetta Zimmerman's house in *Sophie's Choice*, which is both façade and structure) encapsulates the narrative's meaning, while being inside its process, thus mirroring the narrative from inside. The opening description of the temple in *The Confessions of Nat Turner*, its associations with light, solidarity, and yet with emptiness—and repetition—seems to answer this need:

> *There again I see what I know I will always see, as always. In the sunlight the building stands white and serene against a blue and cloudless sky. It is square and formed of marble, like a temple, and is simply designed, possessing no columns or windows but rather, in place of them, recesses whose purpose I cannot imagine, flowing in a series of arches around its two visible sides. The building has no door, at least there is no door that I can see.* (*Darkness*, 4)

Linda Hutcheon, in *Irony's Edge*, speaks of "archeological fiction" (167), identifying this imparting of three-dimensional solidity to the visionary, all part of the passage to naming irony as a trope, fiction's consciousness of its fictionality. The placement of structure within a text is a process of miniaturization, so the whole exchange between great and small (Stingo's placing of Sophie's story inside the more mundane story of coming to authorship) is representative of a creative addiction. We begin to see how a history of an impalpable catastrophe, an impossible act of story telling, gets confused with a more-or-less egocentric *Künstlerroman* drama. We also need to observe that this same self-consciousness, as a ploy to shrink (de-realize) the world to toy dimensions, a place of debauched innocence, is an act of violence. The violence of Stingo's narrative demand of Sophie—verging on the voyeuristic—of his generalized erotic desire is not different from Nathan's, or for that matter Höss's, just as Yetta Zimmerman's house replicates Höss's house in the death camp. In both cases, violence lies in direct relationship with pastoral, as if pastoral is the form *par excellence* adopted by warfare, by recollected guilt—it is the language of the obsessive work of mourning.

We have seen that Styron plays with notions of perspective, that the dissolving of perspective is closely linked to the development of counter-narratives, multiple narratives. Play with perspective connects with the flattening of the real world at times into a two-dimensional space, character into caricature, which also links to the eroticizing of the world. Yet Styron's uncovery of shape within dream, an architecture of memory, may represent the ultimate synthesis of reality and imagination—history and fiction—and so madness and sanity. For it brings trope within the cognizance of textual memory, so that the meanings of the fiction are made functions of the drama. Styron mediates between reading and writing by making the text a reader of itself, and while this does not distinguish madness and sanity, or purge one from the other, it makes them complicit and therefore keeps writing—as a means of living—going indefinitely. Styron extricates his life from the overwhelming, totalizing control of death not by offering his life as a gift to his mother's death but by receiving her initial gift of life—again.

Works Cited

Baudrillard, Jean. 1996. *The Perfect Crime*. Translated by Chris Turner. London and New York: Verso.

——. 1993. *Symbolic Exchange and Death*. Translated by Iain Hamilton Grant with an "Introduction" by Mike Gane. London: Sage.

Burke, Kenneth. 1945. *A Grammar of Motives*. Berkeley: University of California Press.

Derrida, Jacques. 1973. *Speech and Phenomena: And Other Essays on Husserl's Theory of Signs*. Translated with an "Introduction" by David B. Allison and "Preface" by Newton Garver. Evanston: Northwestern University Press.

Freud, Sigmund. *Psycho-Analytic Notes on an Autobiographical Account of A Case of Paranoia (Dementia Paranoides)*. *The Standard Edition of The Complete Psychological Works of Sigmund Freud*. 24 vols. Translated under the General Editorship of James Strachey. London: The Hogarth Press and the Institute of Psycho-Analysis, 1953–1960. Vol XII, 1–82.

Hadaller, David. 1996. *Gynocide: Women in the Novels of William Styron*. Cranbury, NJ: Associated University Presses.

Hutcheon, Linda. 1995. *Irony's Edge: The Theory and Politics of Irony*. London and New York, Routledge.

Ondaatje, Michael. 1982. *Running in the Family*. Afterword by Nicole Brossard, Toronto: McClelland and Stewart.

Styron, William. 1990. *Darkness Visible: A Memoir of Madness*. New York: Random House.

——. 1979. *Sophie's Choice*. Toronto and New York: Bantam.

——. 1966. *The Confessions of Nat Turner*. New York: Random House.

West, James L.W. III. 1998. *William Styron, A Life*. New York: Random House.

12

"The Divine Intoxication": Emily Dickinson's Linguistic Addiction

Cindy MacKenzie

The subjects of pain, loss and death along with the numerous ellipses, pervasive disjunction and extreme tensions in Emily Dickinson's poetry have prompted many of the poet's biographers to speculate on the psychological "crisis" underlying such a tortured expression and to attempt posthumously an analysis of her mental condition. It seems, moreover, that these attempts are determined to support the already persistent stereotype of a frustrated and lonely spinster, an eccentric and reclusive woman dressed in white, dubbed the "myth of Amherst" and a "half-cracked" poetess.[1] So numerous and varied are these speculative analyses—manic-depressive, agoraphobic, alcoholic, to name a few—that in the end, they become fatuous and can be categorized as little more than "medical fiction." Admittedly, however, we must allow some basis for these diagnoses, for the movement between moods of dark despair and manic joy dramatized throughout Dickinson's poetry can be viewed as characteristic of the mercurial temperament of the alcoholic/addict. But feminist scholars have insisted that a much more fruitful analysis can be made by considering the poet's experience as a nineteenth-century woman caught between an identity constructed by patriarchal society and yet fully conscious of another "authentic" if unexpressed self. Living as a split female subject, as Adrienne Rich recognizes, is "an extremely painful and dangerous way to live; that is, split between a publicly acceptable persona, and a part of yourself that you perceive as the essential, the creative and powerful self, yet also as possibly unacceptable, perhaps even monstrous" (175). The stresses of this split, Rich continues, have often resulted in madness, loneliness, and depression—states of mind that are frequently the subject of Dickinson's work and have been emphasized in much of the ongoing biographical stereotyping. But while the poet's *oeuvre* may

---

1. In a letter to his wife after meeting with Dickinson, Thomas Wentworth Higginson, her friend and editor, referred to Emily as his "half-crack'd poetess" (Sewall, 566). Dickinson's neighbour and editor, Mabel Loomis Todd, described Emily as "the myth of Amherst" in a letter to her parents (Sewall, 216).

reveal her psychic struggles, it also expresses her love of language as the space where she can live most freely, for as Suzanne Juhasz points out in *The Emily Dickinson Handbook*, she is the poet of whom it is now quite commonplace to say that she "'lived in language'...[as] language for Dickinson was a 'world'—a context as important to her as Amherst, Massachusetts" (439). In letters to her editor, T.W. Higginson, Dickinson proclaims her love for language in terms that personify the words and humanize her relationship to them: "for several years, my Lexicon—was my only companion—" (L261); and to her friend, Mrs. Holland she exclaims: "How lovely are the wiles of Words" (L555)—emphasizing the seductive lure of language. To call her relationship to language an "addiction" not only emphasizes the intense relationship she has with it but also the movement between lack and excess—between deep despair and manic joy that characterizes the poet's mode of expression. That Dickinson's life was subject to the pain of loneliness and loss enters the text obliquely, for the biography does not constitute the *subject* of the poetry so much as its hermeneutics. Within language, the repressed self, unsuccessful in its yearning for the unified self, fractures the textual landscape with disjunction, dashes and gaps, the visual "wounds" analogous to the fragmented self. However, at the same time, the excesses of language—the sentimentality and melodrama, the hyperbolic rhetoric— that constitute the manic element of this linguistic addiction are evident throughout the canon. Arising from pain but also offering relief from it, Dickinson ultimately finds in the act of writing an analogue for living with the pain of a split self and, paradoxically, a vehicle for salvation.

In one of the numerous poems in which Dickinson relates a painful psychological moment, "I felt a Cleaving in my Mind / As if my Brain had split," the experience could well be related to the highly conflicted tension of the schismatic female self to which Rich refers. The speaker's attempts to match the split seams of "the thought behind" and the "thought before" are futile. Unable to achieve "Sequence," thought ravels "out of Sound / like Balls— opon a Floor"—the resultant silence caused by a failure in sequencing thought in the manner of phallocentric linearity:

> I felt a Cleaving in my Mind—
> As if my Brain had split—
> I tried to match it—Seam by Seam—
> But could not make them fit.
>
> The thought behind, I strove to join
> Unto the thought before—
> But Sequence ravelled out of Sound
> Like Balls—opon a Floor. (F867)

The poem expresses the anxiety of the poet's inability to express freely her thoughts and feelings in conventional forms so that she suffers psychically from the pain of repression, contributing to her sense of madness. Her awareness of a powerful, yet submerged self silenced by a lack of language emphasizes the existence of this inner self—what I will call an "other-in-the-self." The nature of this "self" ranges from an intuited presence—"Conscious am I in my Chamber—/ Of a shapeless friend (F773)—to the articulation of a repressed self lying quiescent beneath the tradition of the "honorable work / Of Woman and of Wife" (F857). Moreover, in the latter poem, the metaphor of submersion established by the images of "Pearl" and "Weed" in the last stanza—"as the Sea/Develop Pearl, and Weed, /But only to Himself—be known/ The Fathoms they abide"—products of the sea, can be read as images of the submerged erotic expression of the wife, an expression known only to herself and held under "Fathoms" of water constituting the volcanic power of the submerged female self. The deep division between the hidden inner self and the restricted public self contribute to the profound tension that exists within her.

Dickinson's idiosyncratic expression is, according to Cristanne Miller, noting the "politics of Dickinson's poetics generally," an expression of the "falseness of the order she perceives so that she can imagine no alternative reordering or new system working from the same parts, and so demonstrates graphically and linguistically the chaos she at least occasionally would prefer to the prescribed apparent order she must live within" (105). I would add that the political implications of a shift of this kind by a female poet facilitates the subsequent excesses of her language in a way that echoes Hélène Cixous's exhortations to women writers:

> *If woman has always functioned "within" the discourse of man, a signifier that has always referred back to the opposite signifier which annihilates its specific energy and diminishes or stifles its very sounds, it is time for her to dislocate this "within," to explode it, turn it around, and seize it; to make it hers, containing it, taking it in her own mouth, biting that tongue with her very own teeth to invent for herself a language to get inside of. And you'll see with what ease she will spring forth from that "within"—the "within"—where once she so drowsily crouched—to overflow at the lips she will cover the foam.* (343)

Stepping "outside" the dominant order involves a paradigm shift that opens the floodgates of the imagination with overwhelming excess, an image in Dickinson's poetry frequently expressed by volcanic eruptions and flooding. In the following poem, for example, the floods caused by a shift in the "brain's flow" are not necessarily volitional but certainly unstoppable.

> *The Brain, within its Groove*
> *Runs evenly—and true—*
> *But let a Splinter swerve—*
> *'Twere easier for You—*
>
> *To put a Current back—*
> *When Floods have slit the Hills—*
> *And scooped a Turnpike for Themselves—*
> *And trodden out the Mills—* (F563)

When the "Brain," Dickinson's word for imagination, stays "within its Groove," it "Runs evenly—and true," the adverbs emphasizing the undeviating uniformity of the flow. But if the tiniest piece splinters from that "Groove," the flow will "swerve" and deviate from its course. The habitual course of ideas can also become an unconscious "groove" or indeed, one that seems "natural" in the view of the majority. Therefore, if one deviates from that course, by changing one's mind or perspective, what changes, the speaker says, is everything. The poem raises the idea of going beyond the predictable, going beyond the expected, so that the subsequent overflow of the imagination becomes transgressive. The "Floods" of her own linguistic excesses do not run within a groove but instead, having "trodden out the Mills," the manufacturers of conventional thinking, they have "Scooped a Turnpike for Themselves," found their own path, their own voice, their own means of expression.

In much the same way, the image of fire in the following poem expresses the unwavering progression of its course as it runs on its own power, once ignited:

> You cannot put a Fire out—
> A Thing that can ignite
> Can go, itself, without a Fan—
> Opon the slowest night—
>
> You cannot fold a Flood—
> And put it in a Drawer—
> Because the Winds would find it out—
> And tell your Cedar Floor— (F583)

The humour in the poem's second stanza drives the point home even more emphatically—the notion of "folding a Flood" up like a piece of dry paper (perhaps the paper on which her own poems are written) and placing it in a "Drawer" sets itself up to be subverted by the last two lines of the stanza as the futility of your attempts would soon be evidenced on your wet "Cedar Floor." Once ignited, the fire of passion is relentless in its journey; once opened, the floods of creativity cannot be contained.

Discovering this boundless space, Dickinson "falls in love" with it—her self-abandon occasionally recorded in terms that emphasize the self-parodic characteristics of giving herself up to it:

> If this is "fading"
> Oh let me immediately "fade"!
> If this is "dying"
> Bury—me, in such a shroud of red!
> If this is "sleep,"
> On such a night
> How proud to shut the eye!
> Good evening, gentle Fellow men!
> Peacock presumes to die! (F119)

Dickinson's "performance" describes her abandonment to language—going to the limits and beyond—languishing in a state of *jouissance* as she goes to her poetic death. The self-mocking naming of her speaker as "Peacock" connotes the showy performance of the poet/bird's seduction and death. The saucy invitation to "gentle Fellow men!" to come and watch continues the suggestion of playful deception created by the words offset by quotation marks and the exclamation marks that follow them. The use of the verb "presumes" further undercuts the seriousness of the event as we can only suppose it to be true. Moreover, another meaning of the verb—"to go beyond what is right or proper"—suggests the transgressive nature of the act. The male gendering of the poet/bird is one such transgression as is the provocative "red shroud" in which the body is buried.

Another little poem with a similar strategy features a speaker who indulges in a mischievous if not hammy performance of her death:

> *Dying at my music!*
> *Bubble! Bubble!*
> *Hold me till the Octave's run!*
> *Quick! Burst the Windows!*
> *Ritardando!*
> *Phials left, and the Sun!* (F946)

Music is orchestrated for this overly dramatized event, music that fairly reels with the excess of drunken abandon. This time, every line ends with an exclamation mark. The words themselves often yield to nonsense, particularly those that suggest the sounds and the pace of such abandon— "Bubble, bubble!" and "Ritardando!" The imperative to "Burst the Windows!" expresses the need to provide for the overflowing excesses of the poem. The image of the final line is one of brilliant effect: that is the light of the sun as it plays on the vessels left behind—or perhaps on the broken glass of the window!

In "I taste a Liquor never brewed," the speaker clearly confesses and indulges in the destabilizing effects of her drunken state:

> *I taste a liquor never brewed—*
> *From Tankards scooped in Pearl—*
> *Not all the Frankfort Berries*
> *Yield such an Alcohol!*
>
> *Inebriate of Air—am I—*
> *And Debauchee of Dew—*
> *Reeling—thro' endless summer days—*
> *From inns of Molten Blue—*
> *When "Landlords" turn the drunken Bee*
> *Out of the Foxglove's door—*
> *When Butterflies—renounce their "drams"—*
> *I shall but drink the more!*
>
> *Till Seraphs swing their snowy Hats—*

> *And Saints—to windows run—*
> *To see the little Tippler*
> *From Manzanilla come! (F207)*

As Cristanne Miller points out, the poem "draws on an analogy likening poetic vision to the state of intoxication" (19). The defiant speaker is unabashed-
ly delighted by her gaiety and, with the bravado of the drunken braggart,
declares her immense capacity for endless "drams" of a mysterious liquor:
"When Butterflies—renounce their "drams"—/ I shall but drink the more!"
The mysterious "liquor" is described in ethereal imagery—it comes from
"Tankards scooped in Pearl—," the "Pearl" suggesting one of Dickinson's
images for poetry. She is drunk on the very air, dew, and sky: she is "Inebriate
of Air," "Debauchee of Dew," and staggers, "reeling ... from inns of Molten
Blue." The disjunction that characterizes the poem—and drunkenness
itself—is intensified in the final stanza when the speaker moves from a romp
with nature to consorting with more heavenly company. Her reeling drunkenness entices even the "Seraphs" who toss their "snowy Hats" in comrade-
ly spirit, and the "Saints," who run to the window to "see the little tippler /
From Manzanilla come!" "Manzanilla," a kind of sherry, is now the name of
her home town, but the strangeness of the word itself plays up the possibility of it being a geographic reality in a way that parallels the speaker's ine-
briated condition.

However, like the "high" of inebriation, these moments do not last but
they can act as "stimulants" for future inspiration. The speaker's shift from
the celebration of a rare moment of bliss to an understanding of the paralyzing ramifications of such an experience are developed from a retrospective
viewpoint in this philosophical poem:

> *Did Our Best Moment last—*
> *'Twould supersede the Heaven—*
> *A few—and they by Risk—procure—*
> *So this Sort—are not given—*
>
> *Except as stimulants—in*
> *Cases of Despair—*
> *Or Stupor—The Reserve—*
> *These Heavenly Moments are—*
>
> *A Grant of the Divine—*
> *That Certain as it Comes—*
> *Withdraws—and leaves the dazzled Soul*
> *In her unfurnished Rooms— (F560)*

The memorable final image of the instantaneity of our "Best Moment," a
"Heavenly Moment" that "leaves the dazzled Soul / In her unfurnished
Rooms—," powerfully merges the idea of the moment as both plenitudinous
and empty. For the soul, dazed by the enchantment of the moment, is left
desolate and paralyzed in the "unfurnished Rooms" of the moment's aftermath. Moreover, according to Dickinson, the potential for calling on the

power of that moment remains as she explains in a letter to her friend, Otis Lord: "The withdrawal of the Fuel of Rapture does not withdraw the Rapture itself. Like Powder in a drawer, we pass it with a Prayer, it's Thunders only dormant" (L842).

Dickinson's speakers, moreover, are not always enchanted by the pleasures of intoxication at all. In poem F312, its disorienting effects can be considered offsetting and even debilitating:

> I can wade Grief—
> Whole Pools of it—
> I'm used to that—
> But the least push of Joy
> Breaks up my feet—
> And I tip—drunken—
> Let no Pebble—smile—
> 'Twas the New Liquor—
> That was all!
>
> Power is only Pain—
> Stranded—thro' Discipline,
> Till Weights—will hang—
> Give Balm—to Giants—
> And they'll wilt, like Men—
> Give Himmaleh—
> They'll carry—Him! (F312)

The poem clearly associates power and pain—pain and the wounding as well as the liberating of consciousness. For Dickinson, pain becomes the paradoxical power that generates her artistic potential. Without pain, she asserts, we would not develop our potential, could not become "Giants," for if we are given an easier way, given "Balm," it would make us "wilt, like Men—." The "new Liquor" cannot be used as a balm as the metaphor emphasizes the falsity of its capacity to produce a high. Faithfulness to the art of poetry, to the integrity to self, to faith in an audience of future readers, requires the renunciation of one kind of life for another. This is the "disciplined pain" that Dickinson equates with power.

Dickinson's poetic expression acts as a hermeneutical analogue of this philosophy in the way that she recognizes the possibility for a site of pleasure that corresponds with Barthes's "pleasure of the text": "what pleasure wants is the site of a loss, the seam, the cut, the deflation, the dissolve which seizes the subject in the midst of bliss" (7). Hence, the gap, "split" or "wound" becomes the site of pleasure in the text—a space that Dickinson works to increase, thereby enlarging the "possibility" of meaning. It would follow then that despite the enormous tensions they produce, oppositional devices offer pleasurable play in Dickinson's text where, according to Barthes, "the opposing forces are no longer repressed but in a state of becoming: nothing is really antagonistic, everything is plural" (31). This plurality of possibility has the capacity to create a paradigm shift or in the poet's words, "a Conversion of the mind" (F627). The paradigm of inner and exter-nal power is reversed so that when the poet becomes aware of the immensi-ty of her self-discovered powers, she "sneers softly" in the realization. Most importantly, however, the reversal repositions the value assigned to inner and outer worlds, freeing the nineteenth-century woman from the limitations of existing roles by positioning itself within her as a "deep and irreplaceable knowledge of [her] capacity for joy [that] does not have to be called mar-riage, nor god, nor an afterlife" (Lorde, 57). Dickinson's personal realization of this opportunity is expressed in this pivotal poem:

> A solemn thing—it was—I said—
> A Woman—white—to be—
> And wear—if God should count me fit—
> Her blameless mystery—
>
> A hallowed thing—to drop a life
> Into the purple well—
> Too plummetless—that it return—
> Eternity—until—
>
> I pondered how the bliss would look—
> And would it feel as big—
> When I could take it in my hand—
> As hovering—seen—through fog—
>
> And then—the size of this "small" life—
> The Sages—call it small—
> Swelled—like Horizons—in my vest—
> And I sneered—softly—"small"! (F307)

Dickinson's excesses, representative of her attempt to close the gap between signifier and signified, between the expression of inner and outer states, are highly transgressive in that they go beyond the conventional bound-aries in which Dickinson was restricted. At the same time, the poetic persona is protected by the armour of "too-muchness," so that, even in her most con-fessional gushings, the sentimentality and melodrama of her voice undercut its seriousness. Such hyperbolic expression clearly belies the absence that resides beneath it so that Dickinson again sets up a kind of oxymoron that juxtaposes fullness (excess) against absence, pain against joy in a way that re-enacts the interstitial moment between life and death. Dickinson's excesses, moreover, create sites of pleasure in the text in the way that Barthes describes:

> The brio of the text (without which, after all, there is no text) is its will to bliss: just where it exceeds demand, transcends prattle, and whereby it attempts to overflow, to break through the con-straint of adjectives—which are those doors of language, through which the ideological and the imaginary come flowing in. (13)

For once again, the language of excess reveals the text's cracks and fissures, the sites of loss that mark the pleasure of the text. So Dickinson's hyperbolic stylistics swell and burst out of the confining word, line, or stanza to flood the page with sumptuous excess. The effect on the reader, which includes the poet herself, bathed in such excesses, is intoxicating. Moreover, the resultant disjunction in the poem is a representation of "excess verbal pleasure," to quote Barthes again, a place where

> the author seems to say to them I love you all (words, phrases, sentences, adjectives, discontinuities: pell-mell: signs and mirages of objects which they represent); a kind of Franciscanism invites all words to perch, to flock, to fly off again: a marbled, iridescent text; we are gorged with language, like children who are never refused anything or scolded for anything or, even worse, "permitted" anything. [This] is the pledge of continuous jubilation, the moment when by its very excess verbal pleasure chokes and reels into bliss. (8)

The final stanza of the following poem effectively illustrates Barthes's theory as the poem bursts open to spill out a series of enticing words:

> The Love a Life can show Below
> Is but a filament, I know,
> Of that diviner thing
> That faints upon the face of Noon—
> And smites the Tinder in the Sun—
> And hinders Gabriel's Wing—
>
> 'Tis this—in Music—hints and sways—
> And far abroad on Summer days—
> Distils uncertain pain—
> 'Tis this enamors in the East—
> And tints the Transit in the West—
> With harrowing Iodine—
>
> 'Tis this—invites—appalls—endows—
> Flits—glimmers—proves—dissolves—
> Returns—suggests—convicts—enchants—
> Then—flings in Paradise— (F285)

The disjunction between the first two stanzas and the last is echoed in the final phrase of the poem, "flings in Paradise," the object pronoun "me" elided from the phrase. Dickinson uses the unusual verb "flings" (at least unusual in this context) to describe the movement of disjunction; that is, the movement from one level of experience to another. But the entire poem manifests the speaker's inability to find the language to describe her subject, and as such, expresses the intense doubleness of her feelings. For despite the exhilarating awareness of divine love, as mortals, we must suffer at the same time in our awareness that we are incapable either of experiencing it or expressing it. In the end, then, Dickinson's "bliss" is always composed of a tempered joy, a mingling of pain and bliss, as the poem's imagery and the alternating meanings of the list of verbs in the last stanza reveal: "invites—appalls"; "endows—Flits"; "glimmers—proves"; "dissolves—Returns"; "suggests—convicts."

In another gesture of excess, the polyvocality of Dickinson's speakers attests to the poet's device of veiling the self—"Tell all the truth but tell it slant." But the protective devices the poet uses—such as the child mask—also increase the danger of self-annihilation. As Gilbert and Gubar point out,

> While freeing her from the terrors of marriage and allowing her
> to "play" with the toys of Amplitude, the child mask (or pose or
> costume) eventually threatened to become a crippling self, a self
> that in the crisis of her gothic life fiction locked her into her
> father's house in the way that a little girl is confined to a nurs-
> ery. What was habit in the sense of costume became habit in the
> more pernicious sense of addiction, and finally the two habits led
> to both an inner and outer inhabitation—a haunting interior and
> an inescapable prison. (591)

The "pernicious" side of addiction leads to self-destruction so that the attendant self, that "other-in-the-self" can be terrifying in its vigilance. When Dickinson writes "Ourself behind Ourself / Should startle most" (407), she calls up this idea by raising the notion of the *unheimlich*.

Thus when Dickinson discovers that the artistic and personal fulfillment she seeks is not situated outside herself, she begins to transform conventional ideas about language and life:

> A loss of something ever felt I—
> The first that I could recollect
> Bereft I was—of what I knew not
> Too young that any should suspect
> A Mourner walked among the children
> I notwithstanding went about
> As one bemoaning a Dominion
> Itself the only Prince cast out—
>
> Elder, Today, A session wiser,
> And fainter, too, as Wiseness is
> I find Myself still softly searching
> For my Delinquent Palaces—
>
> And a Suspicion, like a Finger
> Touches my Forehead now and then
> That I am looking oppositely
> For the Site of the Kingdom of Heaven— (F1072)

But by the very nature of this insight the process towards fulfillment is not linear and is fraught with mystery. It is not possible to follow a chronological order of poems in order to identify the order of the process. Nor is it possible to fix the identity of her speakers but as such, according to Paul Crumbley, "Dickinson fuels our perception of the self as uncontainable, perpetually thwarting any impulse to stabilize meaning or ... identity" (15). In the following complex poem, Dickinson de-centres the "Centre" so that the pursuit of the goal is not linear but dialogical. The "goal" is "adored with caution":

> Each Life Converges to some Centre—
> Expressed—or still—
> Exists in every Human Nature
> A Goal—
>
> Embodied scarcely to itself—it may be—
> Too fair
> For Credibility's presumption
> To mar—
> Adored with caution—as a Brittle Heaven—
> To reach
> Were hopeless, as the Rainbow's Raiment
> To touch—
>
> Yet persevered toward—surer—for the Distance—
> How high—
> Unto the Saints' slow diligence—
> The Sky—
>
> Ungained—it may be—by a Life's low Venture—
> But then—
> Eternity enable the endeavoring
>
> Again. (F724)

The poem destabilizes, indeed, "de-centres" the meaning of the word "Centre," so that it becomes as dynamic as the process of working towards it. In the first three stanzas, the process of persevering toward a goal is shown to resist linearity by raising the possibility that it may not even be expressed though latent and "still." Moreover, even if a goal has been expressed, it is nonetheless extremely fragile, as the crabbed syntax in stanza two suggests. For in the line "Embodied scarcely to itself—it may be—," Dickinson exposes the insubstantiality of "the goal"—it has "scarcely" any embodiment, and may not be attached to anything but "itself." However, in a way, this also gives it substance, solidity, because it cannot be attached to a body; it is not external and therefore it cannot be "marred." We must "cautiously" adore the goal because it is fragile, like a "Brittle Heaven" and elusive like the "Rainbow's Raiment." Therefore, the only certainty we have of knowing it is provided by its distance from us—"yet persevered toward—sure—for the Distance." Although we may not reach it during our earthly existence—"A Life's low Venture—," the striving begins again in "Eternity." Dickinson's eternity, always an equivocal term, dwells in the legacy of the poems and in their ability to stimulate the reader.

The poem is important in its statement of the mechanism of desire and in its locating of that mechanism within the self. The goal is the object of desire, but in Dickinson's text, the meaning of the word is greatly amplified by the image in the first line. For the "Centre" (the goal) of "Human Nature" is the point at which "Life" itself converges; as such, it is a point of immense concision. On the other hand, the path of the self's movement through life towards the goal is limitless, guided as it is by the hand of awe: "Awe is the first hand that is held to us ... though there is no Course, there is Boundlessness" (L871). Thus, the poem—as life itself—moves in both directions, outward and inward, from and to a centre that is neither fixed nor defined but as certain as our own existence.

As a result of the instability of the "I," the poet's use of language also becomes destabilized in a way that Joanne Fiet-Diehl insightfully observes:

> by insisting upon the articulation of her own version of experi-
> ence, she develops rhetorical strategies that break with tradition
> as they depend increasingly upon indeterminacies, upon the dis-
> ruption of linguistic structures that would otherwise provide rec-
> ognizable, coherent meanings. (38)

Indeed, Dickinson's manipulation of language works toward its destabiliza-tion in a way that corresponds to the admonitions of Hélène Cixous: "beware of the signifier that would take you back to the authority of the sig-nified" (347). Furthermore, Barthes's conclusion that "the pleasure of the text is value shifted to the sumptuous rank of the signifier" (65) offers a way of understanding the disjunctive, dissonant Dickinson text. Accordingly, the poet's addiction to language is inscribed in her language by way of her alter-ation of the function of poetic devices such as oxymoron—by sustaining and enlarging the space between terms—and analogy. As Suzanne Juhasz points out in "The Irresistible Lure of Repetition and Dickinson's Poetics of Analogy," analogy is the device that is central to Dickinson's poetics; the use of analogy "referring particularly to her habit of repeating" (23) points "to the compulsion to repeat unconscious conflicts, wishes and experiences that is due primarily to their having remained under repression" (25). This "compul-sion to repeat," continues Juhasz, is understood "not as duplication but cre-ation, using the same elements of the original, constantly destroying or break-ing it down and reforming it, so that its new form is, in fact, an analogue" (25). The repetition here—the mastery and pleasure that come from the repetition—is "not only re-creation but transformation" (29). Thus, analogy, and indeed the tendency in Dickinson to repeat the same idea or wrestle with the same problem as witnessed in the variants of a poem, arises from

> her very love of language and her submission to its lure [so that]
> her creation of a world of linguistic experience ... is neither imi-
> tation nor elimination of the well of psychic experience inside her,
> the source of her need and her art. Analogy is repetition with a
> difference. Telling it again and again but in the process recreat-
> ing it is at the crux of her artistic endeavor. Of course that
> process is an aspect of her personal self, produced from needs and
> desires that stimulate her urge to taste those "signal esoteric
> sips," to experience the irresistible "Rapture" that is language.
> (31)

In the end, by healing the split self through language Dickinson must sustain the terrible tensions of human experience, but by so doing, she finds a creative rather than destructive means of living with them.

Forfeiting the "Bliss," the "Rapture" of fulfillment, because it would mean the end of life and the end of the pursuit of language becomes Dickinson's goal, as she points out with alcoholic images in the following poem:

> *Who never wanted—maddest Joy*
> *Remains to him unknown—*
> *The Banquet of Abstemiousness*
> *Defaces that of Wine—*
>
> *Within its reach, though yet ungrasped*
> *Desire's perfect Goal—*
> *No nearer—lest the Actual—*
> *Should disenthrall thy soul—* (F1447)

Thus part of the aphoristic style is the process, not the end, the philosophy again inscribed in the poetic expression itself. The poet's peculiar use of poetic devices as well as the numerous variants of each poem ensure that her end is not didactic since there is no single guideline or lesson intended. Each of us "learns" from Dickinson according to the way her language affects us. We feel its power as it emanates from the texts, or as this poem states, as the exhalations of the intoxicated poet stimulate the "exhilaration" of others:

> *Exhilaration—is within—*
> *There can no Outer Wine*
> *So royally intoxicate*
> *As that diviner Brand*
>
> *The Soul achieves—Herself—*
> *To drink—or set away*
> *For Visitor—or Sacrament—*
> *'Tis not of Holiday*
>
> *To stimulate a Man*
> *Who hath the Ample Rhine*
> *Within his Closet—best you can*
> *Exhale in offering—* (F645)

The "best you can" do, says the speaker, is to stimulate another, not to offer another by way of overt didacticism, the "Ample Rhine," that royal and divine wine of "Exhilaration." Stimulation can be achieved by "Exhal[ing] in offering"—for your exhilaration is within, not in the material text of the poet, but activated by it. Following her own definition of a good poem, Dickinson emphasizes that like the state of intoxication, an affective, visceral response will ensure its vitality: "If I read a book [and] it makes my whole body so cold no fire ever can warm I know that is poetry. If I feel physically as if the top of my head were taken off, I know that is poetry. These are the only ways I know it. Is there any other way" (L342a). Pushing away from the shores of convention, Dickinson finds unlimited freedom and possibility in the space of her linguistic addiction and the "madness" of her poetic expression ends in a "divine intoxication" that makes "divinest sense" in its assurance of both her personal and her artistic survival:

> *Exultation is the going*
> *Of an inland soul to sea—*
> *Past the Houses—*
> *Past the Headlands—*
> *Into deep Eternity—*
>
> *Bred as we, among the mountains,*
> *Can the sailor understand*
> *The divine intoxication*
> *Of the first league out from Land?* (F143)

Works Cited

Barthes, Roland. 1975. *The Pleasure of the Text*. Translated by Richard Miller. New York: Hill and Wang.

Cixous, Hélène. 1991. "The Laugh of the Medusa." Pp. 334–49 in *Feminisms: An Anthology of Literary Theory and Criticism*, edited by Robyn Warhol and Diane Price Herndl. New Brunswick: Rutgers University Press.

Crumbley, Paul. 1992. "Dickinson's Dashes and the Limits of Discourse." *Emily Dickinson Journal* 1, no. 1: 8–29.

Dickinson, Emily. 1998. *The Poems of Emily Dickinson*. Edited R.W. Franklin. The Belknap Press of Harvard University Press.

——. 1986. *The Letters of Emily Dickenson*. Edited by Thomas H. Johnson and Thelodora Ward. Cambridge: The Belknap Press of Harvard University Press.

Fiet-Diehl, Joanne. 1981. *Dickinson and the Romantic Imagination*. Princeton: Princeton University Press.

Franklin, R.S. (ed.). 1999. *The Poems of Emily Dickinson*. Cambridge, MA: The Belknap Press of Harvard University Press.

Gilbert, Sandra M. and Susan Gubar. 1979. *The Madwoman in the Attic: The Woman Writer and the Nineteenth-Century Literary Imagination*. New Haven: Yale University Press.

Juhasz, Suzanne. 2000. "The Irrestible Lure of Repetition and the Poetics of Analogy." *Emily Dickinson Journal* 9, no. 2: 23–31.

——. 1999. "Materiality and the Poet." In *The Emily Dickinson Handbook*, edited by Gudrun Grabher, Roland Hagenbuechle and Suzanne Juhasz. Boston: University of Massachusetts Press.

Johnson, Thomas. 1980. *The Letters of Emily Dickinson*. Cambridge, MA: Harvard University Press, Belknap Press, 1980.

Lorde, Audre. 1984. *Sister Outsider*. Freedom, CA: The Crossing Press Feminism Series.

Miller, Cristanne. 1987. *Emily Dickinson: A Poet's Grammar*. Cambridge, MA and London: Harvard University Press.

Miller, Cristanne, Martha Nell Smith and Suzanne Juhasz. 1993. *Comic Power in Emily Dickinson*. Austin: University of Texas Press.

Rich, Adrienne. 1995. *On Lies, Secrets and Silence*. New York: W.W. Norton and Co.

13

The Way of Imperfection

Alison Lee Strayer

*"The idea of language trying to be salvific in some way is central
to a lot of stuff that I've written… In my own work, I feel always
that sort of Lacanian ideal of desire exceeding the object, the
overwhelming need to try to be able to use language to head off
[these kinds of] huge travails and disasters."*

Rick Moody in an interview on *Demonology*[1]

There are innumerable ways of characterizing a writer, but the image that holds most true for me is that of a child confronting death. The decision to become a writer must often coincide with the death of a loved one, or the realization that one is going to lose, to death, all the people one loves, and that they will lose us. An early consciousness of death may also arise in the wake of a separation or departure, the loss of a being or place; it may also arise due to an event that causes shame to oneself or a beloved person, awakening an acute knowledge of injustice. All these are experiences of powerlessness in the face of immensity. And ever after, it seems, beauty and love, and whatever brings joy, somehow refer back to the initial "discovery" of death. I believe the writer while writing, whether 18, 55, 70, becomes that child again. I believe that in one's primitive mind, writing is a way of stopping time, while reliving and rehearsing for loss.

I have written since the age of seven, starting with a diary. At first, the diary was simply part of daily ritual, almost neutral. The year I turned eight, my family and I spent a summer in the countryside of Quebec, and my diary took on a sort of mission. For one, it became a repository for new experience that was always slightly overwhelming. Leaving home almost seemed like something one should not survive. It was a shock to me that in the wake of an event so immense, life could carry on unruffled, even offering up new

---

1. Simon Houpt, "Demon Writer." Interview with Rick Moody on his short story collection *Demonology*. *The Globe and Mail*, February 17, 2001.

pleasures and curiosities. In an unknown place, away from Saskatchewan and the people I had always known, I realized we could all become strangers to each other. I realized that one day I would no longer be a child and would lose the people I loved most. Thus when I wrote my diary, I also wrote to seize the day. No day was entirely real or complete until I had written about it. Then, and only then, once recorded, could the day be done. Finished off. Finally perfect.

Much later it occurred to me that this notion of finishing off the day is somewhat double-edged. To finish off the day is to celebrate it, preserve it from oblivion. But it is also to perform a sort of *coup de grâce*. Fixing something in time is also to remove it from time (as Roland Barthes, in *Camera Lucida*, writes in relation to the photograph, the quintessential *memento mori*). It is both an immortalizing and a "mortalizing": an according of permanence and at the same time a burial.

I have proposed that writing is, at its origin, an endeavour to do something about death. I believe that a task so pressing is fertile grounds for addictive fervour. Addiction, here, I define as the state of being spoken over (bound) to an activity, person or substance. My main interest here is the "addictive" extremes in the writing process, in which one is driven not simply to complete a piece of writing in a way that comes closest to one's original vision, but to carry out tasks ("missions") that are not necessarily within the power of the writing to accomplish.

Indeed, one characteristic shared by all who are spoken over to an activity, person or substance, is the compulsive ("life or death") pursuit of tasks which have to do with Time: for example, fixing time, stopping time, hoarding and going back in time. Secondly, addictive desire, thought and endeavour will settle only for perfection, nothing less. Perfection can be envisaged quite simply as the perfect paragraph or the perfect high. But the more one is taken over by one's quest, the more elusive perfection becomes. Perhaps this is because perfection as an ideal can no longer be projected onto an outer object and worked at outside oneself. Instead, it becomes increasingly directed towards some inner object, and a task it dictates that may result in work, and work, and work that proves limitless.

Now we arrive at the question of melancholy, surely the matrix of all addictive behaviours and missions. Freud explains melancholy as the introjection of a lost love object—person, state, place, thing—that one cannot, or will not, release. This object of insatiable yearning is thus mourned within, taking the form, for example, of a lost paradise. For she or he who is performing addictively, the lost paradise may be a regretted state of wholeness into which no desire to write, or to consume, ever irrupted. Or it could be nostalgia for the original high, which includes so-called peak experiences of writing, when one felt justified in the scheme of Nature, as if carrying out one's essential function, like a pear tree producing pears, as a pear tree will do!

A writer is a melancholic *qui se soigne*, who heals or at least sustains herself by way of writing. Writing gives her mobility and volubility despite the paralysing effects of melancholic contemplation. Though unless she can step out of melancholy's circle of enchantment, she is in an irresolvable bind. Melancholy, a threat to writing, is also its wellspring and thus must, to some degree, be sustained. Melancholy deems—and for me, the voice of melancholy is female—that only through perfection may she be appeased and perhaps (but only perhaps) healed. Like a sphinx with her riddle, like Medusa with her fixed gaze, she immobilises, making it extremely difficult to carry out any task, much less accomplish it to perfection! Melancholy has the habit of wanting to survive, like the addictions to which she gives birth.

The most familiar addict archetype is without question that of the substance addict, also a melancholic, who sustains herself via her intoxicant of preference. By consuming, she joins the lost love without whom life is unliveable. She recovers a state of otherwise impossible union with All, and her goal—and this is where any addiction becomes potentially fatal—is never to leave that inner person, state or landscape again. This in turn requires that she never stop consuming. She too may step out of melancholy's circle of enchantment, by ceasing to consume (though some addiction theory would tell us she will never be cured, and always remain "in recovery"); there is no doubt that the best fortification against melancholic take-over is learning to stop, which means truly agreeing to stop. That is no simple matter, and certainly not painless. The fantasy of never stopping is highly seductive.

The quest for perfection and nothing less gives us a sound pretext for never stopping. And so, with each poem, each book, we pursue perfection; but the farther we advance in our addictive process, the true character or definition of "perfection" chillingly reveals itself. Perfection is not simply a matter of making concrete, in every detail of a work, the ideal and vision that engendered it, but means doing it for once and for all. It means the end. This is perfection in the grammatical sense of the word, perfective tenses referring to completed actions, imperfective tenses to ongoing or incomplete actions. If not perfected, the endeavour must be repeated and repeated, no stopping allowed. Perfection (with its stage-mother Melancholy, standing just behind) cracks its whip. Only then do we discover that all along, the desire to never stop has been a desire for its own opposite. There is, in this desire to never stop, a need to outrun a powerful counteracting fatigue, a desire for rich, still being, better than words—to be a prairie, a tree, merged with all around—to be in eros, in the perfection of sheer being.

— • —

"I cannot hold this—I cannot express this—I am overcome by it—I am mastered."

In "Evening Over Sussex: Reflections in a Motor Car," Virginia Woolf describes the experience of contemplation and the vagaries to which it is prone (82–85). This, at least, is how the essay starts, before making a volte-face halfway through. On a summer evening's drive, Woolf's narrator contemplates the land and sky of Sussex by evening. She is moved, struck with awe—though she also admits to a pique of irritation. The clouds are pink, the fields "mottled, marbled." The observer's perceptions "blow out rapidly like air balls [balloons] expanded by some rush of air…"

Suddenly, "a pin pricks." The writer protests: "I cannot hold this—I cannot express this—I am overcome by it—I am mastered." Consciousness cleaves down neatly, putting an end to contemplation and awe:

> So far as I could tell the pin had something to do with one's own impotency … one's nature demands mastery over all that it receives; and mastery here meant the power to convey what one saw … so that another person could share it.

The pin pricks not once, but twice. The first pin-prick having burst the balloon, the second alerts us that "torrents" of beauty are flooding into oblivion before our eyes: "beauty spread at one's right hand, at one's left; at one's back too."

Suddenly, the narrative self splits in two—"a well-known occurrence, in such circumstances," comments the unruffled narrator. On one hand is the "eager and dissatisfied self" (whom I will henceforth refer to as Eager), the poetic self who yearned to capture this evening over Sussex. On the other hand is the "stern and philosophical self" (henceforth, Stern) who advises Eager simply to give up!

> Relinquish these impossible aspirations; be content with the view in front of us… It is best to sit and soak; to be passive; to accept; and do not bother because nature has given you six little pocket knives with which to cut up the body of a whale.

What follows Stern's command to relinquish is a series of further splittings, producing something akin to a party atmosphere. The stern and the eager selves "hold a colloquy about the wise course to adopt in the presence of beauty." Another self, called "I," declares its presence. "I" stands apart (or rather sits apart: we are in a moving car, after all). "Aloof and melancholy," she envies Eager and Stern their chattering complicity, their freedom to look out the window and take note of a haystack, a rust-red roof, a pond, the colours of sky and earth. "I" herself can only look back and regret what has been left behind. "Gone, gone; over, over; past and done with," says she, but is roused from her melancholy by a new "erratic and impulsive" self who points at a star and evokes the future: Sussex in 500 years to come, full of modern appliances "charming thoughts and quick effective beams."

In the end when the landscape is in total darkness, "I" rallies the selves for an inventory of the evening's trophies ("great beauty; and then disappearance and death of the individual; past and future"), before one last voice pipes up, that of the body who clamours for "eggs, toast, tea, a fire, bath, and bed." "And the rest of the journey was performed in the delicious society of my own body."

Thus the story winds down to a tranquil and organic ending, as day has wound down into night. All's well that ends well. But one cannot forget that for the writer-narrator, this journey has not necessarily begun well, or at least, starts out evenly, becomes febrile, untenable, and must suddenly change course. At this point, the essay invites another sort of reading, whereby we discover, in the account of contemplation and the vagaries to which it is prone, a sort of navigational map of its perils, with the suggestion of an alternative route.

In order to identify the perils of contemplation, let us return to the moment where the narrator, as she beholds pink clouds and mottled fields, notes how the perceptions "blow out like air balls." What is conveyed here seems not only outward beauty, but an inner state as well, a fullness of being. The twilight's beauty waxes also within the observer ("all seems blown to its fullest and tautest, with beauty and beauty and beauty"). One suspects that the swelling of the outward landscape echoes bodily sensations such as indrawn breath, a surge of feeling in the heart. It is a moment of full being, of communion, of unimpeded eros.

But we understand, too, that this is a potentially imperilled state; we sense distress in the proclamation: "I cannot hold this—I cannot express this—I am overcome." If we do not hear the narrator's distress with the first pin-prick, we cannot miss it the second time, when "one was wasting one's chance; for beauty spread at one's right hand, at one's left; at one's back too." Not only has the narrator to admit to the failure to "hold" and "express"—in other words, the failure of her writing and of her responsibility to the reader—but also acknowledge that this failure may lead to her own depletion and demise. Or so it would seem, if we assume that flooding-away beauty is probably flooding-away time as well; hence, "[Time] was escaping all the time; one could only offer a thimble to a torrent that could fill baths, lakes." In other words, in the inflamed perceptions of the poetic self, the expression of this experience is a matter of life or death.

Another peril of contemplation (and of writing about it) lies in the fact that the tasks of holding and expressing are mutually exclusive. "Holding" requires that the "air balloon" perceptions remain inflated; "expressing" requires the balloon to be punctured so that what is within may be expelled, then shaped. In other words, one might say that to be in a state of whole being is irreconcilable with writing, which requires separation and distance. Marrying the two is an impossible task; and impossible tasks invite takeover.

Peril, the presence of a threat, may also be indicated by the abruptness with which the narrator puts an end to contemplation. ("The self splits"; Stern suddenly tells Eager to relinquish—and Woolf has Eager immediately obey!) We might see this as a reaction against a "taken-over" state, dangerous to both writer and writing. And indeed, though perhaps not threatened while writing this text in particular, the author herself knew the state well, as biography, journals, and other works of Woolf's confirm.

Finally, that there is considerable peril here is underscored by the strong, not to say violent language employed in the supposedly philosophical advice of Stern: "be content with the view in front of us … and do not bother because nature has given you six little pocket knives with which to cut up the body of a whale."

The whale, at first, we readily accept as a metaphor. The image of this great sad bloated body is reminiscent of the deflated balloon: Beauty, the ideal of perfection that drove the first part of the essay, is pricked twice and collapses. Then, on a second look at the image of the whale, we are struck with its cruelty. It strongly suggests rage, the presence of some enemy we cannot see, but to whose threatening existence the rage bears testimony, and brings to mind the strangling of the Angel in the House in "Professions for Women" (written four years later, in 1931) of whom the narrator writes: "I turned upon her and caught her by the throat... . Had I not killed her she would have killed me. She would have plucked the heart out of my writing" (237–38). But the killing of the whale is far more graphic and barbarous than that of the Angel. A whale is a sympathetic and maternal creature from the point of view of some, yet its body is to be cut to pieces with pocket knives—that is, small and probably not very sharp knives—thus, necessarily, hacked, sawed, gouged to pieces.

One might object: "but no cruelty has actually been committed!" Indeed, in telling Eager to relinquish, Stern is advising her to not even attempt to cut up the body of the whale. But the image is riveting, power-ful, telling : one gets the impression that this cutting up has happened, in fantasy. Certainly, it has happened figuratively, without carnage, on the page before us: when the self splits (is cut up?) into multiple characters/selves.

But let us return to the matter of rage. What could possibly provoke such violent feeling, if not something, someone, some force that threatens life, in the sense of mobility, and ability to express? I believe this threaten-ing entity has something to do with what the whale represents: some sort of immensity (death, injustice, love, loss) that renders one powerless, inarticu-late; a reality that "exceeds the ability of language to express it," in the words of Rick Moody.

What is striking, too, in the "Relinquish!" passage is a rather ceremonial language and a tone that suggests soliloquy, as if Woolf herself were making a statement and also listening to herself: as it were, trying on an idea for size. It is as if, through Stern, the author is addressing her own "eager and dissat-isfied self," a perennially young self, the eternal child in face of death, the one that never learns.

The ceremony performed in the "Relinquish!" passage also calls to my mind a drama I have, on a couple of occasions, played out with myself dur-ing highly charged moments of writing. Fired by zeal to complete and say it all, right away, but also feeling I am headed towards a block (standstill, paral-ysis), I sit at my desk, tugging my hair, and cry out: "I give up!" The words must be cried out loud, after all: in self-pity, as a welcome release and an *in extremis* appeal to some force that is threatening to take me over.

Finally we come to the question of the "alternative route" that I believe is proposed in "Evening over Sussex." According to my reading, the writer's task has been first characterized as something that if left unaccomplished, may lead to her own depletion and demise. An alternative approach is explicitly introduced in the "colloquy about the wise course to adopt in the presence of beauty." The colloquy takes place between a self that is fully engaged, and one that is detached and philosophical. One might, for example, characterize this as a dialogue between the older and younger writer: the one who has learned from experience versus the other who never learns.

Indeed, splitting the narrative self is essential to this alternative approach, which one might say sidesteps the quest for perfection and traces out a "way of imperfection." Here, obviously, the word "imperfection" is by no means a qualitative judgement, but refers to an approach towards Time that deflects "addictive" desire, the yearning for the once-and-for-all. The first part of the essay seems to suggest that one-on-one contemplation of a single object by a single subject carries with it a danger of paralysis, fixation. If Beauty had not collapsed, if the balloon hadn't burst and the self not split, in principle both writer and text would have stopped right there.

Through the splitting of the narrative self, the writer steps out of the circle of paralyzing enchantment (takeover). Indeed, she has done exactly what she says she would not do: she has put the "little pocket knives" to work by way of new characters (six, if you include the original narrator). When the self splits, and splits again, the narrative is brought into the scheme of time, moves from one event or moment of consciousness to another. These selves allow for articulation, in both the sense of expression and of flexibility. We might say a similar process was at work in the writing of *The Waves*, where the poetic contemplation of death is mediated by Bernard, Susan, Nigel, Jinny, Louis and Rhoda.

Yet, though having given up the goal of impossible perfection, having stepped out of the range of the Muse's fixed surveillance, the writer must continue to profit from the inspiration and driving force this Muse provides (melancholy; "addictive" desire). We might speculate that the dead whale is a fantasy-image of her lifeless body; but she can be killed only in fantasy for, no matter how malign she may be at times, she is nonetheless a Muse. Perhaps, then, an alternative poetics does not imply avoiding the perils, but coming as close to them as one can without being "spoken over" to them. Surely it is the emotion and desire these perils awaken, the images they generate, that were and continue to be the impetus for the writing. By crying out 'Relinquish!" or "I give up!" one diverts the surveillance of the muse—of one's own expectations of perfection. With this ceremonious admission of defeat, one leaves oneself free to re-enter time, talk with a friend, a child, a lover; go for a walk; read for no other reason but the pleasure of it; cook, eat, sleep. The pressure is off; one is disgraced in the eye of the task-mistress, but the next day, for the next three or four days perhaps (this won't last long), one shall write as one pleases—"imperfectly," ramblingly, playfully…

Having said this, I still believe that as writers and as people who love, we never quite give up striving for perfection. We desire to create a work that measures up as closely as possible to our initial vision; we desire thereby to give back to people we love what we feel we have deprived them of by our absence; we desire to write the book that says everything we have to say, though knowing that doing so would put an end to all future writing. Yet when all is said and done, perhaps the most difficult part is agreeing to stop, agreeing to "sit and soak and not bother"; agreeing to stop and return to the body, whose needs for "egg, bath, fire and bed," whose intelligence and engagement in the creative process one is quick to forget or deny when one is "spoken over."

— • —

"Every day includes more non-being than being. Yesterday for example ... was as it happened a good day; above the average in 'being.' It [the weather] was fine; I enjoyed writing these first pages." (Woolf, "Sketch," 70)

Over the past few years I have read and reread, with pleasure and gratitude, Woolf's *Moments of Being*, composed of three essays published in 1939, two years before the author's death. In the first memoir, "A Sketch of the Past," Woolf presents an image of being that indicates an alternative "way" to the notion of being as paradisiac state that silences the writer. What Woolf describes as being has something to do with what is memorable, due to pleasure or shock, and calls out to be recorded. Thus, her conception of "being" does not exclude writing, which indeed suggests that writing can itself be a moment of being ("I enjoyed writing these first pages...").

Moreover, it would seem that for Woolf, writing can even draw an event out of non-being. In the same memoir, she writes of "shocks" she experienced from the time she was a child. Though for years they were experienced as unpleasant, as "blows," these shocks have the effect of jarring her into "being" and now are welcome: "I go on to suppose that it is the shock-receiving capacity is what makes me a writer. I hazard the explanation that a shock is at once in my case followed by the desire to explain it." The shock, or blow, will eventually "become a revelation of some order; it is a token of some real thing behind appearances; and I make it real by putting it into words. It is only by putting it into words that I make it whole." Thus, in Woolf's view, as she reflects upon some 40 years of writing and almost 60 years of life, writing can salvage a moment from "non-being," the "cotton wool" that obscures a vital truth, a cosmic pattern; writing can retrieve a moment of lost time, those parts of a day that are unrecorded, only half-experienced, and complete them.

Curiously, for all that Woolf presents "non-being" as less desirable than "being," it is described in far more tangible and alluring terms. "Non-being" moments are "as if embedded in a kind of nondescript cotton"; they make up the "cotton wool of daily life." The recurrent image of "nondescript cotton" or "cotton-wool"—what in North America we call absorbent cotton—is very evocative, insistent. When I read the words "cotton wool," my senses seize upon the thing, the palpable object, before my mind digests it as metaphor. I feel it, rough beneath my fingertips. It is both raw and fluffy, it has texture and density. Intact, it is thick and opaque, but can be easily pulled at, stretched so thin one can see through it, yet resists ripping unless one exerts undue tension from either direction. It evokes connective tissue, the binding of wounds, raw material.

Woolf's account of her day continues with a description of her walk by the river, another "moment of being": "The country, which I notice very closely always, was coloured and shaded as I like—there were the willows, I remember, all plumy and soft green and purple against the blue." She read Chaucer with pleasure, and began a biography of Madame de Lafayette that she found interesting. Yet still, at the end of this "day that was better than average in being" she concludes: "These separate moments of being were however embedded in many more moments of non-being. I have already forgotten what Leonard and I talked about at lunch; and at tea…"

I feel a shock of pleasure, a renegade joy when I reread these words, this example by which Woolf evokes all the non-being moments of the day: a conversation over lunch with a beloved person that goes unrecorded, remains embedded in cotton-wool. Is this not Being too?

— To Jean-Philippe

Works Cited

Barthes, Roland. 1982. *Camera Lucida: Reflections on Photography*. New York: Farrar, Strauss Giroux.

Freud, Sigmund. "Mourning and Melancholia," *Standard Edition*, volume 14.

Woolf, Virginia (1927). 1993. "Evening over Sussex." In *The Crowded Dance of Modern Life: Selected Essays*. Penguin.

—— (1931). 1942. "Professions for Women." In *Death of the Moth and Other Essays*. New York: Harcourt, Brace.

——. 1985. "A Sketch of the Past." *Moments of Being*. New York: Harcourt, Brace.

Envois

*Enivrez-Vous**
Charles Baudelaire

*Il faut être toujours ivre. Tout est là: c'est l'unique
question. Pour ne pas sentir l'horrible fardeau du
Temps qui brise vos épaules et vous penche vers la
Terre, il faut vous enivrer sans trêve.*

*Mais de quoi? De vin, de poésie ou de virtue, à votre
guise. Mais enivrez-vous.*

*Et si quelquefois, sur les marches d'un palais, sur
l'herbe verte d'un fossé, dans la solitude morne de votre
chambre, vous vous réveillez, l'ivresse déjà diminuée
ou disparue, demandez au vent, à la vague, à l'étoile,
à l'oiseau, à l'horloge, à tout ce qui fuit, à tout ce qui
gémit, à tout ce qui roule, à tout ce qui chante, à tout
ce qui parle, demandez quelle heure il est; et le vent,
la vague, l'étoile, l'oiseau, l'horloge, vous répondront:
"Il est l'heure de s'enivrez! Pour n'être pas les esclaves
martyrisés du Temps, enivrez-vous sans cesse! De vin,
de poésie ou de virtue, à votre guise."*

---

*   In *Le Spleen de Paris: Petits Poèmes en prose*. Oeuvres Complètes de Baudelaire. Texte
établi et annoté par Y.G. Le Dantec (Bibliothèque de la Pléiade, publiée à la Librairie
Gallimard, 1951), 330.

Get High*
Charles Baudelaire
(Translated by Edward K. Kaplan)

You must always be high. Everything depends on it: it is the
only question. So as not to feel the horrible burden of Time
wrecking your back and bending you to the ground, you
must get high without respite.

But on what? On wine, on poetry, or on virtue, whatever
you like. But get high.

And if sometimes you wake up, on palace steps, on the
green grass of a ditch, in your room's gloomy solitude, your
intoxication already waning or gone, ask the wind, the
waves, the stars, the birds, clocks, ask everything that flees,
everything that moans, everything that moves, everything
that sings, everything that speaks, ask what time it is. And
the wind, the waves, the stars, the birds, clocks, will answer,
"It is time to get high! So as not to be martyred
slaves of Time, get high! get high constantly! on wine, on
poetry, or on virtue, as you wish."

---

*   In *The Parisian Prowler* (The University of Georgia Press, Athens, GA: 1989), 89.

Index

Moments of Being, 156
morphine, 1, 103–4
Morrison, Toni
    Beloved, 87
mother, death of, 126–27
motivations, human, 83–84
Musgrave, Susan, 56, 58, 64
mysticism, 62

Nabokov, Vladimir, 77
National Post, The, 13
nervous breakdown, 108–9
New York Times, The, 115
nicotine addiction, 45
Nietzsche, Friedrich, 67, 70
non-writing, 60
North West Territories Act of 1875, 12
nostalgia, 127, 131, 150
novel writing, 25, 121

obsession, 108–9
Oedipal relationship, 126–27, 129
Ondaatje, Michael
    Running in the Family, 120
O'Neill, Eugene, 83
    Long Day's Journey Into Night, 90
opium addiction, 1, 80–81
Orestes, 127, 130
Orwell, George, 17

paranoia, 118, 120
paranoid schizophrenia, see schizophrenia
Pasternak, Boris, 60
Penrod, 26
Perfect Crime, The, 119
perfection, in writing, 150–51, 154–55
Perkins, Max, 108, 110–12
Plato, 68
Playing Dead: A Reader's Marginalia, 63
Poe, Edgar Allen, 83, 118
poetry, 59, 141
poiesis, 3, 5, 7–8, 60, 64
    as addiction, 58, 63
power
    addictive, 27
    and authorship, 69–74
    of literature, 87–88
    of the self, 67–68, 142
    of words, 81, 147, 150
    and writing, 118, 129
Prins, Gwyn, 37–38
prohibition, 14, 18–19, 21
Psychiatric Annals, 99
psychiatric disorders, 99
psychosis, 131, 133
psychotropic drugs, 86
Purdy, Al, 21, 40

quasi-journal, 50

Rat Man, 127
reconciliation, 46, 49
recovery, 66, 115, 151
Reid, Steven, 56
relationships, alcoholic, 107
repression, 136
Rich, Adrienne, 135
Richler, Mordecai, 21
Roethke, Theodore, 1
Roth, Mary, 100
Roulston, Robert, 103
Running in the Family, 120

sanity, 132
Save Me the Waltz, 97–99, 104, 107, 110
schizophrenia, 99–100, 102, 105–6, 108,
    111–12, 121, 127
    see also insanity; mental illness
Schreber, 121
Schwartz, Delmore, 1
Seberg, Jean, 116
Secrets of the Flesh: A Life of Colette, 15
Sedgwick, Eve, 79
self
    as hierarchy of power, 68
    inner, 136–37, 142, 144, 151
    as multiple, 67
    splitting of, 155
self-creation, 5
self-delusion, 66
self-destruction, 5, 115, 120, 122, 124–26,
    144
Self-Destruction in the Promised Land, 126
self-division, 4, 66, 74–75
self-mastery, 68
self-murder, 129, 132
self-writing, 116
semantics and language, 70
sentimentality, 142
Sexton, Anne, 1
Shaffer, Peter
    Amadeus, 125
Shakespeare, William
    The Taming of the Shrew, 97
Showalter, Elaine
    The Female Malady, 99
sobriety and lost insights, 86, 94
Some Sort of Epic Grandeur, 100
Sophie's Choice, 119–21, 126–28, 131, 133
Speech and Phenomena, 130
St. Vincent Millay, Edna, 1
Steinbeck, John, 83
Steiner, George, 119, 121
    Language and Silence, 120
story, addictive power of, 27
stress, creational, 118
Styron, Pauline, 126
Styron, William, 116–19, 121–34
    Confessions of Nat Turner, 120

Contributors

ALAN BEWELL is Professor of English at the University of Toronto. His primary interest is in the relationship between literature, science, and medicine, particularly during the eighteenth and nineteenth centuries. His publications include *Romanticism and Colonial Disease* (Johns Hopkins, 1999), *Wordsworth and the Enlightenment: Nature, Man, and Society in the Experimental Poetry* (Yale, 1989), and various essays on botany, obstetric theory, and medicine in Romantic writing.

ANTHONY CUNNINGHAM is Professor of Philosophy at St. John's University in Collegeville, Minnesota. He has also taught philosophy at the University of Pennsylvania, the College of William & Mary, and Colby College. He specializes in ethics and has a particular interest in the ethical resources of literature. He is the author of *The Heart of What Matters: The Role for Literature in Moral Philosophy* (University of California Press, 2004), and has published articles and reviews in *The American Philosophical Quarterly, Dialogue, The Journal of Value Inquiry, Mind, and Ethics*.

TRUDY GOVIER lives and works in Calgary, Alberta. She holds a Ph.D. in Philosophy from the University of Waterloo (1971) and was formerly Associate Professor of Philosophy at Trent University. In addition to writing and lecturing on diverse topics in applied logic and social philosophy, Govier has pursued interests in conflict resolution and peace education. She is married and the mother of three children. Her books include *A Delicate Balance: What Philosophy Can Tell us About Terrorism* (Westview, 2002), *A Practical Study of Argument* (Wadsworth, Fifth edition, 2000), *God the Devil and the Perfect Pizza* (Broadview, 1998), and *Dilemmas of Trust* (McGill-Queen's University Press, 1998).

KRISTJANA GUNNARS is a writer and former Professor of English and writing at the University of Alberta. She is the author of six books of poetry, five books of prose, and two collections of short stories. As well, she has edited and translated several volumes. She has won the Georges Bugnet Award for fiction and the Stephan G. Stephansson Award for poetry in Alberta, and the McNally Robinson Award for non-fiction in Manitoba. As well, her book *Zero Hour* (1991) was nominated for the Governor General's Award for non-fiction and *The Prowler* (1989) was nominated for the books in Canada First Novel Award.

ELLEN LANSKY was born in Minneapolis, Minnesota, and grew up in Overland Park, Kansas. She attended The College of St. Catherine in St. Paul (BA), the State University of New York at Binghamton (MA), and the University of Minnesota (PhD). She now lives in Minneapolis, and she writes and teaches literature and composition at North Hennepin Community College. Her fiction has appeared in several regional and national publications, including the first Evergreen Chronicles novella contest, and her scholarly work on literature and alcoholism has appeared in *The*

Languages of Addiction, Literature and Medicine, Dionysos, and at regional and national conferences. She is a regular contributor to *Lavender Magazine,* and when she is not writing, she is a long-distance cyclist.

JEANETTE LYNES has published three collections of poetry: *A Woman Alone on the Atikokan Highway* (Wolsak and Wynn, 1999), *The Aging Cheerleader's Alphabet* (Mansfield Press, 2003), and *Left Fields* (Wolsak and Wynn, 2003). She also edited the anthologies *Words Out There: Women Poets in Atlantic Canada* (Roseway, 1999) and co-edited (with John Fell and David Antilla) *Paradise Frost: The Thunder Bay Poetry Renaissance* (Edgy Writers, 1999). Her poems are forthcoming in *The Windsor Review and Canadian Literature.* After a six-year stint at Lakehead University, she now teaches English at St. Francis Xavier University in Nova Scotia.

CINDY MACKENZIE teaches English at the University of Regina. She is the editor of *A Concordance to the Letters of Emily Dickinson,* published by the University of Colorado Press, 2000. She has also published articles on Dickinson in *The Emily Dickinson Journal.* Her passionate interest in Dickinson has taken her to conferences in the United States and Europe as an active member and participant of the Emily Dickinson Society and of the American Literature Association. She is currently working on a study of pain and consolation in Dickinson's *oeuvre.* She served as chair of the Saskatchewan Book Awards from 1998–2000.

DAVE MARGOSHES is a fiction writer and poet who lives in Regina. His novels *I'm Frankie Sterne* (2000) and *Drowning Man* (2003) are published by NeWest Press. Other books include a 1999 novella, *We Who Seek: A Love Story,* four short story collections and two volumes of poetry. He is also the author of the biography *Tommy Douglas: Building the New Society.* Margoshes has won a number of awards for his writing, including the Stephen Leacock prize for poetry in 1996. His stories and poems have been in numerous anthologies, including four times in the *Best Canadian Stories* volumes. His work has been published in dozens of magazines and been broadcast on the CBC, and he has given readings across the country. He has taught creative writing at the University of Regina and led creative writing workshops at various locations, and for various age groups, and been involved with the Writers in Electronic Residence program. He was writer in residence in Winnipeg in 1995–96, and in Saskatoon in 2001–02.

CRISPIN SARTWELL is Chair of Humanities and Sciences at the Maryland Institute College of Art. He is the author of several books, including *Six Names for Beauty* (Routledge, 2004), *Act Like You Know: African-American Autobiography and White Identity* (University of Chicago Press, 1998) and *The Art of Living: Aesthetics of the Ordinary in World Spiritual Traditions* (SUNY, 1995). He writes regularly for the opinion pages of the *Philadelphia Inquirer* and the *Los Angeles Times,* as well as being occasional essayist for magazines such as *Harper's.* He lives in rural Pennsylvania with his wife, the writer Marion Winik, and their five children.

STEVEN ROSS SMITH (also published as Steven Smith) writes poetry, fiction, book reviews, and presents sound and performance poetry. He has published eight books of poetry and fiction, and several recordings. He is currently at work on *fluttertongue*, a multi-book long poem. *Book 2, The Book of Emmett* was published in 1999 by Hagios Press, and was a finalist for a Saskatchewan Book Award. *Book 3, disarray*, is near completion. Smith is also featured on *Homo Sonorous: An International Anthology of Sound Poetry* (book & CD) just published by the National Centre for Contemporary Art, Kaliningrad, Russia.

ALISON LEE STRAYER was born in Regina and is a writer and translator. Her first novel, *Jardin et prairie*, written in French, was published by Leméac (Montreal) in 1999. The book was a finalist for a number of awards, including the Governor General's award for fiction, the City of Montreal literary award, the Prix Anne Hébert (Centre culturel canadien, Paris), and the Prix France-Québec. She lives in Paris and is working on a second book.

ANDREW STUBBS (PhD York) teaches at the University of Regina. He has written a full-length study of Eli Mandel, and edited *The Other Harmoy: The Collected Poetry of Eli Mandel* (CPRC, 2000). He has also written on other contemporary poets, fiction writers, and on writing from a rhetorical, psychoanalytical, deconstructive perspective. As well, he publishes poetry in various journals.

ARITHA VAN HERK's writing has been praised throughout North America and Europe. She is the author of the novels *Judith* (McClelland and Stewart, 1978), *The Tent Peg* (McClelland and Stewart, 1981), *No Fixed Address* (Red Deer College Press, 1998), *Places Far From Ellesmere* (Red Deer College Press, 1990), and *Restlessness* (Red Deer College Press, 1998), the latter a fictional examination of contemporary melancholia set in the picaresque core of downtown Calgary. Her non-fiction works, *A Frozen Tongue* (Dangaroo Press, 1992) and *In Visible Ink* (NeWest Press, 1991), address questions of reading as a way of life. She has also written *Mavericks: An Incorrigible History of Alberta* (Viking, 2001). She is fascinated with the addictions of others, and is herself addicted to perusing print.

About the Editors

KENNETH G. PROBERT is Associate Professor of English at the University of Regina. He is the editor of *Writing Saskatchewan* (CPRC, 1989).

BÉLA SZABADOS is Professor of Philosophy at the University of Regina and a past president of the Canadian Society for Aesthetics. He is the author of *In Light of Chaos* (Thisledown, 1990), co-author of *Hypocrisy: Ethical Investigations* (Broadview, 2004), and co-editor of *Wittgenstein Reads Weininger: A Reassessment* (Cambridge University Press, 2004).